STUDY GUIDE
TO ACCOMPANY

PSYCHOLOGY: AN INTRODUCTION
THIRD EDITION

BY
JOSH R. GEROW

STUDY GUIDE

TO ACCOMPANY

GEROW

PSYCHOLOGY: AN INTRODUCTION

THIRD EDITION

Prepared by

Glenda Streetman Smith, Ph.d.
North Harris County College

HarperCollins*Publishers*

Study Guide to accompany PSYCHOLOGY: AN INTRODUCTION, 3rdEdition
By Glenda Streetman Smith

Copyright © 1992 by HarperCollins Publishers Inc.

ISBN: 0-673-46641-8
    93 94 95 9 8 7 6 5

PREFACE

You are beginning a wonderful adventure, an introductory psychology course. This study guide is designed to help you succeed. You will benefit most by familiarizing yourself with the design of the study guide and then working through each chapter as you read the chapters in your text.

Each chapter contains learning objectives, lessons on learning the vocabulary of psychology, practice tests in true-false, fill-in, and multiple choice formats, and helpful study tips.

The learning objectives suggest what you should know when you have finished studying a chapter. However, don't limit your knowledge or interest to the objectives.

One of the most difficult tasks in an introductory psychology course is learning the considerable terminology. The section titled Learning Vocabulary is designed to help you with the new terms and definitions that you will encounter - not only in future psychology courses, but in many other courses and in many different contexts. The exercises are in a familiar matching format.

The practice tests consist of true-false, fill-in, and multiple choice questions. Do not limit your studying to the information in these questions. They are intended to be just a sampling of the information in the chapter not a comprehensive test. The answers to all the practice tests and the matching exercises are presented for all chapters at the end of the study guide.

Finally, Dr. G's Best Study Tips are ideas that my students have proven to be effective and efficient. I suggest that you read through the study tips in all fifteen chapters as soon as possible so that you may apply any or all of them right from the beginning of the course.

Use this study guide faithfully, and you will enjoy your successful adventure through psychology.

TABLE OF CONTENTS

HOW TO SUCCEED IN THIS COURSE

FACTORS AFFECTING THE LEARNING PROCESS

The learning process is an important area of concern for psychologists. You will find this out as you study the principles of learning in your psychology course. The purpose of this book is to help you to improve your learning of psychology. As you read the sections below, you will see how the principles of learning apply not only to your psychology course, but also to your other courses as well.

Remember, effective study habits are developed not for their own sake, but to make learning more efficient. You don't go to college to study; rather you go to learn. A good college student is one who knows how to maximize opportunities to learn. You can be a good student if you can put the principles of learning to work for you. In this first section, we'll preview some of these concepts so you can begin to use them right now. We have put these principles in the form of six pieces of advice. If you take this advice, we believe you'll be pleased with the results.

SET GOALS AND MOTIVATE YOURSELF TO REACH THEM

We are all aware that we can learn some things "by accident" without really intending to do so. We may not set out to learn the numbers on the uniforms on the players of our favorite team, but after attending a number of games, we discover that we can identify the players without a scorecard. Our most efficient learning, however, takes place when we intend to learn, when we make a conscious effort to acquire new information. However, to learn more efficiently, we need to be motivated to learn. And we can motivate ourselves to learn through establishing goals.

Difficulties in learning in college tend to arise when students do not have clear goals, do not know why they are there, and do not have the motivation to do well. Therefore, it's a good idea to clarify in your own mind why you are in college—it will help you to make the commitment necessary to be a successful college student. Doing well in college is probably too general a goal. To be most effective, goals and motives should be as specific and concrete as possible. "Doing well" must, therefore, be broken down into manageable pieces. Familiarize yourself with your instructor's requirements and set reasonable goals. Set a schedule for your studying and learning and stick to it.

PRACTICE, PRACTICE, AND PRACTICE SOME MORE

Learning is defined as a relatively permanent change in behavior that occurs as the result of practice or experience. Practice is an integral part of the learning process. Acquiring new information or developing a new skill involves working with the material, studying it, and practicing. The more you practice the material, the longer it will be retained.

In addition, how you distribute your practice over time is extremely important. Experiments have shown that more learning occurs when material is studied in four 15-minute sections separated by breaks than when the same material is studied in a one-hour session, even though overall study time is the same each case. So take short breaks. Get up and stretch, walk to the window and look out, get a drink of water, and so on. But be careful; don't overdo it—15 minutes of study followed by a four-hour break is not going to work for you!

GET FEEDBACK ON YOUR LEARNING

A very important concept to efficient learning is referred to as knowledge of results, or feedback. A person who has little knowledge of how their learning is progressing is at a distinct disadvantage when compared to the person who is informed. Imagine learning how to shoot basketball foul shots while blindfolded. With little information about how you are doing or where the ball is really going, you can hardly expect to improve your shooting skill. The same argument holds true for any kind of learning.

Some of the feedback you receive in college comes when your instructor evaluates your work. Use your returned exams and papers as feedback. Review them. Note errors you have made. Decide how your study/learning habits need to be changed. You can also provide yourself with valuable feedback by becoming involved in discussions with other students, by constantly appraising and testing yourself, and by using the Study Guide that accompanies your textbook.

MAKE THE MATERIAL YOU LEARN MEANINGFUL TO YOU

If you have never studied French, you would certainly find it easier to memorize a list of twelve common English words than to memorize a list of twelve common French words. The reason is quite clear: you know what the English words mean, you associate them with other things; you can imagine some use of them. The French words, on the other hand, strike you as nonsense. You cannot relate to them in a meaningful way.

This example can be generalized about many other areas. The learning of any information is made easier to the extent that the information can be made meaningful, personal, or useful. To a large degree, this implies fitting the new information in with your past experience and future plans. The Study Questions in your Study Guide make you think about concepts and relate them to familiar situations. They help you learn how to relate psychological concepts to everyday life.

GIVE YOURSELF REWARDS FOR LEARNING

One of the major foundations of the psychology of learning is the Law of Effect. This law holds that behavior will be repeated (that is, learned) or will be dropped (that is, forgotten) depending on the effect that behavior has on the individual. Quite simply, what the law says is that we tend to continue with those activities that make us feel good and tend not to continue with those that provide no satisfaction. This observation, or law, can be applied in many situations.

We all know the satisfaction that comes when our goals are attained. As with anything in life, that great exhilarating feeling of doing well on a quiz, term paper, or laboratory report will do more to insure your doing well again than anything else. Many rewards will also come from instructors, friends, and members of your family like praise and tokens for a job well done. These rewards provide reinforcement for your behavior from others you care about.

However, you can't always depend on rewards from others to maintain your studying. You should develop the habit of providing meaningful rewards for yourself for work well done. Study hard for 50 minutes. Then, reward yourself for putting in the effort. Get something to eat or drink. Watch television. Do something to make yourself feel good—to reward yourself for a job well done. It is likely you will be surprised at how something so simple could have such a significant impact on your behavior.

WORK TO IMPROVE YOUR PERFORMANCE

We must now make a distinction between two related processes. Learning is a process that takes place inside an individual. We cannot see learning take place. We cannot plot its course. We cannot directly observe knowledge increasing. What we must do is infer that learning has taken place by measuring the individual performance. You may think because your little nephew can play a tune on the piano, that he has learned to play. But if he can not (for whatever reason) demonstrate his new skill to you, how are you to know whether he has learned anything? In order to demonstrate that learning has taken place, he must perform. Much the same situation exists in the college classroom.

You may have learned a great deal about a subject, but if you cannot demonstrate what you have learned, as on an examination, why should anyone assume that learning has taken place? Put rather simply, learning involves acquiring new information; performance involves retrieving that information when it is needed. And justifiably or not, it is your performance that is evaluated. Your performance, not your learning, earns your grades in the classroom, or your raise or promotion in the workplace.

The experience of any college course involves two phases of information processing. In the first phase, information must be acquired or learned, which involves practice. In the second phase, learned information must be retrieved from memory, a process which also takes practice. It is this latter kind of practice that too many students neglect. Practice your performance by self-testing before your instructor tests your performance on an exam. The many items on the Practice Tests in your Study Guide perform this function very well. Take them as you would a real exam. Then find the correct answers in the book; this will help you determine whether you are on the right track.

In the sections that follow we will elaborate on these general principles by giving you specific advice on how to get more out of class, how to use your textbook more effectively, and how to prepare better for examinations.

LEARNING IN THE CLASSROOM

"But I never missed a class!" is the claim teachers often hear from students who have not done well on an exam, and who have not yet learned the difference between simply attending a class and taking an active part in class. The difference has a great effect on how well students learn. Just going to class, although a step in the right direction, seldom does anyone very much good.

It is important that you go to class with some expectations about what is going to take place there. No two classroom experiences in college are going to be exactly the same. Instructors will handle their classrooms according to their own individual designs and desires. Even so, classes tend to have more in common than you might expect. In this section we will outline some of the common denominators of classroom instruction and point out some steps you can take to maximize the benefits derived from going to class. Try to put the following advice into practice; you'll be pleasantly surprised.

PREPARE FOR CLASS

It is extremely important to be prepared for class. It is always easier to listen and understand information you are somewhat familiar with than it is to listen and understand totally unfamiliar information. To be sure few lectures and class activities are designed to be about something you knew before you took the class. The material will have to be something new; that is what you are paying for. But if you carefully plan and prepare, lectures or class discussions will not sound alien to you.

Once the term is underway, preparing for class will become relatively easy. You will have had time to "feel out" your instructor. You will find that some instructors lecture from the book, which means that they will spend most of the class time reviewing and expanding on the material found in your textbook. If topics are covered in order, then preparing for class largely amounts to keeping ahead of your instructor in the book so that you know before hand what will be happening. Even those instructors who do not lecture from the book may lecture on materials related to the assigned text (or to another available text) so that you should be able to anticipate a good deal of the class activities for any given day. Instructors who use class discussion expect you to listen to what is going on and to make contributions. Your task here is essentially the same as for lectures—be ready.

Remember, for any class, and for any instructor, the important thing is to avoid going to class unprepared. At least you should have reviewed recent lecture notes and previewed the textbook so that you are familiar with most of the vocabulary words that your instructor will use. The content of introductory psychology courses is largely devoted to learning new vocabulary. If you are familiar with terms before going to class, your listening for new ideas and concepts will be easier because you will not have to think about new words. You will have a chance to think, organize what is being said, and summarize your thoughts in coherent notes.

Most good listening is a matter of attitude. To be an effective listener and user of information, you must be in the proper frame of mind. As you enter the classroom and take your seat, you have to consciously rid your mind of all the trivial activities of the day. You cannot listen well to a lecture if you are thinking about last night's date and this afternoon's lunch. You can't contribute to a discussion if all you want to talk about is last weekend's game. You must be thinking about psychology. Get your mind warmed up. What's the instructor going to talk about? What contributions will you be expected to make? How will it fit with material you already know? How can you relate this to your own experience?

The importance of preparing adequately for discussion/recitation classes and seminars should be especially apparent to you. You should be prepared not only to listen intelligently, but also to participate and carry your weight in the discussions. Having assignments completed is a necessity for participation. It is bad enough not knowing what your instructor is talking about; however, not understanding a discussion among your classmates is a frustrating and potentially embarrassing experience. When you find yourself surprised at what is being said in class, you have not prepared correctly.

DEVELOP YOUR LISTENING SKILLS

Listening is essentially an active process in which you relate what is being said to what you have already stored in your memory.. It is a process of taking in new information, organizing it, and storing it in such a way that it can be used at some later time. Given the large amount of information in the classroom, this active process will require considerable concentration on your part.

We do not often think of it as such, but listening is a skill, a skill that can be developed just like typing, bicycle riding, or reading. Proficiency in listening can be increased through practice. Listening in class for new information is different from listening in casual conversation or listening to a hard-rock radio station. This is because a larger portion of the information will involve new or technical vocabulary terms, and you will be expected to recall the information (on examinations) at some later time. Every time you listen in class you are practicing a very basic skill.

TAKE USEFUL NOTES

Class attendance and careful listening are important in lecture classes because lectures are presented to you only once. You will, therefore, need some written record of the information presented orally in class to study and review later. You will need a record of this information to integrate with material found in your textbook and outside readings. Good lecture notes written in your own words are as valuable as a summarized and organized compilation of classroom information.

Principle 1: Select and Organize the Material Presented to You

It will soon become apparent to you, if it is not already, that there is no way you can write everything your instructor says in class. This can be an advantage. Notetaking should be an active process where you select and organize the material you write down. Although it is generally better to take too many notes than to take too few, you must be an active listener who participates in class—not just a mechanical writer.

Good notetaking can be enhanced by good preparation. Get ready for class. Know what to expect. Familiarize yourself with vocabulary terms from the textbook. Your class notes will be the tangible product of good listening habits.

The notes will be your notes. Put them in a form that you can use. Except for technical terms and new vocabulary use your own words. Relate what your instructor is saying to your own experiences. In this way, your notes will become more meaningful to you when you review them later. Copying information is not learning it.

In the course of taking notes, you should develop some shortcuts, some alternatives to writing everything out in longhand. The key here, once again is flexibility. Feel free to abbreviate. But abbreviate only if you will be able to understand your own symbols when you go back to your notes for study at some later time. Illegible or incoherent notes are worse than useless: you have wasted valuable listening time taking them.

You should also be aware that there will be times when it is best not to take notes at all. Participating in a classroom discussion or asking questions may provide you with the sort of information you will remember best. The reason for this involves your being an active participant in the proceedings as opposed to a passive notetaker sitting on the sideline. Once again, one of the best ways to learn new material is to get involved, work with it, and make it personal.

Principle 2: Edit and Review Your Notes

When the class is over and the instructor has left the room, only part of your work is done. During the class period you have been listening, selecting, organizing, participating, thinking and writing. Now you must go back over your written record of the class, edit, and review your notes. This should be accomplished in three stages.

Stage 1 Immediately after class, while the material is still fresh in your mind, review your notes fill in gaps, underline for emphasis, note unclear sections that will require further work, and generally prepare the notes for further use. You should use your margins to add information from the lecture that you simply did not have the time to record. By rereading your notes immediately after class, you should be able to spot sources of possible difficulty; that is places in your notes that are hard to understand. If your notes are hard to understand right after you have written them, they will probably be impossible to interpret later.

Stage 2 Several times a week as part of your study for each course, continue the editing process. Use your textbook, other notes, outside readings, or consult with your instructor and other students to check spellings, complete lists, note relationships with other lectures, and clarify sections that are not readily understandable. The outline which appears in Part 6 of this book should provide you with a structure to do this. Use them to put your notes together in a meaningful whole.

Because you will be participating in classroom discussion, and what is said will usually be fragmented, stages one and two are particularly important for discussion, recitation, and seminar classes. As you continue to work with your notes and other sources, you will build an integrated set of study resources. If this is done, you are ready to begin reviewing several days before each exam. Final preparation for the exam is done in an orderly and calm fashion. You are not frantically searching and cramming, thus you avoid a primary reason for test anxiety.

Stage 3 A very important stage in reviewing your notes should occur following each examination in a course. After taking an exam, you should go back and critically evaluate your notebook. To what extent did your notes help? How might they be improved? Did you write too much? Too little? Was the format the best you could have used? Did you spend too much or too little time on your notes?

Always remember, good notes can be the difference between success and failure in class. Don't depend on other students' notes; they were written for someone else and may not make much sense to you. At any rate, they will be less useful to you because good notes are not separable from all the other things a good student does to learn class material.

IMPORTANCE OF TEXTBOOK STUDY

There is more information about psychology in your textbook than you could ever get in class. Since this is the case, learning how to get information from your textbook is one of the most important lessons you can learn in college. This is not to de-emphasize the role of your instructor or lessen the value of attendance. In many cases instructors will update textbook material, will interject personal experience and points of view, and will emphasize what they feel are the most important sections of assigned readings. Your instructor, having studied widely in psychology, is aware of more points of view than those presented in your text and is available to answer questions and discuss ideas that result from your textbook study.

Even after you graduate from college, you will find textbook study skills useful in your daily life. Much of the information you will need can be gained through reading. Whether you are reading a cookbook, an operator's manual for a piece of equipment, a business report, or a weekly news magazine, the textbook study skills you develop and practice in college can be applied. Use the following techniques to make your textbook study more efficient and productive.

READ YOUR TEXTBOOK DIFFERENTLY FROM OTHER BOOKS

Perhaps the most significant insight about textbook study is the realization that it is quite different from casual reading. "Reading the chapter" or "moving your eyes over the page" is not studying.

Studying is an active process. It is the active accumulation of information. Studying a text involves a great deal more concentration and mental effort than reading fiction for pleasure. You should look for major ideas and evidence to support those ideas. What is the author trying to say? How are the conclusions supported? You should look for ways to relate what you are reading to your previous experience. How does the information pertain to what you have read elsewhere, to what was said in lecture, or to your own personal experience? How can you make the information in the text relevant and meaningful?

There are times while studying when you should look up from the book, pause and consider what you have read. You should be able to quickly summarize in your own words the paragraphs you have just read. Stop and think about the significance of the material you have just read. Just getting through a given number of pages or chapters in an allotted amount of time is not studying. Speed may be fine, but speed without comprehension is a waste of time.

Works of fiction are rarely accompanied by extensive illustrations. Perhaps this accounts for why pictures, drawings, figures, graphs, and tables are often overlooked in textbook study. Ignoring textbook illustrations is a mistake, since these drawings, figures, and graphs are constructed with great care and are included in the text to provide a pictorial summary. Very often a passage in a textbook cannot be understood without referring to accompanying illustrations. Imagine trying to understand the structure of the nervous system without having the illustrations, too. Don't be surprised if you have to refer back and forth between the written text and the illustrations a number of times before you can fully understand either. This is what study is: an active search for understanding.

To prepare for an examination through effective textbook study, you should study your assignment at least once from your instructor's point of view. That is, imagine that it is your job to write an examination covering the material you are studying. What sorts of questions would you ask? And, more importantly, could you provide adequate answers? This is one of the most effective techniques for self-evaluation.

Effective textbook study is a skill that can be learned by anyone. It it will not be learned automatically. It takes hard work and practice to develop textbook study skills. The rewards for your work, however, should be almost immediate. You should be able to feel the difference in your reading efficiency. Your test grades should improve and your understanding should increase.

PREPARE FOR TEXTBOOK STUDY

Because textbook study is so important, it is an activity that you should think about before beginning. Develop some expectations about the material that you are going to read by reading through the chapter summary and by glancing at the headings, subtitles, and illustrations. From this preview, you should be able to assess the content of the chapter. How important does the material appear to be? How does it compare with material read elsewhere? Does the assigned reading contain considerable detail, perhaps requiring more study time than you had originally planned? How much do you plan to cover in your allotted time? Very basically, you should begin your textbook study by surveying the assignment and developing a feeling for what you are going to read.

Before you actually begin studying your text, you should have a series of questions in mind. Preview the TOPIC Summaries and headings and pay particular attention to the Learning Objectives for each TOPIC that appears in the Study Guide, which was written to help you study your textbook. In addition to providing you with hints about what the chapter will cover in detail, they often give rise to a number of questions. Your questions may be very simple ones. For example, if a TOPIC heading makes no sense to you at all, your questions may be "What in the world is that all about?" Often, however, the summary, headings, italicized terms, or illustrations will remind you of points raised in class, covered in some other reading, or related to your own experience. A very basic question in this case may be, "What are the relationships between what I know about this and what the textbook says?" The more you know about any TOPIC covered in the text, the more detailed your questions. Developing a set of questions about the material you are going to read and thinking about these questions before you begin your reading will give you a framework for evaluating and understanding the assignment.

MAKE TEXTBOOK STUDY AN ACTIVE PROCESS

When we say textbook study is an active process, we mean that it is a mental activity. You must be mentally active and alert while studying so that you can search, question, and think. The textbook and its accompanying Study Guide are designed to facilitate this active process. Use the features built into them; they are based on proven principles from the psychology of learning.

A simple and effective way to make textbook study an active process is to turn chapter and unit headings into questions. For example, by using the heading "Make Textbook Study an Active Process," questions can be formulated. What is active textbook study? What are the individual elements that make textbook study active? Another example in your text includes material on the autonomic nervous system. Here the questions become: What is the autonomic nervous system? What does "autonomic" mean? How does this system function? What parts make up this system? How is it related to other systems studied? You would typically begin this process as you prepare for textbook study. The Study Questions in the Study Guide that accompanies your textbook should help you with this process. They identify key issues by relating psychological concepts to your experience.

As you proceed and become more familiar with the subject matter, your questions will become more specific. This process becomes enhanced when you distribute your allotted study time over days and weeks. You begin moving from the general to the specific, building understanding. This process cannot take place in a short time. For this reason, cramming seldom works because you have to deal with the general and specific all at once, often resulting in confusion rather than understanding.

One of the most helpful study aids you can devise for yourself is an accurate vocabulary list. This can be two types. You should certainly make a practice of looking up the meanings of all words that you don't understand. Making a list of these and practicing their use will add to your personal working vocabulary. In addition, you might find it helpful to make a listing of important or technical terms, their meanings, and/or significance for inclusion in your notebook. If you do not know the meaning of the words used to explain an important concept you are certainly going to have difficulty understanding the concept itself. Pay attention to the terms defined in the margin of your textbook and use the Glossary at the back of your textbook—both are valuable resources for understanding the terminology of psychology. The psychology vocabulary exercises in your Study Guide are designed to help you to learn the over 500 terms contained in your textbook. Use them.

Underlining in textbooks is a common practice. Unfortunately, this practice is often misused. The purpose of underlining is to highlight or emphasize a particular passage of the text so that the essential points of a chapter can be quickly reviewed by simply rereading the underlined passages. The mistake that many students make is to underline too much. When 80 percent of a page is underlined for emphasis, the remaining 20 percent usually appears more striking. Remember that you are underlining to highlight major areas so that you can review your textbook without having to read it all again. Underlining is a summarizing process and should not be used indiscriminately.

You can increase the value of your textbook for studying by using the margins of the pages for your own personal notation. Make your text a storehouse of references. Cross reference textbook material with information in your notebook by jotting down in the margin the date of the lecture covering the same material that is found on the particular page of the book. Similarly, note any other sources of related information you are familiar with , such as library readings or laboratory manuals. Any questions that arise in your reading should also be noted in the margin. It's your book—use it; write in it. For library books, which are not your property, such notations cannot be made in the book. In this case, taking notes on the reading (in your notebook) will be the best method of preserving information.

Your textbook includes "Before You Go On Questions" throughout each topic. By thinking about these questions, you slow down your reading and give yourself time to learn better. This helps you to discover what you know and what you don't know about the reading assignment. The Study Guide contains practice test questions for each topic. They are designed to help you check your knowledge of textbook material. These questions provide a method of self-evaluation that is particularly useful when preparing for examinations. We next consider examinations—what students typically dread most about college.

EXAMINATIONS

Almost everyone associated with the college experience finds examinations distasteful. Graduates commonly list exam taking among their most unpleasant memories of college. Exams call for hard work and a lot of preparation, and they often generate a great deal of anxiety. Even instructors rarely find much enjoyment in trying to formulate and grade an honest, comprehensive test of student's learning. But no matter how "progressive," "modern," or "liberal" the college you attend, you can probably count on taking examinations. They have become a fact of educational life. It is our hope that by following the suggestions presented here, you can make taking examinations a useful, meaningful learning experience. Exams can be viewed in a positive light. They may provide you with new information or help you view information in new and different ways. Moreover, exams give students feedback about their progress.

PREPARING FOR EXAMINATIONS

Few occasions are quite as pleasant as the one you experience when you walk into class to take a big exam fully prepared, confident that you know the material and that you are going to do well. We also know from personal experience how absolutely miserable you feel when you face an exam unprepared, doomed before you begin, unable even to understand, much less answer the first question. The key lies in being fully prepared. Proper preparation for examinations helps to furnish the kind of positive reinforcement that education is supposed to provide. Preparing for exams is not an easy, automatic process; it involves scheduling your time, self-testing your progress, and continuous active reviewing.

Before we deal with how to prepare for examinations it is important to consider briefly how information is acquired and what "study" really means. Study is an active process, not significantly different from acquiring new information and new skills in daily life. Simply spending time with your books, your notes, and passively sitting in class is not learning. You learn things by listening to experts, watching others perform, reading, and practicing. All of these require active thought and application on your part.

If you want to learn how to tune your car's engine or how to sew, you will probably watch and ask questions of those who can already sew or tune engines. You will read about the task, even if what you read is just the owner's manual to your new car or sewing machine. Then you will practice, making some errors at first, but sooner or later you will acquire the skill and simultaneously develop a certain understanding of the principles of auto mechanics or sewing. This means that you have "passed the exam." As you continue to listen, read, and practice, you will be able to undertake more difficult or complex tasks and your understanding will deepen.

The very same processes are involved in acquiring academic skills and understanding. You have to take an active role in the process. You should listen carefully to your instructor, ask questions, and seek additional information from your textbook. You should try to relate the new information to what you already know. Once you understand the principles involved, you should be able to answer exam questions. In fact, you should be able to apply psychological information to a wide range of situations, but the only way to know if you can is by practicing. If you discover that you do not understand a concept, you will have to go back to your notes, books, or instructor for insight into the solution. Again, you will have to be actively involved. You will have to think about the information presented.

Rule 1: Prepare on a Daily Basis - Don't Cram

In almost every case, you will be notified of an upcoming examination well in advance. Often, scheduled exams are noted on the course outlines distributed on the first day of class. Most of your exams should then come as no surprise to you. We often hear students complain that they have two, or even three final exams scheduled for the same day, which they feel allows them only one day to study for each. Nothing could be more untrue. The students have had the whole term to prepare for each of the exams. What they fail to realize is that daily preparation is needed. They should have begun preparing (studying) for their examinations on the first day of class.

To be truthful, preparing daily is not an easy task. It is difficult to sit down today to study for an examination that won't take place for three more weeks. With so much time before the exam, it seems that there will be plenty of opportunities for studying later.

Daily preparation for examinations is exactly what was discussed earlier about gaining understanding, developing new skills, and forming new concepts. To prepare for exams, you do not have to do anything new. Preparing for and carefully listening in class is daily preparation, as well as taking good class notes and reviewing and editing them soon after class. A crucial step in preparing for exams is to make and adhere to a realistic schedule. If you study your textbook on a regular schedule, you will avoid the need for cramming. Using the library when necessary will also help you prepare. A more practical way of viewing these procedures is to consider them as ways of getting ready to do the best possible job of taking an examination. Doing all of these things throughout the term will enable you to sidestep the unpleasant effects of cramming: loss of sleep, anxiety, missed work, cancellation of social activities, and poorer grades.

Rule 2: Find Ways to Test Yourself

As examination day approaches, you will want some indication of how well your studying has been progressing. To be effective, the process of self-testing must begin well in advance of the examination date. If you wait until the night before and find you are having trouble, there is little time to study the areas you do not know well. There are many different techniques for evaluating your own achievement, all of which involve constructing, taking, and grading your own test on the assigned material. For example, if you think that you may have to identify the important structures of the eye, draw a picture of one, labeling all of the structures you can think of and then check your drawing with the one in your book. Did you leave out any parts? Did you put in any that don't belong? If know that your next exam will ask you for the definitions of all the new terms in a chapter, see if you can write out a definition for the terms in your own words and then simply check to see if you have made errors. Even for an essay exam you should test yourself on the factual information involved. It will be help to work out a few practice outlines without referring to your book or notes. Having the factual information in mind and thinking through several different answers to anticipated questions should make writing the essay itself relatively easy.

Self-testing means that you test yourself before your instructor does. The Practice Tests for each TOPIC in this study guide are a good way to get started. Use them to get a feel for what your instructor's examinations will be like. The practice test items in the study guide, were developed from the same material your instructor will be testing you on. Your instructor will likely phrase the questions differently and might emphasize some material more than other material, but your instructor will probably not ask you anything greatly different. If you find yourself struggling to come up with reasonable questions on your own, you certainly need more studying. Go back to your notes, textbook, study guide, the library, your instructor; study some more and try again until you can construct your own test—and pass it.

Rule 3: Build Learning by Reviewing

If you have maintained a schedule of daily preparation and have consistently evaluated your own performance, you should be able to approach the examination day with confidence. There is no way that everything you need to know for an exam can be assimilated on the night before. You cannot digest and understand large amounts of difficult material in a few hours. Attempting to do so will only result in confusion and in a poor performance on the exam. However, it is well worth your time to review the material to be covered. Review means " look at again." You should certainly review just before each examination. But a more helpful procedure is to review on a regular basis; that is, throughout the term. You should be constantly reviewing what you have learned. You should look back over material either on a weekly basis or at the completion of a meaningful unit, such as the assigned topic. Experimental evidence and common sense suggest that most forgetting takes place soon after learning. Frequent review, however can significantly improve retention over a period of time. By definition, review will not introduce new material to be learned, it will simply refresh your memory of familiar material.

A Final Word One final word about preparing for exams. When you take an examination, you are being asked to perform on the basis of what you have learned. Although the effects of anxiety on learning are often subtle, the effects of anxiety on performance are evident and well-known.

Your performance will be poor if you become overly anxious, upset, and uptight—even if you have learned the material reasonably well. Just realizing that anxiety may reduce your efficiency does little to reduce anxiety. Anxiety is one of those things that is very difficult to eliminate by sheer force of willpower. The most effective way to reduce anxiety is to deal with its cause. If you have conscientiously applied yourself to the job of preparing for an exam, you should have reduced, if not eliminated the most common cause of anxiety. If being overly nervous about taking exams becomes a source of concern for you, you should consider talking to someone in the counseling center or the psychology department who can help you overcome this problem

TYPES OF EXAMINATIONS

During your college years you will experience a wide variety of examinations. If you really know and understand the material to be examined, the type of test you are given should be of small consequence. Nonetheless, each different type of exam should be approached with a slightly different method of preparation. You should find out early in the term what type of exams you will be taking in your psychology course so that you can prepare properly from the outset.

As a rule of thumb, you will probably discover that in a large class the exam will be objective tests. In such tests, you indicate your answer by circling a number or a letter or by writing one or two words. These exams are objective because there is little doubt about the correctness of your answers. They are right, or they are wrong. The advantage of such tests is that they can be easily and quickly scored (often by machines), which makes their use in large classes virtually mandatory. Subject areas with a great deal of terminology, such as introductory psychology, are most often tested by objective examinations.

Subjective exams, where your answer will be interpreted and evaluated by a grader, seldom have just one correct answer to a question. Factors such as clarity of expression, logic of organization, and accuracy of factual information all play a part in determining your grade. With subjective examinations, you will be expected to organize, criticize, analyze, interpret, explain, and define. More writing is called for with subjective exams than with objective exams. Because of the time required to grade subjective examinations, you can expect a greater number of these exams in small classes. A few examples of objective and subjective exams are described below.

Objective Examinations

Obtaining a complete understanding of the material to be tested is surely the best way to prepare for any examination. However, if you know that you will be given an objective exam, the questions that you ask yourself while studying your notes and your text should be the same type that you might expect to find on the exam. Try actively to anticipate your instructor's questions. Most of the questions on objective exams are geared toward facts. A good examiner, however, can ask about all sorts of things in an objective way. Objective test items are generally of the following varieties.

True/False A true/false test is simply a listing of statements that you must judge as being either true or false. Occasionally, you will have a space to justify your answer. True/false items should generally be considered at face value. That is, do not try to over-interpret a statement; do not read into an item more than what is there. For example, the statement "The sun rises in the east" should probably be considered true, even if you understand that the sun does not rise but rather the earth's rotation makes the sun appear to rise. You should also be on the lookout for some key words in true/false tests. In general, words like "only," "never," and "always" are clues that the statement is probably a false one. Unless you know you will be penalized for incorrect responses, never leave an item unanswered. If all else fails, guess. A rule of thumb, developed through the experience of taking and constructing true/false examinations, is that unusually long statements are more often than not true, while short statements tend to be false ones. (The rationale here is that instructors don't like to waste time writing a long untrue statement about their subject matter.)

Multiple Choice Multiple choice items present the examinee with a number of alternative ways of completing the statement. One of the alternatives will result in a correct statement. Multiple choice questions appear easier than true/false questions because the correct answer is included among the alternatives and may be discovered by the process of eliminating the incorrect choices. On the other hand, multiple choice items are more difficult than true/false items because there are more ways to make an error.

There are several "tricks" to taking multiple choice tests. We'll consider five. First, even if you're not really sure which of the choices provides the best answer you can usually narrow your choice to two or three alternatives. If all else fails, you should then guess; and unless you remember something that suggests you have guessed incorrectly, you are generally best off sticking with your first guess. Second, if you have absolutely no other information to go on, experience suggests that the longest alternative in a multiple choice item is often the correct one. Third, avoid the two common mistakes students make in taking multiple choice exams. These are reading too much into the question (the same as with true/false exams) and choosing the first alternative that seems reasonable without even reading the other choices. Your job will be to indicate the best alternative, something you cannot do without reading all of them. Fourth, as is true with all objective tests, you are well advised to skip over those items you cannot answer at first reading. You may well find that the answer to an item is revealed to you in a question appearing later in the test. Finally, before handing in your paper, check to be sure that you have supplied an answer to every question.

Completion A completion, or "fill-in-the-blank," exam item is somewhat similar to a multiple choice item except that you must provide the word or phrase that best completes a statement. There is little substitute here for knowing the correct answer. Be sure to put something reasonable in each blank and check to see that the answer you provide is grammatically correct; that is, it results in a complete sentence. If you can think of nothing at all to put in a blank, you might be better off skipping the item. Inserting a word or phrase that is utterly ridiculous will only serve to flaunt your ignorance of that item.

Matching Matching questions may take on a number of forms, but all questions of this type call for you to put complementary items together. You are to associate items on one list with items on another list. Material found in matching questions almost always involves specific factual material, such as matching names with dates, events with dates or names, words with definitions, and so forth. It is particularly important with this type of exam to read and understand the directions. For example, you will need to know if any of the alternatives can be used more than once. Again, be sure to match all the items unless there is a penalty for guessing incorrectly.

Subjective Examinations

As stated above, subjective exams will involve interpretation and evaluation by a grader. These exams are subjective because there is not just one correct answer to each question. A grader will have to interpret and evaluate your response by the organization of information, the clarity of expression, and the accuracy of the facts you supply.

Essay This is a general term used to describe tests calling for such things as explanation, analysis, criticism, comparison, outline, enumeration, description, and summarization. Notice the differences among these words- each one calls for a distinct approach to the question. For example, explaining something is not the same thing as outlining or describing it. A common error in essay exams is the failure to answer the question in the manner specified. A complete description of a phenomenon in response to a question calling for criticism of that phenomenon will be considered as a wrong answer. If you are not already aware of the subtle differences among the above mentioned key words, it would be worth the time to check and learn the definitions of each.

You might be lucky on a multiple choice test and guess the correct alternative for an item or two. Luck has little to do with essay exams. The only way to do well is to be prepared, and the best way to prepare is obviously to anticipate the exam by studying the material to be covered so that you can describe it, evaluate it, criticize it, or analyze it. If you have completely thought through all of the material in these terms, you should be able to handle any question that appears on the exam. Regardless of the form your answer takes, the quality of your response will be in a large part determined by your understanding of the information. You can hardly evaluate a phenomenon when you do not know the facts involved. Most graders have had enough experience to spot an answer filled with many words and few facts. Padding an answer with excess verbiage is more likely to detract from your grade than add to it.

The first thing to do when you get your test paper is to read it carefully. Pay particular attention to the instructions. You may find that you need only answer a percentage of the questions instead of every one. You will seldom be required to answer the questions in the order in which they are asked, so choose what you consider to be an easy item to begin with. Avoid the very common mistake of writing your answer without thinking about it first. If you have time, it would be helpful to sketch a brief outline of your answer before you attempt to write it out. When you have completed your paper, take a minute to read through what you have written. You may think of new information to add or find an error to correct.

Short Answer   A short answer test is a variety of the common essay exam. The questions are generally more specific and therefore call for shorter, more concise answers. If a question can be answered in a short paragraph of four or five sentences, it would qualify as a short answer question. Preparing for and taking a short answer test is essentially the same as preparing for and taking an essay exam: anticipate questions, read all the questions and directions, think before you write, and review your answers before you hand in your paper.

Take Home   You may encounter the sort of examination where you will be given a series of questions or problems to complete at home, using whatever resources you can find to help you answer the question. These take-home exams are qualitatively different from the usual in-class subjective exams. Because there is little time constraint, answers will generally be longer. Because you will have your books to use, a higher degree of precision and accuracy will be expected in your answers. The examiner is looking for a unique, personalized response to a question that does not have a specific solution. Copying or paraphrasing from your books or notes will not be sufficient. You will have to demonstrate that you understand the material that you find in these sources. Preparation should be the same as for other subjective examinations, with the added dimension that you must be familiar enough with the resources at your disposal that you can quickly find whatever information you don't know.

Open Book   These exams are given in class, but you have the opportunity to bring some resource material with you to consult during the exam. Too often students get the impression that because they can bring their books to the exam that they don't have to prepare for the test. Nothing can be further from the truth. Open-book exams are usually constructed so that you will have little time to spend looking through your book. Preparation for this exam is virtually the same as for other essay exams. In addition, you must be familiar enough with your book so that your information can be rapidly retrieved. The less time you have to spend referring to your book, the better off you-will be. Your answers to an open-book exam should be different from simple essay exam answers. You cannot expect to gain much credit for simply restating the facts found in your book. You must analyze, interpret, and organize these facts, perhaps with examples, in ways that are not spelled out in your text. The factual information you present will have to be complete and precise.

AFTER THE EXAMINATION

Independent of the grade you earn, you should consider every examination as a potential learning experience. This may be difficult to do. A natural reaction to a low grade on an exam is to throw it away and forget it. But a low grade implies that you haven't adequately learned the material. The first thing to do is to note which questions you have missed and do whatever is necessary to discover the correct answer. You may "correct yourself" by simply referring to your notes or your textbook. If, after trying on your own, you still do not understand your error, see your instructor. Before you put an exam away, be sure that if you were given the very same exam again that you would be able to answer correctly every question. Failure to review each exam may lead to future errors because some questions on subsequent exams may presuppose your understanding of material on which you were previously tested.

You should also use your examinations to help you evaluate your study habits. If you consistently do well on exams for your psychology course, you should continue to do whatever you are doing, or you may even want to reduce the time spent on psychology to devote more time to another course. (But, of course, it can be dangerous to mess with success.) If you are not achieving the grades you want on your exams, you should certainly change the way you are studying. The first and the simplest thing you should do is to provide yourself with more time to study and to schedule that time accordingly. You will need to evaluate each and every aspect of your study habits. Perhaps you will discover that you have been spending too much time studying your text and not enough time studying your notes or vice versa. Perhaps you should develop a different style of notetaking. There are any number of changes which you can make in the ways you study. Failing to change your study habits when you are not doing well in a course is the worst mistake you can make.

A FINAL WORD ABOUT SITTING DOWN TO STUDY PSYCHOLOGY

The best place to study is the place that has the fewest distractions for you. We can outline, in general, what some of these distractions might be, but it is your job to determine which ones interfere with your study.

Effective study involves concentration. Anything that interferes with your concentration is a distraction. There are two kinds of distractions. The first is mental. By this we mean that your mental attention must be focused only on the task at hand. You must put out of your mind all irrelevant thoughts and daydreams. You can't effectively study psychology while you are thinking about a poor grade on an English theme. If your mind drifts to a conversation you overhear in the hall, you might be better off joining the conversation than straining to hear what is being said, thereby distracting yourself from your study. If during a study period you find your mind wandering, this is an indication that it is time to take a break so that you can then return to study fresh and free from mental distraction

A second type of distraction is physical. In most instances, physical distractions are easier to avoid than mental distractions. It is best to find a quiet environment to study. Experience has shown that learning is diminished when background noise increases. Maybe you "got by" in high school studying by the sound of your stereo or radio, but the odds are that music playing in the background will interfere with the learning of more difficult material encountered in college. It is a wise practice to face your desk to the wall rather than to the window. If you study at home, see to it that other members of your family understand that you need to be left alone. The same goes for roommates.

Some of the most common distractions are social activities that take you away from your studies during scheduled study periods. It takes willpower to turn down invitations to go to the movies or to join a card game in the lounge. These activities are fine when they are done during your free time. When you are distracted from study time by extracurricular activities you find yourself losing free time, losing sleep, cramming, and performing poorly.

What was said above was basically common sense. To make it possible for you to study, it should be obvious that you need to find yourself a comfortable, quiet place where you can concentrate. Although it is true that you should develop the habit of studying any place, you should establish a home base where most of your work will be done. This is generally in your room, but it can be in some other location. Wherever it might be, you will want your home base to be well equipped. Once you begin to study, you shouldn't have to get up and search for things you need for studying. If possible, use a desk that can be reserved just for your studying. A desk is designed for studying, as opposed to the kitchen table, which is often used for other purposes. Your desk has a place to keep a sufficient supply of paper, pencils, erasers, pens, and anything else you will need. It is very easy to waste a whole hour hunting for a ruler that should have been in your desk.

Your home base should serve as your own private library. All of your textbooks and assigned reading books should be kept here, as should reference books such as a good dictionary, a thesaurus, and those books you have checked out of the library. Depending on the courses you are taking, you may find it necessary to purchase some specialized supplies. As was noted above, your term schedule should be clearly in view in your home base. You should get into the habit of using your study area only for studying. Try to avoid using your study environment for paying bills, writing letters, or talking with friends. By so doing, you will immediately establish the proper frame of mind upon entering your home base, thereby fully utilizing the hours you spend there.

As you learn more about psychology you will see that this advice is based on sound psychological theory and research. If you put what you've read here into practice, we believe the results will be positive for you.

CHAPTER 1—THE NATURE OF PSYCHOLOGY
TOPIC 1A—TOWARD A DEFINITION

LEARNING OBJECTIVES TOPIC 1A

Psychology has a broad appeal because it is relevant and dynamic. It is defined as the scientific study of behavior and mental processes. Students should be able to:
1. Know which two points must be demonstrated in order to claim that psychology is a science.
2. Describe the subject matter of psychology and the use of operational definitions.
3. Discuss how Descartes, Locke, Fechner, Darwin, and von Helmholtz influenced psychology.
4. Describe when and where psychology began and who should be credited with its origin.
5. Describe behaviorism and psychoanalysis as approaches to psychology.
6. Describe the two approaches that have challenged behaviorism, humanism and gestalt psychology.
7. Discuss the ways in which Sir Francis Galton, and Alfred Binet, shaped psychology in its early history.
8. Describe the different areas of psychology, what sort of work a psychologist in each area would do, and how employment patterns of psychologists have changed over the past twenty years.
9. Discuss the interaction of nature and nurture.
10. Define phenomenology.
11. Discuss the claim that psychology is one of the most applied sciences.

LEARNING TOPIC 1A VOCABULARY

On your own paper, write the definition for each of the following key terms. Your learning will be facilitated by writing the definition in your own words rather than copying the exact definition from your text.

PSYCHOLOGY	SCIENCE
SCIENTIFIC METHODS	HYPOTHESIS
BEHAVIOR	PUBLICLY VERIFIABLE
MENTAL PROCESSES	COGNITIONS
AFFECT	OPERATIONAL DEFINITION
INTERACTIVE DUALISM	BRITISH EMPIRICISTS
INTROSPECTION	FUNCTIONALISM
BEHAVIORISM	PSYCHOANALYSIS
HUMANISTIC APPROACH	GESTALT
PHENOMENOLOGY	

MATCHING

Match the following key terms from your textbook with the appropriate definition.

_____ 1. psychology   _____ 2. publicly verifiable

_____ 3. science   _____ 4.. mental processes

_____ 5. scientific methods   _____ 6. cognitions

_____ 7. hypothesis   _____ 8. affect

_____ 9. behavior   _____ 10. operational definition

_____ 11. interactive dualism   _____ 12. psychoanalysis

_____ 13. British Empiricists   _____ 14. humanistic psychology

_____ 15. introspection   _____ 16. gestalt

_____ 17. functionalism   _____ 18. phenomenology

_____ 19. behaviorism

a. Descartes' position that a separate body and mind influence each other and are thus knowable.
b. The scientific study of behavior and mental processes.
c. An approach to psychology emphasizing the person or self as a central matter of concern.
d. What an organism does; an action of an organism that can be measured.
e. A technique in which one examines one's own mental experiences and reports them in the most fundamental, basic way.
f. The feelings of mood that accompany an emotional reaction.
g. A tentative proposition or explanation that can be tested or rejected.
h. The study of events as they are experienced by the individual; that experience is reality.
i. Internal activities of consciousness, including cognitions and affect.
j. An organized body of knowledge gained through application of scientific methods.
k. Philosophers who claimed that the contents of the mind come from experience.
l. The agreement of observers that an event did or did not take place.
m. Whole, totality, configuration; where the whole is seen as more than the sum of its parts.
n. Systematic procedures of discovery that include observation, description, control and replication.
o. An approach to psychology emphasizing the study of the mind and consciousness as they help the organism adapt to the environment.
p. The mental processes of knowing, perceiving, thinking, remembering, and the like.
q. A Freudian approach to psychology emphasizing the influence of the unconscious and instincts.
r. An approach to psychology emphasizing the overt, observable, measurable behavior of organisms.
s. A definition of a concept given in terms of the methods used to measure that concept.

TRUE-FALSE PRACTICE TEST 1A

_____ 1. Psychology has its formal roots in the fields of philosophy and history.

_____ 2. One might say that the followers of Locke and the followers of Descartes would differ significantly in the emphasis placed on the role that experience plays in our thinking.

_____ 3. In the mid 1800s, both physicists and physiologists made significant contributions to the field of psychology.

_____ 4. Child psychology, educational psychology, and industrial psychology all have a common origin in structuralism.

_____ 5. Though popular in the early years of psychology, both structuralism and behaviorism are virtually nonexistent in the current study of psychology.

_____ 6. A real strength of Sigmund Freud was his research ability as a laboratory scientist.

_____ 7. Carl Rogers and Abraham Maslow founded the humanistic approach to psychology.

_____ 8. Humanism focuses on the self, whereas behaviorism focuses on the unconscious.

_____ 9. The gestalt psychologists focused their study on perception.

_____ 10. Alfred Binet advanced the work on psychological testing begun by Sir Francis Galton.

_____ 11. The Stanford-Binet Intelligence Test is named for the two men who developed it.

_____ 12. An industrial psychologist is likely to be involved as a consultant to an advertising company.

_____ 13. Questions in psychology which concern nature or nurture are not seen as either or questions because most psychologists agree that nature plays the dominant role in influencing human behavior.

_____ 14. The current thinking among most psychologists is that human behavior represents an interaction between nature and nurture.

_____ 15. The study of events as they are experienced by the individual is referred to as phenomenology.

FILL-IN PRACTICE TEST 1A

1. The founder of British Empiricism is _____ _____.

2. Descartes suggested that the mind and the body influence each other. This position became known as _____ _____.

3. Psychology has its roots in two other disciplines, _____ and _____.

4. One's feelings, mood, or emotional state are referred to as _____.

5. One's perceptions, thoughts, and memories are referred to as _____.

6. Psychologists study mental processes and _____.

7. _____ definitions define concepts in terms of the procedures used to measure them.

8. _____ was a German physicist who used his science to study the psychological process of sensation.

9. The man we would most likely credit as being the first psychologist is _____ _____.

10. _____ _____ was the psychologist who shifted the focus from the structure of the mind to the function of the mind.

11. The psychologist who was responsible for psychology shifting from the study of the mind to the study of behavior was _____ _____.

12. Many psychologists believe that the dominant approach to psychology in existence today is _____.

13. Freud founded an approach to psychology that became known as _____.

14. The best meaning for the word "gestalt" is _____.

15. The founder of psychological testing was _____.

MULTIPLE CHOICE PRACTICE TEST 1 TOPIC 1A

1. Psychologists believe that the best explanations of behavior can be derived from
   a. common sense
   b. great works of art
   c. scientific methods
   d. historical perspective

2. Psychology is considered to be a science because
   a. it does not rely on common sense
   b. scientific methods are used in research
   c. there is no body of organized information
   d. laws have been developed to explain behavior

3. A tentative explanation of some phenomenon that can be tested and then either supported or rejected is a/an
   a. hypothesis
   b. theory
   c. rule of common sense
   d. law of nature

4. A student complains to his teacher that he really knows the subject matter of psychology, even though he has failed the first exam. The teacher is interested in the exam performance because it represents behavior that is
   a. publicly verifiable
   b. indicative of common sense
   c. hypothetical
   d. related to mental processes

5. Cognition is to _____ as affect is to _____.
   a. belief; thought
   b. mood; belief
   c. feelings; perception
   d. thinking; feeling

6. The problem of defining "intelligence" in order to compare students who have attended a preschool program and those who have not is a problem that could be solved by
   a. common sense
   b. formulating a good scientific hypothesis
   c. an operational definition
   d. scientific methods

7. The beginning of psychology is generally linked to the work of
   a. Sigmund Freud
   b. John Locke
   c. William James
   d. Wilhelm Wundt

8. The study of animals was introduced to psychology by the
   a. functionalists
   b. British Empiricists
   c. structuralists
   d. followers of Charles Darwin

9. The psychologist who was responsible for psychology shifting from the study of the mind to the study of behavior was
   a. William James
   b. John Watson
   c. Wilhelm Wundt
   d. Edward Titchener

10. The psychological approach that focuses on the individual and suggests that the self should be the central concern of psychology is
    a. functionalism
    b. behaviorism
    c. humanism
    d. psychoanalysis

11. Psychoanalysis is to _____ as humanism is to _____.
    a. unconscious; self
    b. thought; feeling
    c. mind; behavior
    d. experience; environment

12. Which of the following is NOT a correct match?
    a. humanism — self
    b. psychoanalysis — animals
    c. behaviorism — environment
    d. gestalt — perception

13. Which of the following approaches in psychology would most likely be associated with this statement, "the whole is more than the sum of its parts?"
    a. humanism
    b. psychoanalysis
    c. gestalt
    d. structuralism

14. The telephone company has decided to make its offices "smoke-free" environments and wants a psychologist to teach smoking cessation classes for its employees. The type of psychologist most likely to do this job is a/an
    a. developmental psychologist
    b. educational psychologist
    c. clinical psychologist
    d. counseling psychologist

15. Jane and John are having marital difficulties. They are most likely to seek help from a/an
    a. health psychologist
    b. clinical psychologist
    c. counseling psychologist
    d. social psychologist

MULTIPLE CHOICE PRACTICE TEST 2 TOPIC 1A

1. Which of the following does NOT belong with the other three?
    a. behaviorism
    b. psychoanalysis
    c. phenomenology
    d. gestalt

2. Which of the following best describes the subject matter of psychology?
    a. perceptions, behavior, mental health
    b. affect, behavior, cognition
    c. thoughts, feelings, sensations
    d. behavior, cognition, perception

3. Which of the following pairs is a mismatch?
    a. Binet-Simon
    b. Wundt-Titchener
    c. Rogers-Maslow
    d. Skinner-James

4. Loisann's son is almost two years old and is not yet talking. Which of the following psychology specialists would she most likely consult about this problem?

   a. physiological psychologist

   b. clinical psychologist

   c. health psychologist

   d. developmental psychologist

5. The difference between clinical psychologists and counseling psychologists is primarily in

   a. the severity of the problems they encounter

   b. the different methods that each employs

   c. their graduate training

   d. the work settings where they are employed

6. Which of the following best describes the current thinking in psychology on the nature vs. nurture controversy?

   a. nurture is the best explanation for most phenomena

   b. nature is the best explanation for most phenomena

   c. behavior and mental processes are best explained by considering both nature and nurture

   d. the influence of nature and nurture is interpreted differently according to the particular psychological approach

7. A definition of a concept given in terms of the methods used to measure that concept is a/an

   a. hypothesis

   b. phenomenological theory

   c. operational definition

   d. verifiable behavior

8. Descartes is to interactive dualism as _____ is to _____.

   a. Locke; British Empiricism

   b. Binet; behaviorism

   c. Terman; introspection

   d. Rogers; gestalt

9. The idea that a person forms his/her own reality from the events experienced is a basic principle of

   a. behaviorism

   b. interactive dualism

   c. phenomenology

   d. psychoanalysis

10. The psychological approach that emphasizes the role of the unconscious and instincts is
    a. humanism
    b. interactive dualism
    c. phenomenology
    d. psychoanalysis

11. A significant contribution of the behaviorist approach was the emphasis placed on
    a. measurable observations
    b. unconscious motives
    c. interpreting experience
    d. sensations and perceptions

12. The Gestalt approach to psychology was founded by
    a. Wundt
    b. Wertheimer
    c. Watson
    d. James

13. Sir Francis Galton developed the notion of psychological testing to satisfy his curiosity about
    a. human perception
    b. deviant behavior
    c. individual differences
    d. the role of the unconscious

14. The psychologist who believed that behavior is most influenced by changes in the environment was
    a. James
    b. Skinner
    c. Maslow
    d. Freud

15. Such matters as love, hate, will, concern, and intention are worthy of scientific study according to the
    a. behaviorists
    b. empiricists
    c. functionalists
    d. humanists

CHAPTER 1—THE NATURE OF PSYCHOLOGY TOPIC 1B—THE GOALS AND METHODS OF PSYCHOLOGY

LEARNING OBJECTIVES TOPIC 1B

It is necessary to understand the goals of psychology in order to understand what psychology is. Student objectives for TOPIC 1B are listed below.

1. List psychology's two major goals.
2. Define naturalistic observation and discuss the potential problems with its use.
3. Explain how surveys and case history studies can be used to understand R-R relationships.
4. Explain why correlation is used, what data are needed to calculate a correlation coefficient, and the meaning of positive, negative, and zero correlation coefficients.
5. Understand the essence of doing an experiment and be able to identify and define independent, dependent, and extraneous variables.
6. Explain how random assignment, baseline design, and double-blind procedures help control extraneous variables.
7. Discuss ethics in psychological research.

LEARNING TOPIC 1B VOCABULARY

On your own paper, write the definition for each of the following key terms. Your learning will be facilitated by writing the definition in your own words rather than copying the exact definition from the text.

SCIENTIFIC LAW	NATURALISTIC OBSERVATION
OBSERVER BIAS	SURVEY
SAMPLE	CASE HISTORY
CORRELATION	CORRELATION COEFFICIENT
EXPERIMENT	INDEPENDENT VARIABLES
DEPENDENT VARIABLES	EXTRANEOUS VARIABLES
EXPERIMENTAL GROUP	CONTROL GROUP
RANDOM ASSIGNMENT	BASELINE DESIGN
SINGLE-BLIND TECHNIQUE	DOUBLE-BLIND TECHNIQUE
META-ANALYSIS	DEBRIEF

MATCHING

Match the following key terms from your textbook with the appropriate definition.

_____ 1. independent variables   _____ 2. control group

_____ 3. baseline design   _____ 4. sample

_____ 5. single-blind technique   _____ 6. debrief

_____ 7. meta-analysis   _____ 8. correlation

_____ 9. scientific law   _____ 10. survey

_____ 11. observer bias   _____ 12. experiment

_____ 13. dependent variables   _____ 14. experimental group

_____ 15. double-blind technique _____ 16. random assignment

_____ 17. extraneous variables   _____ 18. case history

_____ 19. correlation coefficient _____ 20. naturalistic observation

a. A statement about one's subject matter thought to be true, based on evidence.
b. The method of observing and noting behaviors as they occur naturally.
c. When one's own motives, expectations, and past experiences interfere with the objectivity of one's observations.
d. A means of collecting observations from a large number of subjects, usually by interview or questionnaire.
e. The portion of a larger population chosen for study.
f. An intensive, retrospective, and detailed study of some aspects of one (or a few) individual(s).
g. A largely statistical technique used to determine the nature and extent of the relationship between two measured responses.
h. A number that indicates the nature and the strength of the relationship between measured responses.
i. A series of operations used to investigate relationships between manipulated events (independent variables) and measured events (dependent variables), while other events (extraneous variables) are eliminated.
j. Those events in an experiment that are manipulated by the experimenter that are hypothesized to produce changes in responses.
k. Those responses measured in an experiment, whose values are hypothesized to depend on manipulations of the independent variable.
l. Those factors in an experiment that need to be minimized or eliminated so as not to affect the dependent variable.
m. Those participants in an experiment who receive some treatment or manipulation—there may be more than one in an experiment.
n. Those participants in an experiment who do not receive any experimental treatment or manipulation.
o. The selection of members of a population in such a way that each has an equal opportunity to be assigned to any one group.
p. A method in which subjects' performance with an experimental treatment is compared with performance without that treatment (the baseline).
q. A protection against bias in which subjects are kept from knowing the hypothesis of an experiment.
r. A protection against bias in which both the subjects and the data collector/analyzer are kept from knowing the hypothesis of an experiment.
s. A statistical procedure of combining the results of several studies to see more clearly any relationships among observations that may be present.
t. To fully inform a subject about the intent and/or hypothesis of one's research once data have been collected.

TRUE-FALSE PRACTICE TEST 1B

_____ 1. One advantage of the case history method is that it can provide a wealth of information about a few individual cases.

_____ 2. A second advantage of the case history method is that the information learned can be easily generalized to other cases.

_____ 3. The actual value of a correlation coefficient can never be zero.

_____ 4. Correlation studies are widely used to demonstrate cause-effect relationships.

_____ 5. Predictions cannot be made for individual cases even when two responses are well correlated.

_____ 6. One advantage of using laboratory animals such as rats is that control of extraneous variables is often easier.

_____ 7. Most of what we know in psychology has been learned by conducting experiments.

_____ 8. There is no problem with using animals in research either in terms of generalizing results or in terms of ethical considerations.

_____ 9. Random assignment and matching are both techniques used to control extraneous variables.

_____ 10. Random assignment and matching techniques should be applied after the data is collected.

_____ 11. Double-blind techniques are superior to single-blind techniques in controlling observer bias.

_____ 12. Meta-analysis is a technique used to establish relationships between dependent and independent variables.

_____ 13. Ethical considerations are so important in the field of psychology because the subjects for research are usually living organisms.

_____ 14. The ethical standards in the field of psychology are dictated by the American Medical Association.

_____ 15. In psychological research, safety is of great concern, but confidentiality does not really matter.

FILL-IN PRACTICE TEST 1B

1. _____ is a statistical procedure that can be used to assess the nature and degree to which sets of observations are related.

2. In a _____ correlation, high scores on one set of responses are associated with high scores on the other.

3. In a _____ correlation, low scores on one set of responses are associated with high scores on the other.

4. Most of what we know today in the field of psychology has been learned through the research method of _____.

5. The research method intended to discover cause/effect relationships is _____.

6. The variable that the researcher manipulates is called the _____ variable.

7. The variable that is measured by the researcher is called the _____ variable.

8. Variables that should be eliminated from consideration are referred to as _____ variables.

9. Subjects who receive some treatment or manipulation are said to be members of the _____ group.

10. Subjects who do not receive a treatment constitute the _____ group.

11. _____ _____ means that each research participant has an equal chance of being assigned to the control group or any of the experimental groups.

12. In a _____ research technique, the subjects are not aware of the purpose or the hypothesis of the experiment.

13. In a _____ research technique, neither the subject nor the person collecting the data knows what the purpose or hypothesis of the experiment is.

14. _____ is a statistical procedure for combining the results of many studies to analyze the relationship between independent and dependent variables.

15. _____ occurs when the participants in an experiment are told the true nature and intent of the research.

MULTIPLE CHOICE PRACTICE TEST 1 TOPIC 1B

1. A statement about one's subject matter that one believes to be true defines a/an
    a. hypothesis
    b. scientific law
    c. theory
    d. scientific method

2. In the science of physics, the statement " a gas expands when heated," is an example of a/an
    a. scientific law
    b. application
    c. hypothesis
    d. theory

3. Which of the following are the two important characteristics of scientific laws?
    a. describe relationships and develop theories
    b. predict events and explain hypotheses
    c. make predictions and describe relationships
    d. suggest theories and prove hypotheses

4. Most psychologists who are practitioners are _____ psychologists.
    a. counseling
    b. health
    c. school
    d. social

5. In which of the following areas is psychology most different from other sciences?
    a. making predictions
    b. developing research hypotheses
    c. attempting to discover scientific laws
    d. attempting to control observed phenomena

6. The two goals of psychology are
    a. discovering and proving psychological laws
    b. forming and proving psychological hypotheses
    c. discovering and applying psychological laws
    d. conducting research and observing behavior

7. The biggest problem with applying common sense to interpret our observations about behaviors is that
    a. naturalistic observation is a better method
    b. common sense observations are often not true
    c. scientific laws cannot be developed from common sense observations
    d. some things cannot be interpreted using common sense

8. The work of Dianne Fossey, the researcher who studied gorillas in their own environment, is an example of
    a. single-blind design
    b. correlation
    c. case history
    d. naturalistic observation

9. In which type of research is observer bias more likely to present a problem?
    a. naturalistic observation
    b. single-blind technique
    c. experimental design
    d. correlation

10. Which of the following is NOT a problem associated with naturalistic observation?
    a. observer bias
    b. the desired behaviors are not exhibited during the observation period
    c. the organism may act differently with knowledge that he/she/it is being watched
    d. the variables are difficult to manipulate

11. Which of the following is the best example of naturalistic observation?
    a. studying chimps at the zoo
    b. studying children in a day care center
    c. conducting sleep research in a laboratory
    d. observing children with their families in a park

12. The best research method for gathering information about a large group of subjects is a/an
    a. experiment
    b. survey
    c. case history
    d. correlation

13. A subset of a larger group that is chosen to be studied is referred to as a
    a. population
    b. control group
    c. sample
    d. questionnaire group

14. The study of one person in an in depth manner over a long period of time is a research method called
    a. survey
    b. case history
    c. experiment
    d. naturalistic observation

15. The research technique which Freud used almost exclusively in developing his theories was
    a. experiment
    b. correlation
    c. case history
    d. naturalistic observation

MULTIPLE CHOICE PRACTICE TEST 2 TOPIC 1B

1. Correlation coefficients may range in value from _____ to ____
    a. 0 to 2
    b. -1 to +1
    c. 0 to +1
    d. -1 to 0

2. As a person's cholesterol level increases, the risk for heart disease also increases. This is an example of

   a. case study

   b. naturalistic observation

   c. negative correlation

   d. positive correlation

3. The best interpretation for a correlation coefficient of zero is that the two sets of responses

   a. are not related

   b. are positively correlated

   c. are negatively correlated

   d. none of the above

4. The research method responsible for most of our knowledge in the field of psychology is

   a. experiment

   b. case history

   c. correlation

   d. survey

5. A researcher conducts a study in which he exposes women to different fear conditions and then measures their desire to affiliate. In this experiment, the various fear conditions would be the

   a. dependent variables

   b. independent variables

   c. extraneous variables

   d. effect

6. The quality of an experiment depends most on the researchers ability to control the

   a. dependent variables

   b. independent variables

   c. extraneous variables

   d. outcome

7. Which of the following is NOT a method for controlling the effects of extraneous variables in experiments

   a. baseline design

   b. matching

   c. single-blind design

   d. random assignment

8. You conduct a study in which you wish to determine the effects of blood-doping on athletes. You have the athletes run a five mile course without the blood-doping. The following week, they run the same course after blood-doping. The method you have used for controlling extraneous variables is

    a. random assignment

    b. matching

    c. correlation

    d. baseline design

9. The purpose of single-blind and double-blind research techniques is to control

    a. observer bias

    b. calculation errors in the statistics

    c. extraneous variables

    d. treatment effects

10. Which of the following is/are ethical considerations for psychological research?

    a. The subjects' confidentiality must be guaranteed.

    b. Participation in research should be totally voluntary.

    c. Subjects must give advised consent.

    d. All of the above.

11. A researcher wishes to know a limited amount of information about a large number of subjects. The best research method for this purpose would be

    a. case history

    b. survey

    c. correlation

    d. experiment

12. A researcher has established a relationship between GPA and SAT scores such that high SAT scores usually predict that a student will earn a high GPA. This information was most likely established with the _____ research method.

    a. case history

    b. survey

    c. correlation

    d. experiment

13. A study is being conducted to determine the effects of vitamin C on IQ. The researcher who is analyzing the data has hired an assistant to determine which subjects will get the actual vitamin C and which will get an orange flavored sugar tablet. The subjects are unaware of who gets the vitamin C and who does not. This experiment is using a method for controlling observer bias known as

    a. baseline design

    b. single-blind

    c. double-blind

    d. debriefing

14. The study of a woman named Sybil who had multiple personalities represents an example of which research method?

    a. case history

    b. survey

    c. correlation

    d. meta-analysis

15. Random assignment is done in an experiment as a means of

    a. establishing a correlation

    b. controlling observer bias

    c. controlling extraneous variables

    d. making predictions about a set of responses

Dr. G's Best Study Tips #1

The following questions will help you determine if your study habits are similar to those of successful students. Answer as honestly as you can. Then check your answers to learn which of your habits could be improved.

A = always

U = usually

N = never

TIME MANAGEMENT

DO YOU . . .???

A	U	N	1.	Study every day including the weekends?
A	U	N	2.	Study at regularly scheduled times?
A	U	N	3.	Know how much time you spend studying?
A	U	N	4.	Turn assignments in on time?
A	U	N	5.	Only study when an exam is near?
A	U	N	6.	Study after 10 o'clock at night?
A	U	N	7.	Review frequently?
A	U	N	8.	Procrastinate and try to get things done at the last minute?
A	U	N	9.	Take short breaks every hour or so?
A	U	N	10.	Find time for fun?

ANSWERS

1. Always or usually are the answers that successful students give. Establishing studying as a part of your regular routine is important for two reasons. First, it helps get you started. As with other positive habits such as exercise, routine creates the attitude of expectation that you will do what has to be done. Second, research tells us that we learn more efficiently if we study for shorter sessions spaced over several days rather than cramming at the last minute.

2. Always or usually are the answers that successful students give.

3. Always know how much time you spend. What other way is there to determine whether your study methods are effective and efficient? As a general rule of thumb, an average student should plan to spend two hours of study time for every hour of class. On a semester hour basis, most introductory psychology courses would consist of three hours of class per week. Therefore, MINIMUM study time should be at least six hours per week.

4. Always turn assignments in on time. It is senseless to turn an assignment in late and risk losing points when you are doing the work anyway. Do it on time.

5. Never. More successful students study well in advance of exams so that their study time can be distributed over many study sessions. Cramming may be reinforced because it works in some cases. However, you will find that as the amount of material increases and the complexity increases, cramming is a less and less effective learning strategy. I believe this is a crucial adjustment that students must make in the transition from high school study skills to college study skills.

6. Either seldom or never unless you have no other choice. For most people, general alertness and mental efficiency decline late at night. Studies have shown that some students can accomplish in one hour earlier in the day what will take them an hour and a half to do later at night.

7. Always. Frequent reviewing is one of the keys to learning large amounts of complex information.

8. Never or seldom. Successful students enjoy getting assignments and studying for exams done ahead of time and then relaxing when they know they are fully prepared.

9. Usually or always. Studies indicate that the most efficient timing is to study for about fifty minutes to an hour and then take a short break of five or ten minutes. There are two exceptions to this: either writing a paper, or solving a complex problem in math or logic will benefit more from periods of continuous work (say two to three hours) without the interruptions of a break.

10. Always. Successful students find time for fun because they use efficient strategies that leave them time to do so and because they know the wisdom of the old adage, "All work and no play makes Jack a dull boy."

CHAPTER 2 —THE BIOLOGICAL BASES OF BEHAVIOR
TOPIC 2A—BASIC STRUCTURES AND FUNCTIONS

LEARNING OBJECTIVES TOPIC 2A

It is necessary to understand the basic fundamentals of the nervous system in order to understand behavior and mental processes. Students should be able to:
1. Discuss the basic concepts involved in the genetic transmission of physical characteristics.
2. Describe three ways of studying the influence of genes on behavior, cognition, and emotion.
3. Describe the main structural features of the neuron, and the role of myelin.
4. Discuss the basic process involved when a neuron fires and what the all-or-none principle states.
5. Explain how neural impulses are transmitted at the synapse.
6. Name four neurotransmitters and indicate some psychological reaction when each is involved.
7. Explain how the nervous systems are structured.
8. Discuss the methods used to study the brain including observation of injury, lesioning, CAT scan, PET scan, and NMI.

LEARNING TOPIC 2A VOCABULARY

Write the definition for each of the following key terms. Your learning will be facilitated by writing the definition in your own words rather than copying the exact definition from your text.

GENETICS	GENE
CHROMOSOME	DOMINANT GENE
RECESSIVE GENE	NEURON
CELL BODY	DENDRITES
AXON	MYELIN
AXON TERMINALS	NEURAL IMPULSE
ION	RESTING POTENTIAL
ACTION POTENTIAL	ALL-OR-NONE PRINCIPLE
NEURAL THRESHOLD	SYNAPSE
VESICLES	NEUROTRANSMITTERS
SYNAPTIC CLEFT	CENTRAL NERVOUS SYSTEM
PERIPHERAL NERVOUS SYSTEM	SOMATIC NERVOUS SYSTEM
AUTONOMIC NERVOUS SYSTEM	SYMPATHETIC DIVISION
PARASYMPATHETIC DIVISION	ENDOCRINE SYSTEM
HORMONES	LESION
ELECTRODE	CAT SCAN
NMI	PET SCAN

MATCHING

Match the following key terms from your text book with the appropriate definition.

_____ 1. myelin

_____ 2. neurotransmitters

_____ 3. all-or-none principle

_____ 4. axon terminals

_____ 5. sympathetic division

_____ 6. CAT scan

_____ 7. lesion

_____ 8. central nervous system

_____ 9. somatic nervous system

_____10. endocrine system

_____11. resting potential

_____12. synapse

_____13. gene

_____14. cell body

_____15. neuron

_____16. action potential

_____17. parasympathetic division

_____18. autonomic nervous system

_____19. peripheral nervous system

_____20. electrode

_____21. hormones

_____22. neural threshold

_____23. neural impulse

_____24. ion

_____25. vesicles

_____26. synaptic cleft

_____27. genetics

_____28. axon

_____29. dendrites

_____30. NMI

_____31. PET scan

_____32. recessive gene

_____33. chromosome

_____34. dominant gene

a. The science that studies the transmission of traits or characteristics from one generation to the next.

b. The basic mechanism of hereditary transmission; that which gets passed from one generation to the next.

c. Literally, "colored body," that thin, threadlike structure found in 23 pairs in human cells that carry genes.

d. A gene that carries a trait that will be expressed regardless of the gene it is paired with.

e. A gene that carries a trait that will be expressed only if it is paired with another similar recessive gene.

f. A nerve cell, the basic building block of the nervous system that transmits neural impulses.

g. The largest mass of a neuron, containing the cell's nucleus, and which may receive neural impulses.

h. Branchlike extentions from a neuron's cell body where most neural impulses are received.

i. The long, tail-like extension of a neuron that carries an impulse away from the cell body toward the synapse.

37

j.   A white fatty covering found on some axons that serves to insulate and protect them, while increasing the speed of impulses.

k.   The series of branching end points of an axon where one neuron communicates with the next in a series.

l.   A sudden and reversible change in the electrical charges within and outside the membrane of a neuron, which travels from the dendrite to the axon end of a neuron.

m.   An electrically charged (either + or -) chemical particle.

n.   The difference in electrical charge between the inside of a neuron and the outside when it is at rest.

o.   The short-lived burst of a change in the difference in electrical charge between the inside and the outside of a neuron when it fires.

p.   The fact that a neuron will either fire and generate a full impulse (an action potential) or it will not fire at all.

q.   The minimum amount of stimulation required to produce an impulse within a neuron.

r.   The general location where an impulse is relayed from one neuron to another by means of neurotransmitters.

s.   The small containers, concentrated in axon terminals that hold neurotransmitter molecules.

t.   Chemical molecules released at the synapse which will, in general, either excite or inhibit neural impulse transmission.

u.   The space between the membrane of an axon terminal and the membrane of the next neuron in a sequence.

v.   Those neurons in the brain and spinal cord.

w.   Those neurons not found in the brain or spinal cord, i.e. those found in the periphery of the body.

x.   Sensory and motor neurons outside the CNS that serve the sense receptors and the skeletal muscles.

y.   Those neurons of the PNS that activate the smooth muscles and glands.

z.   Those neurons involved in states of emotionality.

aa. Those neurons involved in the maintenance of the states of calm and relaxation.

bb. A network of glands that secrete hormones directly into the bloodstream.

cc. A variety of chemical compounds, secreted by the glands of the endocrine system, many of which have effects on behavior or mental states.

dd. A cut or incision that destroys specific areas of tissue.

ee. A fine wire used to either stimulate or record the electrical activity of neural tissue.

ff. A method of imaging brain structures through the computer enhancement of x-ray pictures.

gg. A process that provides clear, detailed pictures of the brain by recording energy from cells when the brain has been placed in a magnetic field.

hh. A method of imaging the brain and its activity by locating small amounts of radioactive chemical injected into the brain.

TRUE-FALSE TEST TOPIC 2A

_____   1.   Chromosomes are found only in the reproductive cells of organisms.

_____   2.   The nucleus of all human cells contains 23 pairs of chromosomes.

_____   3.   Our self-image is at least partially determined by genetic factors.

_____   4.   When traits tend to show up more consistently within groups that are genetically related than they do in unrelated groups, a logical assumption is that the trait has a genetic basis.

_____   5.   The role of genetics is fairly well established in diseases and disorders such as Alzheimer's, alcoholism, and schizophrenia.

6. It has been clearly demonstrated by research that in some populations, depression is genetically based.

7. The neurons or nerve cells in the brain, although different from other cells in the nervous system, are essentially identical.

8. In the brain, the white matter is composed of myelin which is lacking in the gray matter.

9. Myelinated fibers can carry neural impulses 100 times faster than unmyelinated ones.

10. The longer the nerve fibers in the body, the more likely they are to be myelinated.

11. The time in our lives when we possess the greatest number of neurons is at birth.

12. Alcohol kills brain cells.

13. One unique characteristic of neurons is that lost ones are not replaced.

14. The term neural impulse is synonymous with refractory period.

15. A higher intensity stimulus will cause more neurons to fire than a low intensity stimulus.

16. The sole function of neurotransmitters is to excite the transmission of neural impulses.

17. It is likely that diseases such as Alzheimers' are related to the presence or absence of neurotransmitters.

18. Hormones are secreted into the bloodstream by the endocrine system.

19. Many hormones and neurotransmitters are similar and can have similar effects.

20. Unlike the nervous system, the endocrine system has no effect on behavior.

FILL-IN PRACTICE TEST TOPIC 2A

1. The _gene_ is the basic mechanism of hereditary transmission.

2. A _dominant gene_ is one whose characteristics will be expressed in the organism.

3. A single nerve cell is called a _neuron_

4. The cell body contains the _nucleus_ of the cell.

5. The _Axon_ is the long thin fiber in the neuron that sends neural impulses to other neurons.

6. _Myelin_ is a white, fatty substance found on about half of the neurons.

7. _Myelin_ is the feature of neurons that is undeveloped at birth.

8. Axons end in a branching series of points called _axon terminals_ that communicate with other neurons.

9. A _neural impulse_ is a sudden and irreversible change in the electrical charges within and outside a neuron.

10. The tiny chemical particles which carry the electrical charge in the brain are called _ions_

11. The small electrical charge present when a neuron is at rest is called *resting potential*.

12. The time during which the neuron cannot fire is known as the *resting* period.

13. The minimum level of stimulation required to get a neuron to fire is called *neural threshold*.

14. A neural impulse is relayed from one neuron to another at a location called the *synapse*.

15. The complex chemicals in the brain are referred to as *neurotransmitters*.

16. The natural pain suppressors in the brain are called *Endorphines*

17. Acetylcholine is a neurotransmitter which affects *memory*.

18. The *central nervous system* is made up of all the nerves and nerve fibers in the brain and spinal cord.

19. The endocrine system secretes *hormones* into the bloodstream.

20. The recording of brain activity was first done by a German psychiatrist named ~~Hellman~~ *Hans Berger 1929*

MULTIPLE CHOICE PRACTICE TEST 1 TOPIC 2A

1. The first person to study genes was
    a. Gregor Mendel
    b. Charles Darwin
    c. Rene Descartes
    d. Sir Francis Galton

2. Which of the following statements is true of a child with brown eyes?
    a. The child could have had two brown eyed parents.
    b. The child's father could have had blue eyes and the mother could have had brown eyes.
    c. The child's parents could not have both had blue eyes.
    d. All of the above.

3. A gene whose characteristic is transmitted to the individual regardless of the gene with which it is paired is referred to as a
    a. recessive gene
    b. master gene
    c. dominant gene
    d. trait-bearing gene

4. A good explanation for the relationship between heredity and environment is that
    a. a favorable environment allows genetic input to reach its full potential
    b. hereditary input dominates environmental influence
    c. environment has limited influence on inherited characteristics
    d. only a bad environment restricts the development of genetic characteristics

5. Sir Francis Galton concluded that certain traits have a genetic basis through his study of
   a. eye color
   b. genius
   c. musical talent
   d. schizophrenia

6. There are several approaches to studying the influence of heredity. The one used to study the hereditary influence on schizophrenia is
   a. twin studies
   b. inbreeding studies
   c. family history studies
   d. adoption studies

7. In family history studies the role of the environment is considered to be
   a. limited and thus is given little attention
   b. mildly influential but uncontrollable
   c. important because most siblings have similar environments
   d. irrelevant because hereditary characteristics are dominant

8. Which of the following diseases or disorders is least likely to be influenced by genetics?
   a. Alzheimer's
   b. alcoholism
   c. epilepsy
   d. depression

9. The best explanation of what we actually inherit from our parents is
   a. behaviors
   b. chemicals
   c. physical characteristics
   d. personality traits

10. The function of the dendrites is
    a. receiving neural impulses
    b. sending neural impulses
    c. storing neural impulses
    d. unknown

11. Which of the following is NOT a function of myelin?
    a. speeds the transmission of neural impulses
    b. aids the production of neurotransmitters
    c. insulates the nerve cell
    d. acts as a protective covering for the axon

12. Which of the following represents the correct path of a neural impulse?
    a. dendrites-axons-terminals
    b. axons-nucleus-terminals
    c. dendrites-cell body-axon-terminals
    d. nucleus-dendrites-terminals-myelin

13. The time in our lives when we will possess the greatest number of neurons is
    a. at birth
    b. during childhood
    c. in adolescence
    d. in early adulthood

14. Which of the following is most similar in meaning to the term neural impulse?
    a. refractory period
    b. resting potential
    c. ion charge
    d. action potential

15. When a neuron is stimulated, it either transmits an impulse along, or it doesn't. This fact is described as the
    a. refractory phenomenon
    b. action potential
    c. myelination process
    d. all-or-none principle

MULTIPLE CHOICE PRACTICE TEST 2 TOPIC 2A

1. Neurotransmitters are contained in the
    a. vesicles
    b. cell body
    c. nucleus
    d. axon terminals

2. The tiny space between two neurons is referred to as the
    a. vesicle
    b. nucleus
    c. axon terminal
    d. synaptic cleft

3. Which of the following is the best description of the role of neurotransmitters?
    a. they inhibit the firing of neurons
    b. they enhance the firing of neurons
    c. they have no effect on the firing of neurons
    d. they either enhance or inhibit the firing of neurons

42

4. The neurotransmitter which influences normal memory function is/are
   a. dopamine
   b. acetylcholine
   c. norepinephrine
   d. endorphins

5. The neurotransmitter associated with the impairment of movement responses is/are
   a. dopamine
   b. norepinephrine
   c. acetylcholine
   d. endorphins

6. Endorphins are neurotransmitters which affect
   a. motor skills
   b. level of pain
   c. memory function
   d. anxiety and arousal

7. The neurons and nerve fibers in the brain and spinal cord makeup the
   a. autonomic nervous system
   b. somatic nervous system
   c. central nervous system
   d. peripheral nervous system

8. The skeletal muscles and sense organs are served primarily by the
   a. autonomic nervous system
   b. somatic nervous system
   c. central nervous system
   d. peripheral nervous system

9. Sympathetic nervous system is to excitement as _____ is to _____.
   a. autonomic; spinal cord
   b. somatic; calm
   c. parasympathetic; relaxation
   d. central; arousal

10. The endocrine system is primarily related to behavior in the areas of
    a. motivation and emotion
    b. deviance and disorder
    c. violence and depression
    d. memory and mood

11. Beth has been frightened by a strange noise outside her apartment. Her heart is pounding and her breathing is rapid. Although she may not be aware of it, her body is also producing extra adrenaline. All these changes are in response to the

    a. central nervous system

    b. sympathetic nervous system

    c. parasympathetic nervous system

    d. endocrine system

12. Broca discovered the location in the brain where speech is produced by using a method of study referred to as

    a. lesioning

    b. CAT scan

    c. MRI

    d. accident and injury

13. Which of the following methods of studying the brain would be the most destructive?

    a. MRI

    b. CAT scan

    c. lesioning

    d. electrical stimulation

14. If we want to learn more about overall brain activity rather than about specific functions in exact locations of the brain, which method of study would we most likely use?

    a. lesioning

    b. recording electrical activity

    c. electrical stimulation

    d. accident and injury

15. A method of studying the brain which allows us to examine brain functioning as well as structure is

    a. PET scan

    b. MRI

    c. CAT scan

    d. EEG

CHAPTER 2—THE BIOLOGICAL BASES OF BEHAVIOR
TOPIC 2B—THE CENTRAL NERVOUS SYSTEM

LEARNING OBJECTIVES TOPIC 2B

Psychologists study the major structures and functions of the brain to find out how this important part of the nervous system affects the many aspects of behavior that it does. Students should be able to:

1. Describe the major features of a spinal reflex and explain why spinal cord injury sometimes causes paralysis.
2. Discuss the two brain stem structures, their location and their functions.
3. Describe the cerebellum, its location, and its major function.
4. List the location and functions of the RAS, limbic system, hypothalamus, the basal ganglia, and thalamus.
5. Explain the location of the four lobes of the cerebral cortex and the primary sensory, motor, and association areas of the cerebrum.
6. Describe the split-brain procedure and differentiate the functions of the right and left hemispheres.

LEARNING TOPIC 2B VOCABULARY

On your on paper, write the definition for each of the following key terms. Your learning will be facilitated by writing the definition in your own words rather than copying the exact definition from your text.

SPINAL CORD	SPINAL REFLEX
BRAIN STEM	MEDULLA
NUCLEI	CROSS-LATERALITY
PONS	CEREBELLUM
TREMORS	RETICULAR ACTIVATING SYSTEM (RAS)
LIMBIC SYSTEM	HYPOTHALAMUS
BASAL GANGLIA	PARKINSON'S DISEASE
THALAMUS	CEREBRAL CORTEX
CEREBRAL HEMISPHERES	FRONTAL LOBES
TEMPORAL LOBES	OCCIPITAL LOBES
PARIETAL LOBES	SENSORY AREAS
MOTOR AREAS	ASSOCIATION AREAS
CORPUS CALLOSUM	SPLIT-BRAIN PROCEDURE

MATCHING

Match the following key terms from your textbook with the appropriate definition.

_____ 1. occipital lobes   _____ 2. split-brain procedure

_____ 3. reticular activating system   _____ 4. cerebral hemispheres

_____ 5. thalamus   _____ 6. spinal cord

_____ 7. tremors   _____ 8. cross-laterality

_____ 9. basal ganglia   _____10. frontal lobes

_____11. temporal lobes   _____12. limbic system

_____13. spinal reflex   _____14. pons

_____15. parietal lobes   _____16. corpus callosum

_____17. cerebral cortex   _____18. hypothalamus

_____19. Parkinson's disease   _____20. sensory areas

_____21. motor areas   _____22. brain stem

_____23. cerebellum   _____24. medulla

_____25. association areas   _____26. nuclei

a. A mass of interconnected neurons within the spine that conveys impulses to and from the brain and is involved in some reflex behaviors.
b. An automatic, involuntary response to a stimulus that involves sensory neurons carrying impulses to the spinal cord, interneurons within the spinal cord, and motor neurons carrying impulses to muscles.
c. The lowest part of the brain, just above the spinal cord, comprised of the medulla and the pons.
d. An area of the brain stem that monitors breathing and heart rate, and where most cross-laterality occurs.
e. Small collections or bundles of neural cell bodies.
f. The process of nerve fibers crossing over the brain stem so that the left side of the body sends impulses to and receives impulses from the right side of the brain, and vice versa.
g. A brain stem structure forming a bridge between the brain and the spinal cord that monitors the sleep-wake cycle.
h. A spherical structure at the lower rear of the brain involved in the coordination of bodily movements.
i. Involuntary, trembling, jerky movements.
j. A network of nerve fibers extending from the brain stem to the cerebrum that is involved in maintaining levels of arousal.
k. A collection of structures, including the amygdala and septum, which are involved in emotionality, and the hippocampus, involved in forming long-term memories.
l. A small structure near the limbic system in the center of the brain, associated with feeding, drinking, sex, and aggression.
m. A collection of structures in front of the limbic system that produce and depend on dopamine to control large, slow bodily movements.
n. A disorder of movement caused by damage to tissues in the basal ganglia.
o. The last sensory relay station; it sends impulses to the appropriate area of the cerebral cortex.
p. The large, convoluted outer covering of the brain that is the seat of cognitive functioning and voluntary action.
q. The two halves of the cerebral cortex, separated by a deep fissure running from front to back.

r. The largest of the cerebral lobes, in front of the central fissure and above the lateral fissure.
s. The lobes of the cerebrum located at the temples.
t. The cerebral lobes at the very back of the brain.
u. The lobes of the cerebrum found behind the frontal lobes, in front of the occipital lobes, and above the temporal lobes.
v. Those areas of the cerebral cortex that receive impulses from our sense receptors.
w. The strips at the back of the frontal lobes that control voluntary movement.
x. Those areas of the frontal, parietal, and temporal lobes in which higher mental processing occurs.
y. A network of nerve fibers that interconnect the two hemispheres of the cerebrum.
z. A surgical technique of severing the corpus callosum, allowing the two hemispheres to operate independently.

TRUE-FALSE PRACTICE TEST

_____ 1. Sensory impulses that originate below the neck enter the brain through the spinal cord.

_____ 2. The higher on the spinal cord that injury takes place, the greater portion of the body that will lose function.

_____ 3. Paralysis is often caused by lack of myelin in the neurons of the spinal cord.

_____ 4. We have no voluntary control over the nuclei in the medulla.

_____ 5. Due to cross laterality, a stroke victim who has suffered damage to the left side of the brain is likely to suffer the results in terms of damage to the right side of the body.

_____ 6. The influence of the limbic system on emotional responses is the same for both humans and animals.

_____ 7. Parkinson's disease is related to the health and proper functioning of the basal ganglia.

_____ 8. Sensory and motor processing in the brain occurs proportionally to the size of the body part that receives the original stimulus.

_____ 9. Patients who have undergone split-brain surgery appear quite normal unless they are engaged in laboratory tests.

_____ 10. The difference between white matter and gray matter in the nervous system is related to the amount of myelin coating the cells.

_____ 11. The term lower brain refers only to the location of the particular structures involved.

_____ 12. The split-brain surgical procedure was first done in an attempt to aid schizophrenics.

_____ 13. It is safe to say that in general, language and speech are processed in the left hemisphere.

_____ 14. Emotions appear to be processed in both hemispheres equally.

_____ 15. The right hemisphere is more involved with visual arts and emotionality.

FILL-IN PRACTICE TEST

1. The _____ _____ is a massive collection of neurons within the spinal column that resembles a rope.

2. _____ _____ are simple automatic behaviors that occur without conscious, voluntary action of the brain.

3. The fact that the left side of the body sends impulses to and receives messages from the right side of the brain is a function of _____ _____.

4. The _____ serves as a bridge, relaying sensory messages from the spinal cord and the face to the higher brain centers.

5. The _____ _____ controls the instinctive behavioral patterns of animals.

6. The _____ is the part of the limbic system involved in forming memories.

7. The largest structure in the human brain is the _____.

8. The _____ lobe does not have an association area as all its capacity is used for sensory processing.

9. The series of fibers connecting the two hemispheres of the cerebral cortex is called the _____ _____.

10. The surgical technique that separates the two hemispheres in the cerebral cortex is known as _____ _____

11. The split-brain surgery was first done to improve patients suffering from _____.

12. _____ _____ is a movement disorder caused by damage to the tissues in the basal ganglia.

13. A drug that is used to successfully retard the progress of Parkinson's disease is _____.

14. The _____ controls such functions as eating, drinking and sex drive.

15. The _____ acts as the final relay station for sensory information coming into the brain.

MULTIPLE CHOICE PRACTICE TEST 1 TOPIC 2B

1. The fact that the center area of the spinal cord is made up of dark gray matter indicates that
    a. there are no neurons present
    b. the nerve cells there are undifferentiated
    c. the axons of the nerve cells are unmyelinated
    d. the myelin has fully matured in these cells

2. The brain stem consists of the
    a. spinal cord and motor neurons
    b. medulla and pons
    c. pons and spinal cord
    d. basal ganglia and motor neurons

3. The major functions of the medulla involve
   a. emotions
   b. memories
   c. motor skills
   d. involuntary reflexes

4. Smooth muscle movements such as a golf swing are controlled by the
   a. cerebellum
   b. pons
   c. medulla
   d. cerebrum

5. The amygdala is to increasing emotional intensity as the _____ is to decreasing emotional intensity.
   a. hippocampus
   b. septum
   c. medulla
   d. pons

6. Which of the following is NOT monitored by the hypothalamus?
   a. eating
   b. sleeping
   c. shivering
   d. feeling thirsty

7. The basal ganglia produces a neurotransmitter necessary for large motor movements such as walking. The name of this neurotransmitter is
   a. L-Dopa
   b. adrenaline
   c. dopamine
   d. histamine

8. Which of the following pairs is NOT an appropriate match?
   a. cerebral cortex - information storage
   b. brain stem - reflexes
   c. basal ganglia - speech
   d. thalamus - senses

9. Which of the following is the best description of how the brain really functions.
   a. the left hemisphere controls all voluntary functions and the right controls involuntary functions
   b. association areas each control their own functions
   c. the various lobes operate independently, each controlling certain functions
   d. the brain really functions more as a whole

10. Knowledge of the two hemispheres of the cerebral cortex has increased tremendously because of
    a. split-brain surgery
    b. animal research using CAT scans
    c. case studies like that of Phineas Gage
    d. the work of researchers like Broca

11. For most right handed individuals, speech is controlled in the
    a. right hemisphere
    b. left hemisphere
    c. cerebellum
    d. temporal lobes

12. The areas associated with higher mental processes are known as
    a. motor areas
    b. mental areas
    c. association areas
    d. sensory areas

13. The first split-brain surgical procedures were done to help with the disease of_____.
    a. schizophrenia
    b. Parkinson's disease
    c. autism
    d. epilepsy

14. The largest of the cerebral lobes are the
    a. parietal
    b. occipital
    c. temporal
    d. frontal

15. Small collections or bundles of neural cell bodies are referred to as
    a. basal ganglia
    b. nuclei
    c. corpus callosum
    d. pons

MULTIPLE CHOICE PRACTICE TEST 2 TOPIC 2B

1. Reflexes like eye blinks are controlled by the
    a. spinal cord
    b. medulla
    c. pons
    d. cerebrum

2. Holding your breath is an example of
    a. involuntary reflex
    b. overriding the involuntary control of the medulla
    c. total voluntary behavior
    d. controlling a voluntary behavior

3. Cross laterality takes place initially in the
    a. brain stem
    b. spinal cord
    c. cerebrum
    d. left hemisphere

4. The staggering walk of a drunk is likely produced by the effects of alcohol on the
    a. cerebrum
    b. pons
    c. medulla
    d. cerebellum

5. Level of arousal and activity is controlled by the
    a. cerebellum
    b. brain stem
    c. reticular activating system
    d. central nervous system

6. The major role of the thalamus is processing
    a. sensory messages
    b. motor messages
    c. impulses from the spinal cord
    d. emotional impulses

7. Voluntary action in humans is controlled in the
    a. thalamus
    b. cerebral cortex
    c. hypothalamus
    d. reticular activating system

8. Which of the following pairs is NOT a correct match between brain center and function?
    a. occipital lobes - vision
    b. temporal lobes - hearing
    c. parietal lobes - body senses
    d. temporal lobes - rhythmic movement

9. If someone tickles your right foot, that sensation would be processed in the
   a. left temporal lobe
   b. right parietal lobe
   c. right occipital lobe
   d. left parietal lobe

10. Which of the following is NOT a correct match in terms of hemispheric dominance?
    a. left hemisphere - speaking
    b. left hemisphere - arithmetic
    c. left hemisphere - drawing
    d. left hemisphere - writing

11. Neural impulses enter the spinal cord on
    a. ventral roots
    b. nuclei
    c. dorsal roots
    d. efferent neurons

12. Impulses travel in on sensory neurons, within on interneurons, and out on motor neurons. This describes
    a. simple reflexes
    b. voluntary behavior
    c. involuntary but controllable behavior
    d. higher mental processing

13. Which of the following is NOT considered a part of the lower brain structures?
    a. pons
    b. medulla
    c. reticular activating system
    d. left hemisphere

14. Catherine is outdoors playing and the weather begins to turn cloudy and colder. Since Catherine is without her coat, she will have to rely on part of her brain to initiate some warming responses. The part of the brain that can do this job is the
    a. medulla
    b. hypothalamus
    c. hippocampus
    d. thalamus

15. Joe is returning home to Texas from a trip to Japan. He is likely to experience jet lag and his normal waking and sleeping patterns will go through a period of adjustment. Under normal circumstances, waking and sleeping patterns are controlled by
    a. the pons and the thalamus
    b. the right and left hemispheres
    c. the medulla and the pons
    d. the thalamus and the hypothalamus

Dr. G's Best Study Tips #2

The following questions will help you determine if your study habits are similar to those of successful students. Answer as honestly as you can. Then check your answers to learn which of your habits could be improved.

A = always

U = usually

N = never

DISTRACTIONS

DO YOU . . .???

A	U	N	1.	Eat or chew gum while you study?
A	U	N	2.	Watch TV or listen to the stereo while you study?
A	U	N	3.	Daydream or lose concentration?
A	U	N	4.	Study in the library or other quiet place?
A	U	N	5.	Think about other things you should be doing?

ANSWERS

1. Never is the answer that successful students give. Eating or chewing gum while studying is distracting for two reasons. First, the rhythmical chewing creates a physiological interference. You are likely to begin to read in rhythm with the chewing. This reading rate would be much slower than normal and would interfere with your reading comprehension. Remember the old childhood trick of rubbing your stomach and patting your head at the same time. Each activity interferes with the other. Reading and chewing are related in much the same fashion. The second reason for not eating is that the taste and smell of the food may serve as a reminder of a previous experience and thus send you off into a daydream. You will find it much more difficult to concentrate. If you are truly hungry, both the dining experience and your studying will benefit if you just take a break and eat.

2. Never is the best answer. Many research studies have shown that groups not listening to stereo or television perform better on memory and learning tasks than those groups who do listen. Regardless of how well you are now doing, you could improve by turning off these distractions.

3. Hopefully, you can answer never or seldom. Losing concentration causes you to lose precious study time. If this is a problem for you, refer to Dr. G's study tips on reading a textbook and the importance of generativity emphasized in study tip #1. In addition, you may want to try the pencil cure. Keep a pencil or pen in your hand as you read or study. After every page attempt to write a brief summary of what you have read. You may list only key words or phrases. If you can do this, you know you have been concentrating. If not, you have caught yourself quickly and have only one page to reread.

4. Always is the answer that successful students give. The library not only has the advantage of being quiet, but it keeps you away from numerous other distractions such as phone calls,

interacting with roommates, even seeing your personal effects that may start you daydreaming or thinking of other things.

5. Successful students would answer never or seldom. If interfering thoughts about realistic concerns do distract you while studying, the best solution is to write them down. You will then have the problem preserved so that you can take care of it at a later time. This way, you have no need to keep mulling the problem over while you try to concentrate on studies.

CHAPTER 3—SENSORY PROCESSES TOPIC 3A—VISION

LEARNING OBJECTIVES TOPIC 3A

Everything we know has come through our senses so it is important to know how our senses work. Students should be able to:
1. Define sensation, psychophysics, absolute threshold, difference threshold, and signal detection theory.
2. Discuss the affect of subliminal perception on behavior.
3. Understand how the amplitude, length, and purity of light waves affect psychological experience.
4. Discuss the major eye structures and their functions.
5. Discuss the rods and the cones and differentiate between the visual experiences attributed to each.
6. Compare and contrast the trichromatic and opponent-process theories.

LEARNING TOPIC 3A VOCABULARY

On your own paper, write the definition for each of the following key terms. Your learning will be facilitated by writing the definition in your own words rather than copying the exact definition from your text.

SENSATION	TRANSDUCER
PSYCHOPHYSICS	ABSOLUTE THRESHOLD
SUBLIMINAL PERCEPTION	DIFFERENCE THRESHOLD
JUST NOTICEABLE DIFFERENCE (JND)	SIGNAL DETECTION THEORY
SENSORY ADAPTATION	DARK ADAPTATION
LIGHTWAVE	AMPLITUDE
BRIGHTNESS	WAVELENGTH
NANOMETER (NM)	HUE
MONOCHROMATIC	SATURATION
WHITE LIGHT	CORNEA
PUPIL	IRIS
LENS	CILIARY MUSCLES
ACCOMMODATION	AQUEOUS HUMOR
VITREOUS HUMOR	RETINA
PHOTORECEPTORS	RODS
CONES	OPTIC NERVE
FOVEA	BLINDSPOT
OPTIC CHIASMA	PRIMARY HUES

MATCHING

Match the following key terms from your textbook with the appropriate definition.

_____ 1. primary hues   _____ 2. light

_____ 3. iris   _____ 4. saturation

_____ 5. optic chiasma   _____ 6. pupil

_____ 7. brightness   _____ 8. white light

_____ 9. subliminal perception   _____10. dark adaptation

_____11. JND   _____12. retina

_____13. ciliary muscles   _____14. lens

_____15. blind spot   _____16. nanometer

_____17. hue   _____18. cornea

_____19. sensation   _____20. signal detection theory

_____21. difference threshold   _____22. transducer

_____23. monochromatic   _____24. photoreceptors

_____25. cones   _____26. accommodation

_____27. aqueous humor   _____28. vitreous humor

_____29. optic nerve   _____30. psychophysics

_____31. sensory adaptation   _____32. absolute threshold

_____33. wave amplitude   _____34. fovea

_____35. rods   _____36. wavelength

a. The process of receiving information from the environment and changing that input into nervous system activity.

b. A mechanism that converts energy from one form to another—a basic process common to all our senses.

c. The study of the relationship between physical attributes of stimuli and the psychological experiences they produce.

d. The physical intensity of a stimulus that one can detect 50 percent of the time.

e. The process of responding to, or perceiving, stimuli that are presented at levels below one's absolute threshold.

f. The minimal difference in some stimulus attribute, such as intensity that one can detect 50 percent of the time.

g. The minimal change in some stimulus attribute, such as intensity, that can be detected.

h. The view that stimulus detection is a matter of decision-making, of separating a signal from background noise.

i. The process in which our sensory experience tends to decrease or diminish with continued exposure to a stimulus.

j. The process by which our eyes become more sensitive to light as we spend time in the dark.

k. A radiant energy that can be represented in wave form with wave lengths between 380 and 760 nanometers.

l. A characteristic of waveforms (the height of the wave) that indicates intensity.

m. The psychological experience associated with a lights intensity or wave amplitude.

n. A characteristic of wave forms that indicates the distance between any point on a wave and the corresponding point on the next cycle of the wave.

o. One millionth of a millimeter—the unit of measurement for the wavelength of light.

p. The psychological experience associated with a light's wavelength.

q. Literally one colored; a pure light made up of light waves all of the same wavelength.

r. The psychological experience associated with the purity of a light wave, where the most saturated lights are monochromatic and the least saturated are white light.

s. A light of the lowest possible saturation, containing a mixture of all visible wavelengths.

t. The outermost structure of the eye that protects the eye and begins to focus light waves.

u. The opening in the iris that changes size in relation to the amount of light available and emotional factors.

v. The colored structure of the eye that reflexively opens or constricts the pupils.

w. The structure behind the iris that changes shape to focus visual images in the eye.

x. Small muscles attached to the lens that control its shape and focusing capability.

y. The process in which the ciliary muscles change the shape of the lens in order to focus a visual image.

z. Watery fluid found in the space between the cornea and the lens that nourishes the front of the eye.

aa. The thick fluid behind the lens of the eye that helps keep the eyeball spherical.

bb. Layers of cells at the back of the eye that contain the photosensitive rod and cone cells.

cc. Light-sensitive cells of the retina that convert light energy into neural energy.

dd. Photosensitive cells of the retina that are most active in low levels of illumination and do not respond differentially to different wavelengths of light.

ee. Photosensitive cells of the retina that operate best at high levels of illumination and are responsible for color vision.

ff. The fiber of many neurons that leaves the eye and carries impulses to the occipital lobe of the brain.

gg. The region at the center of the retina, comprised solely of cones, where acuity is best in daylight.

hh. The small region of the retina, containing no photoreceptors, where the optic nerve leaves the eye.

ii. The location in the brain where impulses from light in the left visual field cross to the right side of the brain and similarly for light from the right visual field.

jj. Red, green, and blue; those colors from which all others can be produced.

TRUE-FALSE PRACTICE TEST

_____ 1. The terms sense receptor and transducer are synonymous.

_____ 2. Absolute threshold is absolute, and is not affected by such things as motivation or attention.

_____ 3. Subliminal stimuli can produce dangerous and harmful behaviors after repeated exposures.

_____ 4. To reach a threshold, stimuli must be detected at least fifty percent of the time.

_____ 5. A just noticeable difference and a difference threshold are essentially the same.

_____ 6. According to what we know about sensation of light, it would be better to paint firetrucks yellow-green instead of red.

_____ 7. Vision actually takes place in the brain, not in the eyes.

_____ 8. The blindspot and the fovea are the same.

_____ 9. Glaucoma is a disorder of the eye related to problems with the vitreous humor.

_____ 10. Nocturnal animals rely heavily on their cones for good night vision.

_____ 11. The three primary colors of light are red, blue, and green.

_____ 12. The trichromatic theory appears to be the most widely accepted theory of color vision.

_____ 13. Rods and cones are the actual transducers for vision.

_____ 14. Damage to the rods will produce color blindness.

_____ 15. The lowest possible saturation of light is white light.

FILL-IN PRACTICE TEST

1. _____ is the converting of physical energy in the environment into the neural energy of our nervous system.

2. _____ is the study of the relationships that exist between the physical attributes of stimuli and the psychological experiences that they produce.

3. When a stimulus registers at a level beyond our conscious awareness, this is known as _____ _____.

4. The smallest difference between stimulus attributes that can be detected is called _____ _____.

5. _____ _____ is a condition in which our sensory experience tends to decrease with the continued exposure of a stimulus.

6. The fact that our visual receptors become more sensitive to light if we spend time in the dark is referred to as _____ _____.

7. When sensory sensitivity increases, threshold _____.

8. The unit of measure for a wavelength of light is a _____.

9. The colored part of the eye is called the _____.

10. The part of the eye where vision actually begins to take place is the _____.

11. Color vision relies heavily on the _____.

12. Red, blue, and yellow are primary colors for pigment; but red, blue, and green are primary colors for _____.

13. According to the concept of negative afterimages, if you stare at a blue figure for a long time and then look away you will see a _____ colored figure.

14. The outermost structure of the eye that protect the eye is the _____.

15. A light made up of light waves that are all the same length is described as
    _____.

MULTIPLE CHOICE PRACTICE TEST 1 TOPIC 3A

1. Which of the following is the best example of a transducer?
    a. a light bulb
    b. your eye
    c. a radio
    d. all of the above

2. Ronda hears the so-called "silent" alarm that is present in many institutional buildings. Most people do not hear this high frequency pitch. It would be most accurate to say that in regard to hearing, Ronda's absolute threshold is
    a. lower than that of most people
    b. higher than that of most people
    c. about the same except for certain frequencies
    d. not functioning appropriately

3. Which of the following best describes the influence of subliminal stimuli?
    a. they have no effect
    b. the effect only relates to eating behaviors
    c. there is an impact, but not directly on behavior
    d. there is no such thing as subliminal stimuli

4. Charlie and Sharon live near an airport. However, they are no longer awakened by the sound of planes flying low overhead. The best explanation for this is
    a. subliminal perception
    b. signal detection theory
    c. sensory adaptation
    d. difference threshold

5. The quality or characteristic of a stimulus that our sense receptors will most likely respond to is
    a. intensity
    b. quality
    c. change
    d. constancy

6. The reason that we cannot see microwaves or radar waves is because
    a. they are invisible
    b. they are beyond the maximum wavelength detectable by humans
    c. they are beyond the minimum wavelength detectable by humans
    d. they have no hue

7. When the aqueous humor cannot escape from the space behind the cornea and causes a build up of pressure in the eye, the resulting problem is
    a. nearsightedness
    b. farsightedness
    c. accommodation
    d. glaucoma

8. The part of the eye where vision actually begins to take place is the
    a. lens
    b. retina
    c. iris
    d. cornea

9. The cones are to color vision as the rods are to
    a. lack of color
    b. low light levels
    c. intense light levels
    d. wavelength differentiation

10. The theory of color vision based on the idea that we possess three distinct receptor areas for the three primary colors of light is the
    a. primary color theory
    b. signal detection theory
    c. opponent process theory
    d. trichromatic theory

11. Which of the following is NOT a correct match?
    a. Young - trichromatic theory
    b. Helmholtz - trichromatic theory
    c. Wundt - signal detection theory
    d. Hering - opponent-process theory

12. Color blindness provides support for the
    a. trichromatic theory
    b. signal detection theory
    c. effects of subliminal stimuli
    d. opponent-process theory

13. The fovea and the blindspot are both features of the
    a. cornea
    b. lens
    c. retina
    d. pupil

14. Which of the following statements best describes visual fields?
    a. the left eye receives light only from the left visual field
    b. the right eye receives light only from the right visual field
    c. both eyes receive light from both visual fields
    d. the visual field depends on the dominance of the left or right hemisphere

15. Which of the following statements best describes the rods and cones?
    a. the rods outnumber the cones twenty to one
    b. they are represented in equal numbers in the eyes
    c. they function similarly
    d. they are found in different parts of the eye

MULTIPLE CHOICE PRACTICE TEST 2 TOPIC 3A

1. Which of the following is the best synonym for difference threshold?
    a. absolute threshold
    b. subliminal stimulus
    c. difference threshold
    d. detected signal

2. Joe asks Tess if the tie he has selected matches the new suit he is buying.   He is concerned with a/an
    a. absolute threshold
    b. just noticeable difference
    c. difference threshold
    d. detected signal

3. According to signal detection theory, experiencing a stimulus is a matter of
    a. background noise
    b. level of attention
    c. subject bias
    d. all of the above

4. Applying the principles related to sensory adaptation, the best way to get attention from an audience to whom you are speaking is to
    a. speak louder
    b. whisper
    c. speak faster
    d. all of the above

5. Spending time in the dark results in the visual receptors
    a. becoming more sensitive to light
    b. becoming less sensitive to light
    c. not responding to light stimuli at all
    d. responding to light about the same as before

6. In light stimuli, wavelength determines
    a. intensity
    b. amplitude
    c. color
    d. brightness

7. Problems such as nearsightedness and farsightedness are the result of
    a. problems with the shape of the lens
    b. disease in the cornea
    c. glaucoma
    d. over accommodation

8. The part of the eye where vision is most acute is the
    a. fovea
    b. iris
    c. cornea
    d. retina

9. Joseph dropped a quarter in the movie theater. Since it is quite dark in there, the part of his eye which will help him most in finding the lost coin is his
    a. cones
    b. rods
    c. lens
    d. cornea

10. Which of the following is NOT one of the visual mechanisms in the opponent-process theory?
    a. blue-yellow processor
    b. black-white processor
    c. red-blue processor
    d. red-green processor

11. Negative afterimages provide support for the
    a. trichromatic theory
    b. signal detection theory
    c. effects of subliminal stimuli
    d. opponent-process theory

12. A pure light made up of wavelengths that are all the same length would be
    a. red
    b. white
    c. invisible
    d. monochromatic

13. The psychological experience associated with a light's wavelength is
    a. hue
    b. brightness
    c. amplitude
    d. intensity

14. The process in which the ciliary muscles change the shape of the lens is called
    a. focusing
    b. accommodation
    c. sensing
    d. transduction

15. The most accurate statement about vision is that it occurs in the
    a. cornea
    b. lens
    c. rods and cones
    d. brain

CHAPTER 3—SENSORY PROCESSES TOPIC 3B— HEARING AND THE OTHER SENSES

LEARNING OBJECTIVES TOPIC 3B

People depend most heavily on their sense of vision but gain a great deal of information about their environments from their other senses. Students should be able to:
1. Discuss the three major physical characteristics of sound and the psychological experiences they produce.
2. Explain how sound passes through the ear.
3. Describe the stimulus, receptor, and primary qualities of the chemical senses.
4. List the cutaneous senses and explain how sensory adaptation is demonstrated.
5. Explain the position senses and how they operate.
6. Explain how the sensation of pain is produced.
7. Discuss gate control theory.

LEARNING TOPIC 3B VOCABULARY

On your own paper, write the definition for each of the following key terms. Your learning will be facilitated by writing the definition in your own words rather than copying the exact definition from your text.

LOUDNESS	DECIBEL SCALE
HERTZ	PITCH
TIMBRE	WHITE NOISE
PINNA	EARDRUM
MALLEUS, INCUS, STAPES	COCHLEA
BASILAR MEMBRANE	HAIR CELLS
TASTE BUDS	PHEROMONES
VESTIBULAR SENSE	KINESTHETIC SENSE
GATE-CONTROL THEORY	PLACEBO

MATCHING

Match the following key terms from your textbook with the appropriate definition.

_____ 1. Hertz   _____ 2. malleus, incus, stapes

_____ 3. placebo   _____ 4. taste buds

_____ 5. loudness   _____ 6. white noise

_____ 7. basilar membrane   _____ 8. pitch

_____ 9. pheromones   _____10. gate-control theory

_____11. decibel scale   _____12. pinna

_____13. timbre   _____14. cochlea

_____15. eardrum   _____16. hair cells

_____17. kinesthetic sense   _____18. vestibular sense

a. The psychological experience correlated with the intensity, or amplitude, of a sound wave.
b. A scale of our experience of loudness in which 0 represents the absolute threshold and 140 is sensed as pain.
c. The standard measure of sound wave frequency that is the number of wave cycles per second.
d. The psychological experience that corresponds to sound wave frequency and gives rise to high (treble) or low (bass) sounds.
e. The psychological experience related to wave purity by which we differentiate the sharpness, clearness, or quality of a tone.
f. A sound composed of a random assortment of all wave frequencies from the audible spectrum.
g. The outer ear that collects and funnels sound waves into the auditory canal toward the eardrum.
h. The outermost membrane of the ear that is set in motion by the vibrations of a sound; transmits vibrations to the ossicles.
i. Three small bones that transmit and intensify sound vibrations from the eardrum to the oval window.
j. Part of the inner ear where sound waves become neural impulses.
k. A structure within the cochlea that vibrates and thus stimulates the hair cells of the inner ear.
l. The receptor cells for hearing, located in the cochlea, stimulated by the vibrating basilar membrane; they send neural impulses to the temporal lobe.
m. The receptors for taste located on the tongue.
n. Chemicals that produce an odor that is used as a method of communication between organisms.
o. The position sense that tells us about balance, where we are in relations to gravity, acceleration, or deceleration.
p. The position sense that tells us the position of different parts of our bodies and what our muscles and joints are doing.
q. The theory of pain sensation that argues that there are brain centers that regulate the passage of pain messages from different parts of the body to the brain.
r. An inactive substance that has its effect because a person has come to believe that it will be effective.

TRUE -FALSE PRACTICE TEST

_____ 1. Vision is considered to be the dominant sense.

_____ 2. The absolute threshold for sound is zero decibels.

_____ 3. Sound that is of greater intensity than 100 decibels is experienced more as pain than as audition.

_____ 4. One similarity between sight and hearing is that in both cases the stimulus energy is represented as waves.

_____ 5. One unique thing about taste buds is that they reproduce or replace themselves when they die.

_____ 6. Pheromones are chemicals that produce very distinctive tastes and warn us about potentially poisonous plants.

_____ 7. In general, there is agreement on seven primary odors that can be detected by humans.

_____ 8. In order to produce a sensation of pain, any kind of stimulus must be very intense.

_____ 9. There is really no such thing as the placebo effect.

_____ 10. The experience of pain is related to both psychological and physical factors.

_____ 11. The gate-control theory suggests an explanation for the experience of pain not at the receptor sites, but in the nervous system.

_____ 12. Pain is usually considered to be a vestibular sense.

FILL-IN PRACTICE TEST

1. The _____ of a sound wave depicts its intensity or loudness.

2. Sound intensity is measured in units called _____.

3. The purity of sound is referred to as _____.

4. A random mixture of sound frequencies produces _____ _____.

5. The outer ear is called the _____.

6. The malleus, incus, and stapes are all _____.

7. Our senses of smell, texture, and temperature contribute heavily to our sense of _____.

8. The sense with the shortest, most direct pathway from the receptor site to the brain is the sense of _____.

9. Chemicals that produce distinctive odors are called _____.

10. Another term for the senses of temperature and pressure is _____ senses.

11. The _____ sense tells us about balance, where we are in relation to gravity.

12. The _____ sense tells us about the movement or position of our joints and muscles.

13. A substance that a person believes will be effective in treating a symptom such as pain is called a/an _____.

14. The neurotransmitters that help reduce pain are the _____.

15. The sense that is partially explained by gate-control theory is our sense of _____.

MULTIPLE CHOICE PRACTICE TEST 1 TOPIC 3B

1. The amplitude of sound is measured in units called
   a. frequencies
   b. Hertz
   c. wavelengths
   d. decibels

2. Dogs hear sounds that are
   a. higher in decibels than humans can hear
   b. lower in frequency than humans can hear
   c. higher in Hertz than humans can hear
   d. about the same as humans hear

3. Which of the following represents similarities between sight and hearing?
   a. in both the stimulus energy is in the form of waves
   b. in both the primary physical structures simply transfer energy to the brain
   c. in both the physical characteristics of the waves correlate to the psychological experience
   d. all of the above

4. The chemical senses are
   a. taste and smell
   b. hearing and smell
   c. sight and touch
   d. movement and balance

5. Pheromones carry messages that are related to
   a. sexual availability
   b. sexual preference
   c. repelling members of the opposite sex
   d. identifying women with PMS

6. Motion sickness is the result of a disturbance of the _____ sense.
   a. kinesthetic
   b. vestibular
   c. visual
   d. cutaneous

7. The one sense that appears to have no one specific center in the cerebral cortex is
   a. vision
   b. cutaneous
   c. smell
   d. pain

8. The gate-control theory of pain proposes that pain actually occurs
   a. at the receptor cite
   b. only in the external receptors
   c. in the central nervous system
   d. only under intense stimulus levels

9. Neurotransmitters that reduce the sense of pain are called
   a. enkaphalins
   b. endorphins
   c. pheromones
   d. hormones

10. The current explanation for our ability to discriminate among different types of cutaneous sensations is that
   a. a unique combination of responses is produced by the many receptor cells reacting to different types of stimuli
   b. there are specialized receptor cells that each produce a specialized type of cutaneous sense
   c. cutaneous senses often occur at levels of intensity beyond our conscious awareness
   d. we have certain types of cutaneous receptors that respond to some types of stimuli and other generalized receptors that respond to all stimuli

MULTIPLE CHOICE PRACTICE TEST 2 TOPIC 3B

1. A Hertz is a measure of sound
   a. wavelength
   b. frequency
   c. intensity
   d. amplitude

2. The psychological experience of the purity of sound is referred to as
   a. frequency
   b. Hertz
   c. timbre
   d. decibels

3. The part of the ear that marks the transition from the middle ear to the inner ear is the
   a. oval window
   b. incus
   c. cochlea
   d. ear drum

4. The actual transducers for hearing are located in the
   a. oval window
   b. incus
   c. cochlea
   d. ear drum

5. Which of the following taste-receptor site pairs is INCORRECT?
    a. sweet-tip of tongue
    b. salty-center of the tongue
    c. sour-sides of the tongue
    d. bitter-back of the tongue

6. The receptors for the kinesthetic sense are located primarily in the
    a. inner ear
    b. skin cells
    c. pheromones
    d. joints

7. Bill has been at his desk studying psychology for several hours. When he gets up to take a break, he realizes his foot has fallen asleep and he has difficulty walking. This will most likely make him appreciate his _____ sense.
    a. vestibular
    b. cutaneous
    c. kinesthetic
    d. position

8. Pain on or near the surface of the skin may be particularly responsive to a pain reducing technique called
    a. counter irritation
    b. hypnosis
    c. placebo effect
    d. endorphin release

9. Which of the following is NOT related to the gate-control theory of pain?
    a. placebo effect
    b. accupuncture
    c. counter irritation
    d. use of local anesthetics

10 Sharon's three-year-old son, Jess, is worried about going to the doctor to get a shot. To help him deal with the pain, Sharon should
    a. give him some apple juice and tell him it has magic power against pain
    b. rub his arm vigorously near the area where he will get the injection
    c. have him repeat the phrase, "It really won't hurt very much".
    d. all of the above

Dr. G's Best Study Tips #3

GET TO KNOW YOUR TEXT BOOK.

1. **Learn about the author.** Do this by reading the preface in the text. Also, look for any information about the author. Does the author specialize in a specific area of psychology? Is the author a faculty member at a college or university? Where? Where was the author educated? Has the author published other texts or scholarly writing?

2. **Learn about the publisher.** What company published the text? Where is the company located? Have you used other texts by this publisher? What did you like or not like about them?

3. **Learn about the book itself.** Read the table of contents to get an overview as to how the book is organized. Find out from your professor if the course organization will follow the structure of the book. Determine from your course calendar about how much of the text you will need to read on a weekly basis. What edition is the text? What does this mean? Look for the date of publication. How current is the text? Scan a few chapters. Look at the figures, tables, charts, graphs, cartoons, and any other illustrations. Note special features such as the running glossary, any appendices, and reference sections. How does the text read?

4. **See Dr. G's Best Study Tips** at the end of Chapter 4 for more information on reading your text book.

CHAPTER 4—PERCEPTION AND CONSCIOUSNESS
TOPIC 4A—PERCEPTION

LEARNING OBJECTIVES TOPIC 4A

Perception is an active process that represents the information presented to us by our senses. Students should be able to:
1. Explain how and why stimulus factors determine our selection of perceptions.
2. Describe how personal factors are involved in perceptual activity.
3. Discuss how stimulus factors and personal factors determine how we organize stimuli in perception.
4. List the cues that provide us with information about depth and distance.
5. Describe how the two illusions of motion are produced.
6. Explain how the types of perceptual constancy operate.

LEARNING TOPIC 4A VOCABULARY

On your own paper, write the definition for each of the following key terms. Your learning will be facilitated by writing the definition in your own words rather than copying the exact definition from your text.

PERCEPTION	CONTRAST
MENTAL SET	GESTALT
FIGURE-GROUND RELATIONSHIP	PROXIMITY
SIMILARITY	CONTINUITY
COMMON FATE	CLOSURE
SUBJECTIVE CONTOURS	RETINAL DISPARITY
CONVERGENCE	ACCOMMODATION
ILLUSION	PHI PHENOMENON
AUTOKINETIC EFFECT	SIZE CONSTANCY
SHAPE CONSTANCY	LIGHTNESS CONSTANCY

MATCHING

Match the following key terms from your textbook with the appropriate definition.

_____ 1. gestalt   _____ 2. common fate

_____ 3. subjective contours   _____ 4. lightness constancy

_____ 5. convergence   _____ 6. autokinetic effect

_____ 7. perception   _____ 8. similarity

_____ 9. accommodation   _____10. shape constancy

_____11. phi phenomenon   _____12. closure

_____13. contrast   _____14. continuity

_____15. retinal disparity   _____16. mental set

_____17. size constancy   _____18. proximity

_____19. illusion   _____20. figure-ground relationship

a. The cognitive process of selecting, organizing, and interpreting stimuli.
b. The extent to which a stimulus is in some physical way different from other surrounding stimuli.
c. A predisposed way to perceive something; an expectation.
d. Whole, totality, configuration, or pattern; the whole being perceived as more than the sum of its parts.
e. The Gestalt psychology principle that stimuli are selected and perceived as figures against a ground or background.
f. The Gestalt principle of organization that claims that stimuli will be perceived as belonging together if they occur together in space or time.
g. The Gestalt principle of organization that claims that stimuli will be perceived together if they share some common characteristics.
h. The Gestalt principle of organization that claims that a stimulus or a movement will be perceived as continuing in the same smooth direction as first established.
i. The Gestalt principle of organization that claims that we group together into the same figure, elements of a scene that move together in the same direction at the same speed.
j. The Gestalt principle of organization that claims that we tend to perceive incomplete figures as whole and complete.
k. The perception of a contour that is not there, but is suggested by other aspects of a scene.
l. The phenomenon in which each retina receives a different view of the same three-dimensional object.
m. The tendency of the eyes to move toward each other as we focus on objects up close.
n. The process in which the shape of the lens is changed by the ciliary muscles to focus an image on the retina.
o. A perception that is at odds with what we know as physical reality.
p. The visual illusion of the apparent motion in which a stationary light is flashing on and off.
q. The visual illusion of apparent motion in which a stationary pinpoint of light in an otherwise dark environment appears to move.
r. The tendency to see objects as being of constant size regardless of the size of the retinal image.
s. The tendency to see objects as being of constant shape regardless of the shape of the retinal image.
t. The tendency to see objects as the same regardless of the intensity of light reflected from them.

TRUE-FALSE PRACTICE TEST

_____ 1. Sensation is more influenced than perception by such things as motivation and experience.

_____ 2. Psychological preparedness for perception is referred to as having a mental set.

_____ 3. Attending to stimuli because of experience or motivation demonstrates bottom-up processing.

72

_____ 4. Proximity is a perceptual stimulus factor that applies only to visual stimuli.

_____ 5. Similarity, closure, continuity, and proximity are all examples of gestalt principles.

_____ 6. The personal factors that influence perception are the same as the ones that influence stimulus selection.

_____ 7. Retinal disparity is a monocular depth cue.

_____ 8. Stereoscopes and 3-D movies illustrate convergence.

_____ 9. We tend to see small objects as moving faster than large objects, even if their speed is the same.

_____ 10. Objects seen against a plain background will be perceived as moving faster than when seen against a patterned background.

_____ 11. Our perception of motion is not influenced by personal factors such as experience and expectation.

_____ 12. A ganzfeld is an environment totally void of depth cues.

_____ 13. When a woman looks in a small lipstick mirror, her lips will appear to be their normal size.

_____ 14. Size constancy depends a great deal on the quality of depth perception cues available and familiarity with the stimulus.

_____ 15. Human perception consists of three different constancies, size, shape, and color constancy.

FILL-IN PRACTICE TEST

1. The selection, organization, and interpretation of stimuli is known as _____.

2. A powerful stimulus factor in determining visual attention is _____.

3. When stimulus selection is based on motivation factors, mental set, and past experience, this is referred to as _____ processing.

4. The _____ psychologists studied factors that influence perception.

5. Our tendency to fill in gaps in our perception is known as _____.

6. Cues about depth and distance that require both eyes are called _____ cues.

7. The difference between what the right eye sees and what the left eye sees is called _____ _____.

8. When our perceptions seem to be at odds with what we know as reality, we are experiencing a/an_____.

9. A roller coaster is outlined with lights that flash on and off in a sequential pattern. This will produce the _____ _____.

10. The apparent movement of a pinpoint source of light in an otherwise darkened environment defines the _____ effect.

11. An environment that is totally void of depth cues is called a/an _____.

12. _____ _____ refers to our perception of objects maintaining their shape even though the retinal image they cast may change.

13. Looking at a car in the rearview mirror would provide an example of _____ constancy.

14. The Muller-Lyer is a well known _____.

15. _____ is the process in which the shape of the lens is changed by the ciliary muscles to focus an image on the retina.

MULTIPLE CHOICE PRACTICE TEST 1 TOPIC 4A

1. The bridge between what our senses record and what we later remember is provided by
   a. sensation
   b. memory
   c. organization
   d. perception

2. In perception, personal factor is to motivation as stimulus factor is to
   a. experience
   b. selection
   c. intensity
   d. sensation

3. Beth is waiting for her brother at the airport. Several times she thinks she sees him but it turns out to be someone with similar physical characteristics. This illustrates
   a. signal detection theory
   b. selective attention
   c. top down-processing
   d. bottom-up processing

4. In top-down processing, which of the following is NOT an influence on selection?
   a. stimulus intensity
   b. mental set
   c. motivation
   d. past experience

5. Events that occur close together in space or time are generally perceived as belonging together. Gestalt psychologists refer to this as
   a. proximity
   b. closure
   c. similarity
   d. continuity

6. While hunting, Charlie unknowingly approaches a well camouflaged snake. He is surprised when the snake slithers away through the grass. His perception of the snake is best explained by the gestalt principle of

   a. proximity

   b. common fate

   c. similarity

   d. figure-ground

7. We are able to experience 3-D movies because of the perceptual phenomenon of

   a. convergence

   b. accommodation

   c. similarity

   d. retinal disparity

8. The distance cue that is limited to "arm's length" is

   a. convergence

   b. retinal disparity

   c. accommodation

   d. linear perspective

9. Ben is standing in the middle of a railroad track. As he looks far ahead, the tracks seem to come together in the distance. This illustrates

   a. linear perspective

   b. interposition

   c. similarity

   d. convergence

10. As you drive by a construction site at night, you notice that a number of stationary, flashing warning lights appear to be moving back and forth. You are experiencing

    a. a primitive, sensory delusion

    b. the autokinetic effect

    c. motion parallax

    d. the phi phenomenon

11. You see two trees which in reality are of equal height. One is 50 feet away from you and the other is 200 feet away. The image that you receive from the farther tree will be_____ than the image from the closer tree, and according to the principle of size constancy, you will perceive the trees as _____ in size.

    a. larger; the same

    b. larger; different

    c. smaller; the same

    d. smaller; different

12. You walk into a dark movie theater wearing a white shirt, and notice that the shirt now looks gray. However, you know that the shirt is still white because of
    a. size constancy
    b. lightness constancy
    c. linear perspective
    d. texture gradient

13. The Muller-Lyer is an example of a/an
    a. illusion
    b. autokinetic effect
    c. phi phenomenon
    d. perceptual constancy

14. Often the difference between what is sensed and what is perceived can be explained by
    a. illusions
    b. impossible figures
    c. perceptual constancies
    d. depth perception

15. Which of the following is NOT an example of perceptual constancy?
    a. size
    b. shape
    c. color
    d. dimension

MULTIPLE CHOICE PRACTICE TEST 2 TOPIC 4A

1. The most important stimulus factor in perception is
    a. contrast
    b. intensity
    c. size
    d. motion

2. Bottom up processing is to stimulus intensity as top-down processing is to
    a. stimulus size
    b. motivation
    c. contrast
    d. stimulus intensity

3. On a cold winter morning, a number of birds fly into the yard. The one that really gets noticed among all the other little brown and gray birds is a bright red cardinal. This illustrates

   a. signal detection theory

   b. selective attention

   c. top down-processing

   d. bottom-up processing

4. Top-down processing is to motivation as bottom-up processing is to

   a. mental set

   b. experience

   c. stimulus intensity

   d. signal detection

5. The Australian koala is perceived as a bear because it looks like one. This illustrates the gestalt principle of

   a. continuity

   b. similarity

   c. closure

   d. contiguity

6. Retinal disparity is to binocular cue as _____ is to monocular cue.

   a. convergence

   b. size constancy

   c. accommodation

   d. continuity

7. Which of the following perceptual cues could not be experienced by a cyclops?

   a. size constancy

   b. accommodation

   c. convergence

   d. linear perspective

8. Which of the following is NOT a pictorial depth cue?

   a. convergence

   b. linear perspective

   c. relative size

   d. interposition

9. As Dorothy traveled down the "yellow brick road", if she looked down at her feet, the bricks would appear their normal size. However, if she looked ahead down the road, the bricks would appear to be smaller. This can be explained by the perceptual phenomenon of
   a. linear perspective
   b. texture gradient
   c. interposition
   d. relative size

10. Pick and Jo are on a cross-country train ride. As night falls and a full moon appears, they notice that the moon seems to follow the train. This can be explained by
    a. convergence
    b. linear perspective
    c. accommodation
    d. motion parallax

11. Early one night, you notice a single star in the sky and at first cannot decide if it is stationary or moving. This is probably an example of the
    a. moon illusion
    b. Purkinje effect
    c. effect of imagination on perception
    d. autokinetic effect

12. A native who has lived all his life in the dense jungle and thus has not perceived any stimulus from a great distance, would most likely NOT have developed
    a. shape constancy
    b. light constancy
    c. size constancy
    d. all of the above

13. Assuming that a cat's visual perception is similar to human perception, a kitten raised in the dark for research purposes would likely be lacking in the perceptual ability of
    a. lightness constancy
    b. shape constancy
    c. size constancy
    d. all of the above

14. Which of the following statements about illusions is NOT true?
    a. Illusions do not depend on our ignorance of the situation.
    b. Gestalt psychologists are able to explain illusions in perceptual terms.
    c. Illusions do not occur at the retina.
    d. The effects of an illusion do not depend on movements of the eye.

15. Impossible figures are examples of
    a. shape constancy
    b. texture gradient
    c. the autokinetic effect
    d. illusions

CHAPTER 4—PERCEPTION AND CONSCIOUSNESS
TOPIC 4B—VARIETIES OF CONSCIOUSNESS

LEARNING OBJECTIVES TOPIC 4B

Consciousness is an integral part of our lives that has resumed its place in mainstream psychology. Students should be able to:
1. Define consciousness, and explain its four basic characteristics.
2. Define an altered state of consciousness.
3. Distinguish between the EEG and EMG.
4. Describe the four stages of sleep.
5. Explain how REM sleep differs from NREM sleep.
6. Discuss the effects of sleep deprivation and the restorative and evolutionary perspectives as explanations for sleep.
7. Define hypnosis, and describe how it affects consciousness.
8. Describe meditation and its affects on relaxation and somatic activity.
9. Discuss the effects of stimulant drugs.
10. Discuss the effects of depressant drugs.
11. Describe the effects of hallucinogenic drugs.
12. Describe the effects of marijuana.

LEARNING TOPIC 4B VOCABULARY

On your own paper, write the definition for each of the following key terms. Your learning will be facilitated by writing the definition in your own words rather than copying the exact definition from your text.

CONSCIOUSNESS	INSOMNIA
ELECTROENCEPHALOGRAM	ELECTROMYOGRAM
ALPHA ACTIVITY	REM SLEEP
ATONIA	MICROSLEEPS
HYPNOSIS	HALLUCINATIONS
MEDITATION	PSYCHOACTIVE DRUG
DEPENDENCE	TOLERANCE
WITHDRAWAL	ADDICTION
DRUG ABUSE	STIMULANTS
DEPRESSANTS	HALLUCINOGENS

MATCHING

Match the following key terms from your textbook with the appropriate definition.

____ 1. meditation   ____ 2. depressants

____ 3. withdrawal   ____ 4. electroencephalogram

____ 5. hallucinations   ____ 6. REM sleep

_____ 7. hallucinogens   _____ 8. drug abuse

_____ 9. dependence   _____10. stimulants

_____11. consciousness   _____12. alpha activity

_____13. atonia   _____14. addiction

_____15. insomnia   _____16. hypnosis

_____17. electromyogram   _____18. psychoactive drug

_____19. microsleeps   _____20. tolerance

a. Our awareness or perception of the environment and of our own mental processes.
b. The chronic inability to get to sleep and to get an adequate amount of sleep.
c. An instrument used to measure and record the electrical activity of the brain.
d. An instrument used to measure and record muscle tension/relaxation.
e. An EEG pattern associated with quiet relaxation and characterized by slow wave cycles of 8 to 12 per second.
f. Rapid eye movement sleep during which vivid dreaming occurs, as do heightened levels of physiological functioning.
g. Muscular immobility—associated with REM sleep—caused by the total relaxation of the muscles.
h. Brief episodes of sleep discernable only by examination of an EEG record.
i. An altered state of consciousness characterized by an increase in suggestibility, attention, and imagination.
j. Perceptual experiences without sensory input; that is, perceiving that which is not there or not perceiving that which is there.
k. The focusing of awareness in order to arrive at an altered state of consciousness and relaxation.
l. A chemical that has an effect on psychological processes and consciousness.
m. A state in which drug use is either necessary or believed to be necessary to maintain functioning at some desired level.
n. In using a drug, a state where more and more of the drug is required to produce the same level of effect.
o. A negative, painful reaction that may occur when one stops taking a drug.
p. An extreme dependency, usually accompanied by symptoms of tolerance and painful withdrawal.
q. Abuse implies a lack of control, a disruption of interpersonal relationships or difficulties at work, and a history of maladaptive use for at least one month.
r. Those drugs (such as caffeine, cocaine, and amphetamines) that increase nervous system activity.
s. Those drugs (such as alcohol, opiates, heroin, and barbiturates) that slow or reduce nervous system activity.
t. Those drugs (such as LSD) whose major effect is the alteration of perceptual experience and mood.

TRUE-FALSE PRACTICE TEST

_____ 1. EEG's measure brain activity and muscle activity.

_____ 2. The best indicator of how much sleep a person gets is a self-report.

_____ 3. Dreams occur in "real" time.

_____ 4. Everybody experiences REM sleep and dreams every night.

_____ 5. The older a person is, the less he/she will tend to sleep.

_____ 6. Sleep deprivation can produce some lasting harmful effects, especially if the person is deprived of REM sleep.

_____ 7. Being deprived of REM sleep produces a rebound effect, but there is no rebound for deprivation of NREM sleep.

_____ 8. Anyone can be hypnotized, even against his/her will.

_____ 9. Research by David Holmes indicated that there is no difference between meditating subjects and subjects who are simply resting in terms of arousal or relaxation.

_____ 10. Many of the claims made about meditation have not been proven by research.

_____ 11. Tolerance and withdrawal are both associated with addiction.

_____ 12. Stopping the intake of caffeine can result in a rebound effect.

_____ 13. Nicotine and caffeine are the most commonly used stimulants.

_____ 14. The effects of a depressant drug is about the same regardless of whether a large or small dose is taken.

_____ 15. Alcohol is the most deadly of all drugs.

FILL-IN PRACTICE TEST

1. _____ is the chronic inability to get to sleep and to get an adequate amount of sleep.

2. _____ waves occur mainly during sleep stages 3 and 4 .

3. _____ sleep is the period during which dreaming occurs.

4. _____ sleep consists mostly of stages 2, 3, and 4 .

5. _____ believed that dreaming provides the opportunity for fantasy and wish fulfillment.

6. During dreams, the muscles are inactive or immobilized. This is called _____.

7. Short sleeps called _____ are found in the EEG records of waking subjects.

8. _____ is a self-induced state of altered consciousness characterized by a focusing of attention and relaxation.

9. A softly spoken or chanted word or phrase used to focus attention during meditation is called a _____.

10. Drugs that create changes in perception, mood, and behavior are referred to as _____ drugs.

11. A condition in which the use of a drug leads to a state where more and more of it is needed to produce the same effect is referred to as _____.

12. _____ is a negative reaction that results when one stops taking a drug.

13. Dependence on drugs can be either physical or _____.

14. Drugs that stimulate or activate the nervous system are called _____ .

15. _____ is the most commonly used depressant drug.

MULTIPLE CHOICE PRACTICE TEST 1 TOPIC 4B

1. According to William James, there are four basic realities associated with consciousness. Which of the following is NOT one of them?

    a. change

    b. stimulus factors

    c. personal experience

    d. continuity

2. Which of the following is NOT a correct match?

    a. alpha waves-altered state produced by drugs

    b. theta waves-stage 1 sleep

    c. sleep spindles-stage 2 sleep

    d. delta waves-stage 3 sleep

3. The psychologist who believed that dreams were the pathway to the unconscious was

    a. James

    b. Kleitman

    c. Freud

    d. Jung

4. Subjects deprived of REM sleep for a few nights and then left alone will spend long periods in REM sleep. This is referred to as

    a. microsleep

    b. REM rebound

    c. atonia

    d. REM exaggeration

5. One problem with Dement's sleep research on the effects of deprivation of REM sleep was that

    a. Dement fell prey to observer bias

    b. subjects were not debriefed

    c. the laboratory controls were not stringently applied

    d. the findings could not be replicated

6. An evolutionary perspective on sleep and dreaming would predict that over a two or three day period, a/an _____ would require the LEAST amount of total sleep time.

    a. newborn infant

    b. college student

    c. rabbit

    d. elephant

7. Which of the following is NOT true of hypnosis?
    a. Avid readers and runners do not make good hypnotic subjects.
    b. People do not do anything under hypnosis that they would not do otherwise.
    c. Hypnosis can be used to alleviate pain.
    d. Hypnosis can not improve memory or learning ability.

8. Which of the following is NOT a factor distinguishing drug abuse from drug use?
    a. An abuser shows a lack of control where the drug is concerned.
    b. An abuser experiences tolerance and withdrawal.
    c. A disruption of interpersonal relationships is usually associated with abuse.
    d. Maladaptive drug use has continued for at least one month.

9. The feeling of relaxation that smokers seem to enjoy can be attributed to
    a. the psychological effects of having something to do with their hands
    b. the effect of nicotine on the brain
    c. the ritual of smoking after meals and at other times when people are normally relaxed
    d. the effects of nicotine on the central nervous system that causes muscle tone to relax

10. Which of these drugs seems to be the LEAST addictive?
    a. cocaine
    b. heroine
    c. barbiturates
    d. marijuana

11. The specific effects of alcohol on the drinker is related most to
    a. the amount consumed
    b. the past experience of the drinker
    c. the temperature at the time the alcohol is consumed
    d. the type of alcohol consumed

12. Being legally drunk is defined as having a blood alcohol level of
    a. 5 percent
    b. 3 percent
    c. 1 percent
    d. 1/10 percent

13. Which of the following drugs is most likely to produce hallucinations?
    a. heroin
    b. nicotine
    c. LSD
    d. alcohol

14. The use of LSD affects the level of the neurotransmitter

    a. dopamine

    b. norepinephrine

    c. serotonin

    d. endorphin

15. Which of the following is NOT associated with long-term marijuana use?

    a. bronchitis and other lung ailments

    b. chromosomal abnormalities in offspring

    c. hallucinations

    d. adverse effects on the immune system

MULTIPLE CHOICE PRACTICE TEST 2 TOPIC 4B

1. An instrument that measures and records the electrical activity of the brain is called a/an

    a. electromyogram

    b. electrocardiogram

    c. electroencephalogram

    d. polygraph

2. Sexual arousal or excitement usually occurs during _____ sleep.

    a. stage 2

    b. REM

    c. NREM

    d. stage 4

3. REM sleep is sometimes referred to as "paradoxical sleep" because

    a. it is a very active time and not peaceful

    b. the brain waves produce sleep spindles

    c. the person may actually be awake

    d. so little is known about it

4. Following a period of several nights during which you are prevented from having REM sleep, you are allowed to sleep undisturbed. Which of the following best describes this sleep following REM deprivation?

    a. You experience REM rebound, having more REM than usual.

    b. You have the same amount of REM that you would normally have, but it occurs right after you go to sleep.

    c. You have the same amount of REM that you would normally have, in the same pattern as usual.

    d. You experience REM suppression, having less REM than normal.

5. Which of the following is NOT true of hypnosis?
   a. It is characterized by an increase in suggestibility.
   b. During hypnosis a person is unaccepting of distortions of reality.
   c. When hypnotized, a person's attention is narrowly focused.
   d. A hypnotized person uses imagination in an exaggerated way.

6. Which of the following is TRUE of meditation?
   a. Meditation heightens awareness.
   b. Meditation decreases somatic arousal better than resting.
   c. People who meditate cope with stress better than those who do not.
   d. Meditation is a self-induced altered state of consciousness that became popular during the 60s.

7. Which of the following is NOT a correct match?
   a. nicotine-tolerance
   b. caffeine-rebound
   c. cocaine-stimulant
   d. marijuana-stimulant

8. Which of the following is NOT true of depressants?
   a. Depressants reduce a person's awareness of external stimuli.
   b. Depressants slow bodily functions.
   c. Depressants cause the user to feel emotions of sorrow and sadness.
   d. Depressants decrease levels of overt behavior.

9. In many ways, the most dangerous of all drugs is
   a. alcohol
   b. LSD
   c. cocaine
   d. nicotine

10. Variations in the effects of alcohol can be explained by
   a. whether the person has eaten or not
   b. cognitive factors such as one's frame of mind
   c. the amount of alcohol consumed
   d. all of the above

11. Drugs which are also called analgesics because they relieve pain are
   a. stimulants
   b. opiates
   c. depressants
   d. hallucinogens

12. The major difference between methadone and heroin is that
    a. Methadone is not addictive.
    b. Heroin and methadone have different psychological effects.
    c. Methadone reaches the brain more slowly.
    d. all of the above apply

13. Death from heroin use is often associated with
    a. long term damage to the nervous system
    b. impaired function of the internal organs
    c. increased dosages causing breathing to stop
    d. weakening of the body's immune system

14. The drugs which have the most unpredictable effect on consciousness are
    a. hallucinogens
    b. barbiturates
    c. stimulants
    d. depressants

15. Which of the following is NOT true of marijuana?
    a. It impairs judgment and reflexes.
    b. Its use can impair memory function.
    c. It produces the release of serotonin and other neurotransmitters.
    d. It is associated with increased numbers of miscarriages.

Dr. G's Best Study Tips #4

HOW TO READ YOUR TEXTBOOK

If you followed study tips #3 from the previous chapter, you should be familiar with your text by now. In this segment, I want to help you develop a system for chapter by chapter reading.

1. **Preread the chapter.**

   a. First read the outline at the beginning. This will give you an idea as to the structure and organization of the chapter. What topics are being covered? Are there issues with which you are already familiar?

   b. Then skip to the end of the chapter and read the summary. This will fill in a little more fully the ideas that will be presented in detail in the chapter. By reading this summary, you are preparing yourself to learn the more detailed information.

   c. Now skim through the chapter examining the charts, graphs, tables, figures, and any other illustrations. Students are tempted to ignore anything that isn't print. This is a big mistake. The author has carefully chosen this type of illustrative material to emphasize and explain important points. See what you can learn from them. Think of them as sign posts indicating important material.

   d. Finally, read through the chapter taking only one section at a time. When you have finished a section, you need to check your comprehension in some way. Try to say out loud the major points or write them down. This is generativity that was mentioned in the first study tips. You must turn the passive process of reading into an active one.

2. **Plan to read the chapter only once.** For most people, rereading an entire chapter is a very inefficient study method. It is far better to do one thorough and comprehensive reading.

3. **Keep a pencil and a highlighter handy.** Use the highlighter to underline important points that you want to return to or emphasize. Use the pencil to make notes to yourself in the form of questions or your own interpretations of what you have read. When you are ready to review, you should be able to review what you have underlined and the notes you have read. Reserve rereading only for the most difficult concepts or ideas which seem unfamiliar or unclear.

4. **Sit at the keyboard.** I often use a strategy of sitting at a typewriter or word processor and typing notes in the form of a summary or outline as I read. Then I study just my notes as I review, going back to the text only for clarification. Typing the notes is at least twice as fast as handwriting, even if you are a poor typist.

CHAPTER 5—LEARNING TOPIC 5A—
CLASSICAL CONDITIONING

LEARNING OBJECTIVES TOPIC 5A

Classical conditioning is a simple form of how we learn and adapt to our environment. Pavlov's work illustrates the basic principles that can be applied to our daily lives. Students should be able to:
1. Define learning and conditioning.
2. Describe the essential features of classical conditioning.
3. Explain what acquisition, extinction, and spontaneous recovery are.
4. Define generalization and discrimination.
5. Describe the sorts of responses that are most readily influenced by classical conditioning.
6. Describe the "Little Albert" experimental demonstration.
7. Define phobic disorders and describe the use of systematic desensitization to treat phobias.
8. Understand what makes an effective CS.
9. Discuss how taste aversion studies relate to the CS-UCS interval.
10. Apply classical conditioning principles to their study behavior.

LEARNING TOPIC 5A VOCABULARY

On your own paper, write the definition for each of the following key terms. Your learning will be facilitated by writing the definition in your own words rather than copying the exact definition from your text.

LEARNING	REFLEX
CLASSICAL CONDITIONING	UNCONDITIONED STIMULUS (UCS)
UNCONDITIONED RESPONSE (UCR)	ORIENTING REFLEX
HABITUATION	CONDITIONED STIMULUS (CS)
CONDITIONED RESPONSE (CR)	ACQUISITION
EXTINCTION	SPONTANEOUS RECOVERY
GENERALIZATION	DISCRIMINATION
PHOBIC DISORDER	SYSTEMATIC DESENSITIZATION

MATCHING

Match the following key terms from your textbook with the appropriate definition.

____ 1. acquisition	____ 2. systematic desensitization
____ 3. unconditioned stimulus	____ 4. conditioned stimulus
____ 5. reflex	____ 6. orienting reflex
____ 7. extinction	____ 8. discrimination
____ 9. learning	____10. conditioned response
____11. classical conditioning	____12. generalization
____13. phobic disorder	____14. spontaneous recovery

____15. habituation   ____16. unconditioned response

a. Demonstrated by a relatively permanent change in behavior that occurs as the result of practice or experience.
b. An unlearned, automatic response that occurs in the presence of specific stimuli.
c. Learning in which an originally neutral stimulus comes to elicit a new response after having been paired with a stimulus that reflexively elicits that same response.
d. In classical conditioning, a stimulus that reliably and reflexively evokes a response.
e. In classical conditioning, a response reliably and reflexively evoked by a stimulus.
f. The simple, unlearned response of orienting toward, or attending to a new or unusual stimulus.
g. A simple form of learning in which an organism comes to ignore a stimulus of no consequence.
h. In classical conditioning, an originally neutral stimulus that, when paired with a UCS, comes to evoke a new response.
i. In classical conditioning, the learned response evoked by the CS after conditioning.
j. The process in classical conditioning in which the strength of the CR increases with repeated pairings of the CS and the UCS.
k. The process in classical conditioning in which the strength of the CR decreases with repeated presentations of the CS alone.
l. The phenomenon in classical conditioning in which a previously extinguished CR returns after a rest interval.
m. The phenomenon in classical conditioning in which a CR is elicited by stimuli different from, but similar to, the CS.
n. The phenomenon in classical conditioning in which an organism learns to make a CR in response to only one CS, but not to other stimuli.
o. A psychological disorder in which a person suffers from an intense, irrational fear of an object or situation that leads the person to avoid it.
p. The application of classical conditioning procedures to alleviate anxiety in which anxiety-producing stimuli are paired with a state of relaxation.

TRUE-FALSE PRACTICE TEST

_____   1. Learning results in a relatively permanent change in behavior.

_____   2. The disappearance of an orienting reflex is caused by habituation.

_____   3. A conditioned stimulus and an unconditioned stimulus can produce responses with equal strength.

_____   4. The more trials that are presented during the acquisition stage, the greater the strength of the conditioned response to the conditioned stimulus.

_____   5. When a CS is repeatedly presented without being paired with the UCS, spontaneous recovery will occur.

_____   6. In classical conditioning, the CR and the UCR are actually the same behavior.

_____   7. One series of extinction trials is usually sufficient to eliminate a response permanently.

_____   8. Extinction in classical conditioning can be considered a type of forgetting.

_____   9. Conditioning trials do not have to be applied over and over again in order for the organism to respond to separate stimuli.

_____   10. All human emotional responses are acquired through classical conditioning.

_____ 11. Phobic disorders are as easily extinguished as they are acquired.

_____ 12. Recent research on classical conditioning indicates that any stimulus can become a conditioned stimulus.

_____ 13. Only humans can be classically conditioned to avoid certain foods.

_____ 14. It is likely that the association between a food stimulus and nausea that occurs hours later may be biologically predisposed.

_____ 15. There really are limited applications of classical conditioning where human behavior is concerned.

FILL-IN PRACTICE TEST

1. The most basic fundamental types of learning are called _____.

2. A _____ is an unlearned, automatic response that occurs in the presence of a specific stimulus.

3. The stage of classical conditioning during which the strength of the conditioned response increases is called _____.

4. The repeated presentation of the CS without the UCS will result in _____.

5. In Pavlov's conditioning research, the conditioned response was _____.

6. When an extinguished response reappears automatically after a rest period, this is called _____ _____.

7. In classical conditioning, an extinguished response is not forgotten, rather it is _____.

8. The process in which an organism learns to make a conditioned response to only one conditioned stimulus, but not to other stimuli is called _____.

9. An intense irrational fear of some object that leads a person to avoid contact with the object is a _____ _____.

10. The most common treatment for phobic disorders is _____ _____.

11. The psychologist who provided the theoretical basis for systematic desensitization was _____.

12. Another name for systematic desensitization is _____.

13. The psychologist who conducted the famous classical conditioning experiment with Little Albert was _____.

14. A simple form of learning in which an organism comes to ignore a stimulus is called _____.

15. A strong dislike for a stimulus that usually produces avoidance of the stimulus is called _____.

MULTIPLE CHOICE PRACTICE TEST 1 TOPIC 5A

1. In Pavlovian conditioning, the relationship between the unconditioned response and the unconditioned stimulus is
   a. learned
   b. reflexive
   c. hereditary
   d. conditioned

2. In the Pavlovian demonstration of classical conditioning, the conditioned response was _____ and the unconditioned response was _____.
   a. food powder; salivation
   b. a bell; food powder
   c. salivation; salivation
   d. food powder; a bell

3. If a conditioned stimulus is repeatedly presented without being paired with the unconditioned stimulus, the behavior will eventually fail to occur. This is known as
   a. conditioning failure
   b. stimulus rejection
   c. extinction
   d. habituation

4. The strength of a response made to a similar stimulus during generalization depends on
   a. the similarity between the new stimulus and the CS
   b. the amount of time that has passed since the acquisition stage
   c. the difference between the new stimulus and the UCS
   d. the number of extinction trials presented prior to generalization

5. As a child, Sharon was attacked by a black labrador retriever. She was only scratched and knocked down, but terribly frightened. Now, as an adult she is afraid of all large dogs. This is an example of
   a. stimulus generalization
   b. stimulus discrimination
   c. spontaneous recovery
   d. reflexive relationships

6. John Watson's conditioning of Little Albert to fear a white rat was based on
   a. Little Albert's natural fear of the rat
   b. the reflexive relationship between fear and loud noises
   c. the child's natural anxiety in the presence of strangers
   d. Little Albert's ability to generalize fear to many different stimuli

7. Phobic disorders are not easily extinguished because

    a. people who suffer them usually refuse treatment

    b. a person with a phobia is usually successful at simply avoiding the feared object

    c. the fear simply generalizes to a different stimulus

    d. emotional responses are impossible to extinguish

8. An anxiety hierarchy is used in

    a. conditioning phobias

    b. extinguishing pleasure responses

    c. creating stimulus generalization

    d. treating phobic disorders

9. Systematic desensitization is most similar to

    a. stimulus generalization

    b. extinction

    c. counterconditioning

    d. spontaneous recovery

10. Systematic desensitization is based on principles introduced by

    a. Wolpe

    b. Watson

    c. Pavlov

    d. Raynor

11. According to recent research on classical conditioning, what matters most in determining whether or not a stimulus will become a conditioned stimulus is

    a. the extent to which the stimulus is generalized

    b. how closely the conditioned stimulus follows the unconditioned stimulus

    c. the degree to which the organism can discriminate the stimulus from other stimuli

    d. the extent to which the stimulus provides information about the occurrence of another stimulus

12. An application of classical conditioning principles to studying for college courses can be found in the notion that

    a. students study best in one place because the environment acts as a conditioned stimulus

    b. students can generalize good study habits and study effectively in many locations

    c. since the library is usually associated with learning, it is the only good place to study

    d. students can discriminate different environments for different behaviors and can study well in different locations

13. Which of the following is the best application of classical conditioning principles to human learning

    a. cognitive maps

    b. phobias

    c. punishment

    d. fear of pain

14. If a person blinks when a puff of air hits his/her eyes, a/an _____ is being exhibited.

    a. conditioned response

    b. generalized response

    c. discriminatory response

    d unconditioned response

15. A basic principle of systematic desensitization is that

    a. emotional responses are not acquired through classical conditioning

    b. stimuli which produce the most intense fear response should be extinguished first

    c. taste aversion can be extinguished using this method

    d. a person cannot be anxious and relaxed at the same time

MULTIPLE CHOICE PRACTICE TEST 2 TOPIC 5A

1. Which of the following is the correct order of stimuli and responses during the acquisition stage?

    a. UCS-CS-CR

    b. UR-UCS-US

    c. CS-UCS-UCR

    d. CS-UCR-UCS

2. Pace lives in a college dorm and has learned that while in the shower, if a toilet flushes, he will immediately be scalded by very hot water. His response to this unpleasant stimulus is to jump out of the way. After a few times of this, Pace jumps as soon as he hears the sound of the toilet flushing. In this example of classical conditioning, the hot water is the _____ and the sound of the toilet flushing is the _____.

    a. unconditioned stimulus; conditioned stimulus

    b. neutral stimulus; conditioned stimulus

    c. learned stimulus; neutral stimulus

    d. unconditioned stimulus; unconditioned response

3. A person blinks when a puff of air is blown into his/her eyes. In classical conditioning, the blink is considered to be a/an

    a. unconditioned response

    b. learned response

    c. neutral response

    d. conditioned response

4. One of Pavlov's students discovered that she could make dogs act in a very nervous, agitated way (referred to by Pavlov as experimental neurosis) by:

   a. first conditioning dogs to salivate to a tone stimulus, and then never again presenting the tone.

   b. putting dogs through a series of extinction trials to totally suppress a conditioned response.

   c. having conditioned dogs spontaneously recover so many times they did not know if they were in acquisition or extinction.

   d. requiring dogs to make discriminations between stimuli that were too similar to differentiate.

5. If spontaneous recovery of a classically conditioned response occurs, it will occur immediately following

   a. the presentation of the UCS

   b. acquisition

   c. a rest period

   d. extinction

6. In John Watson's classical conditioning studies with Little Albert, the rat was the _____ and the loud noise was the _____.

   a. neutral stimulus; conditioned stimulus

   b. generalized stimulus; discriminated stimulus

   c. unconditioned stimulus; conditioned stimulus

   d. conditioned stimulus; unconditioned stimulus

7. A common method of treating phobic disorders is

   a. classically conditioning a new "safe" stimulus

   b. producing extinction of the fear response

   c. systematic desensitization

   d. generalization of nonfear stimuli

8. Rescorla's recent classical conditioning research demonstrated that

   a. rats do not fear electric shock

   b. every stimulus cannot become a conditioned stimulus

   c. lights will not become conditioned stimuli for rats

   d. a tone will not serve as a UCS for fear responses in rats

9. Research on the formation of aversions to certain tastes indicates that

   a. the CS and UCS must be closely paired in time

   b. taste aversions require the CS and UCS to be similar in intensity

   c. the CS and UCS can be separated by longer time periods than previously thought

   d. taste aversions are only formed is association with unpleasant tastes

10. Joseph Wolpe contributed research on the principles of _____.
    a. systematic desensitization
    b. taste aversion
    c. reflexive relationships
    d. stimulus generalization

11. One problem with John Watson's research involving Little Albert is that
    a. the conclusions were misinterpreted
    b. Little Albert was an atypical subject
    c. the research was interrupted and never completed
    d. by today's standards, the research was unethical

12. In systematic desensitization, replacing an old fear response with a new relaxation response is called
    a. aversion
    b. counterconditioning
    c. creating a hierarchy
    d. generalizing

13. Your text suggests that studying at the kitchen table is probably not a good idea because
    a. it will usually be too noisy in such an environment
    b. the table cannot be discriminated from the desk where exams will be taken
    c. studying there may become an unconditioned response toward certain foods
    d. the kitchen is a conditioned stimulus for competing responses

14. To determine whether or not generalization or discrimination has taken place, we need to measure
    a. how long it takes to determine acquisition
    b. the strength of the CR
    c. the reliability of the UCS-UCR pairing
    d. the organism's ability to generalize or discriminate

15. In classical conditioning, the first response made to the neutral stimulus is called
    a. orienting reflex
    b. learned response
    c. reflexive response
    d. unconditioned reflex

CHAPTER 5 —LEARNING TOPIC 5B—OPERANT CONDITIONING AND BEYOND

LEARNING OBJECTIVES TOPIC 5B

The basic premise of operant conditioning is that behaviors are influenced by consequence. Cognitive approaches put more emphasis on mental processes. Students should be able to:
1. Explain the principles of operant conditioning.
2. Discuss how shaping, acquisition, extinction, and spontaneous recovery function in operant conditioning.
3. Understand the operational definition of reinforcer.
4. Define a negative reinforcer and explain how it is used in escape and avoidance conditioning.
5. Distinguish between primary and secondary reinforcers.
6. Explain intermittent schedules of reinforcement and the advantages of using each of them.
7. Describe how generalization and discrimination function in operant conditioning.
8. Explain how instinctive drift limits conditioning.
9. Define learning set.
10. Discuss the notions of cognitive maps and latent learning.
11. Relate the basic concepts of social learning theory and modeling.
12. Use operant conditioning and cognitive approaches to learning to improve study skills.
13. Explain the role of vicarious reinforcement and vicarious punishment in learning.

LEARNING TOPIC 5B VOCABULARY

On your own paper, write the definition for each of the following key terms. Your learning will be facilitated by writing the definition in your own words rather than copying the exact definition from your text.

OPERANT	OPERANT CONDITIONING
LAW OF EFFECT	SHAPING
ACQUISITION	EXTINCTION
SPONTANEOUS RECOVERY	REINFORCEMENT
REINFORCERS	POSITIVE REINFORCER
NEGATIVE REINFORCER	PRIMARY REINFORCER
SECONDARY REINFORCER	CONTINUOUS REINFORCEMENT SCHEDULE

INTERMITTENT REINFORCEMENT SCHEDULES

PUNISHMENT	GENERALIZATION
DISCRIMINATION	INSTINCTIVE DRIFT
LEARNING SET	LATENT LEARNING
COGNITIVE MAP	SOCIAL LEARNING THEORY

VICARIOUS REINFORCEMENT OR PUNISHMENT

MATCHING

Match the following key terms from your textbook with the appropriate definition.

____ 1. vicarious reinforcement   ____ 2. discrimination

____ 3. negative reinforcer   ____ 4. latent learning

____ 5. secondary reinforcer   ____ 6. cognitive map

____ 7. extinction   ____ 8. positive reinforcer

____ 9. operant   ____10. reinforcement

____11. law of effect   ____12. reinforcers

____13. social learning theory   ____14. shaping

____15. intermittent reinforcement   ____16. learning set

____17. primary reinforcers   ____18. operant conditioning

____19. generalization   ____20. acquisition

____21. punishment   ____22. spontaneous recovery

____23. continuous reinforcement   ____24. instinctive drift

a. Behaviors used by an organism to operate on its environment.
b. Changing the rate of a response on the basis of the consequences that result from that response.
c. The observation that responses that lead to satisfying states of affairs tend to be repeated, while those that do not, are not.
d. A procedure of reinforcing successive approximations of a desired response until that desired response is made.
e. The process in operant conditioning in which the rate of a reinforced response increases.
f. The process in operant conditioning in which the rate of a response decreases as reinforcers are withheld.
g. The phenomenon in operant conditioning in which a previously extinguished response returns after a rest interval.
h. A process that increases the rate or probability of the response that it follows.
i. Stimuli that increase the rate or probability of the responses they follow.
j. A stimulus that increases the rate of a response when that stimulus is presented after the response is made.
k. A stimulus that increases the rate of a response when that stimulus is removed after the response is made.
l. Stimuli that increase the rate of a response with no previous experience required.
m. Stimuli that increase the rate of a response because of their having been associated with other reinforcers; also called conditioned, or learned, reinforcers.
n. A reinforcement schedule in which each and every response is followed by a reinforcer.
o. Reinforcement schedules in which responses are not reinforced every time they occur.
p. The administration of a punisher, which is a stimulus that decreases the rate or probability of a response that precedes it.
q. The process by which a response that was reinforced in the presence of one stimulus appears in response to other, similar stimuli.
r. The process of differential reinforcement wherein one stimulus is reinforced while another stimulus is not.
s. The tendency of behaviors that have been conditioned to eventually revert to more natural, instinctive behaviors.
t. An acquired strategy for learning or problem solving; learning to learn.
u. Hidden learning that is not demonstrated in performance until that performance is reinforced.

v. A mental representation of the learning situation or physical environment.
w. The theory that learning takes place through observation and imitation of models.
x. Increasing the rate (with reinforcement) or decreasing the rate (with punishment) of responses due to observing the consequences of someone else's behaviors.

TRUE-FALSE PRACTICE TEST

_____ 1. In operant conditioning, learning is a matter of increasing responses that produce positive consequences and decreasing responses that produce negative consequences.

_____ 2. Classical conditioning applies to animal behavior, whereas operant conditioning applies to human behavior.

_____ 3. Thorndike's work on operant conditioning preceded Skinner's research.

_____ 4. In some cases, operant conditioning does not result in the learning of a new response, but rather it results in a change in the rate of the response.

_____ 5. A positive reinforcer always increases the rate of the response it follows.

_____ 6. A negative reinforcer decreases the rate of the response it follows.

_____ 7. One cannot be sure that a particular stimulus will be a reinforcer until it is actually presented to the organism.

_____ 8. Positive reinforcement is effective in changing behaviors, but negative reinforcement is not.

_____ 9. Primary reinforcers are preferred over secondary reinforcers.

_____ 10. Most of the reinforcers that humans work for are secondary reinforcers.

_____ 11. Secondary reinforcers tend to be biological or physiological in nature and related to the survival of the organism.

_____ 12. To decrease the rate of the response, use negative reinforcement.

_____ 13. Intermittent reinforcement schedules are more effective than continuous reinforcement schedules.

_____ 14. Harlow's research with monkeys demonstrated the value of a learning set, a prepared way of solving problems.

_____ 15. Learning that remains hidden until it is useful is called latent learning.

FILL-IN PRACTICE TEST

1. Approaches that focus more on the mental processes of the learner are referred to as _____.

2. A behavior that an organism uses to operate on its environment is called a/an _____.

3. Operant behaviors are controlled by _____.

4. The psychologist who studied operant conditioning before Skinner was _____.

5. Another name for an operant chamber is _____ _____.

6. The number of times a response is made when it is not being reinforced is referred to as _____ _____.

7. Reinforcing successive approximations of the response that you want to condition is referred to as _____.

8. In operant conditioning the rate of response increases during _____.

9. The return of an extinguished response following a rest period is called _____ _____.

10. The process that increases the rate or the probability of the response it follows is _____.

11. _____ reinforcers do not require previous experience in order to be effective.

12. Learned or acquired reinforcers are called _____.

13. A reinforcement schedule that does not reinforce every response is called a/an _____ reinforcement schedule.

14. When a stimulus decreases the rate of response it is called _____.

15. The Brelands' research led to the discovery of the fact that some animals seem to resist operant conditioning and revert back to their natural behavior patterns. This phenomenon is referred to as _____ _____.

MULTIPLE CHOICE PRACTICE TEST 1 TOPIC 5B

1. Which statement best characterizes operant conditioning?
   a. In the proper setting, learning can override heredity.
   b. Good things tend to happen to good people.
   c. Behaviors are influenced by their consequences.
   d. Behavioral change follows most readily from cognitive change.

2. An approach to learning that focuses more on the mental processes of the learner and less on the nature of stimuli and responses is described as
   a. cognitive
   b. behavioristic
   c. operant conditioning
   d. information oriented

3. Skinner is to operant conditioning as _____ is to _____.
   a. Wolpe; Little Albert
   b. Watson; classical conditioning
   c. Raynor; instrumental conditioning
   d. Pavlov; classical conditioning

4. The primary purpose of an operant chamber is to
   a. provide reinforcement
   b. control the environment
   c. serve as punishment
   d. all of the above

5. A fundamental difference between classical and operant conditioning is that
   a. in operant conditioning, the desired response has to be elicited before it can be reinforced
   b. in classical conditioning, responses are not reinforced
   c. in operant conditioning there is no stimulus generalization
   d. in classical conditioning, extinguished responses do not spontaneously recover

6. A rat is bar pressing at a very high response rate. Then reinforcement is withheld. The predictable outcome is
   a. acquisition
   b. extinction
   c. generalization
   d. spontaneous recovery

7. What is the difference between positive reinforcement and negative reinforcement?
   a. Positive reinforcement is classically conditioned and negative reinforcement is operantly conditioned.
   b. Positive reinforcement increases the probability of a response and negative reinforcement decreases the probability of a response.
   c. Positive reinforcement uses primary reinforcers and negative reinforcement uses secondary reinforcers.
   d. A stimulus is presented after a response in positive reinforcement and a stimulus is removed in negative reinforcement.

8. _____ is to primary reinforcer as _____ is to secondary reinforcer.
   a. money; grades
   b. food; warmth
   c. water; praise
   d. promotions; money

9. Ben got a speeding ticket. However, he took a defensive driving class and did not have to pay the ticket. Having the fine removed is an example of
   a. positive reinforcement
   b. negative reinforcement
   c. secondary reinforcement
   d. primary reinforcement

10. In a token economy, the tokens serve as
    a. secondary reinforcers
    b. primary reinforcers
    c. stimuli
    d. bribes

11. A psychology professor gives ten points of extra credit for each lab project students turn in. This represents a _____ schedule of reinforcement.
    a. variable interval
    b. fixed interval
    c. variable ratio
    d. fixed ratio

12. The removal of a punisher would result in
    a. no behavioral change
    b. positive reinforcement
    c. negative reinforcement
    d. decreased response rate

13. The social learning theory was developed by
    a. Tolman
    b. Bandura
    c. Harlow
    d. Skinner

14. Learning about the consequences of one's behaviors by observing the consequences of someone else's behaviors is called
    a. vicarious reinforcement
    b. modeling
    c. role playing
    d. variable learning

15. Which of the following is NOT an appropriate match?
    a. Breland-instinctive drift
    b. Bandura-modeling
    c. Harlow-learning set
    d. Tolman-vicarious reinforcement

MULTIPLE CHOICE PRACTICE TEST 2 TOPIC 5B

1. The theoretical orientation of classical and operant conditioning is
    a. psychodynamic
    b. behavioristic
    c. humanistic
    d. gestalt

2. The learning that a college student does is best described by the _____ approach.
   a. cognitive
   b. behavioristic
   c. classical conditioning
   d. operant conditioning

3. Thorndike's law of effect states that
   a. operant behaviors are determined by the environment
   b. behaviors are not repeated if they are followed by rewards
   c. responses are learned if followed by a satisfying situation
   d. the effect of consequences on any given response cannot be determined

4. In training your dog to jump over a high hurdle, you begin by reinforcing it for hopping over a small board. You gradually add height to the board, having the dog jump the hurdle to earn a reinforcer with each new height until the hurdle is as high as you would like. The best term to describe the procedure that you have used is
   a. shaping
   b. negative reinforcement
   c. generalization
   d. gradual attainment of a classically conditioned response

5. In operant conditioning, when extinction occurs the response rate
   a. stays the same
   b. returns to the base rate
   c. returns to zero
   d. is unaffected

6. Once acquired, an operant response can
   a. easily be extinguished in one trial
   b. seldom be eliminated in one trial
   c. cannot be eliminated at all
   d. can be eliminated by using punishment

7. You take an aspirin to relieve a headache. It works and you feel better. Your aspirin taking response has been
   a. generalized
   b. extinguished
   c. negatively reinforced
   d. positively reinforced

8. In regard to the extended use of token economies, Skinner hoped that
   a. entire societies would function on token economies
   b. token economies would replace prison systems
   c. individuals would eventually appreciate the intrinsic awards of appropriate behavior
   d. punishment could also be a part of the system so that behavior could be totally controlled

9. Some people are disturbed by the idea of using token economies to manage the behavior of children and compare it to

    a. child abuse

    b. communism

    c. mental cruelty

    d. bribery

10. One problem with a continuous reinforcement schedule is that

    a. the supply of reinforcers is quickly depleted

    b. the acquired response is easily extinguished

    c. the organism never becomes satisfied with the amount of reinforcement

    d. the reinforcer becomes too effective

11. Which of the following reinforcement schedules produces responses that are resistant to extinction?

    a. fixed ratio

    b. fixed interval

    c. variable ratio

    d. all of the above

12. Which of the following is NOT true of punishment?

    a. It is most effective if administered immediately.

    b. It should be administered consistently.

    c. It decreased only the punished response.

    d. It does not give the organism any information about appropriate behavior.

13. A major implication of Albert Bandura's classic study with the BoBo doll is that

    a. children can and do learn all sorts of behaviors from watching television

    b. children will do behaviors that they see others doing even when the others are punished

    c. children will only do behaviors that are modeled by live models

    d. children are most influenced by adult models viewed on television

14. In regard to observational learning, the role of reinforcement and punishment is

    a. still undetermined

    b. demonstrated to be significant

    c. of little importance

    d. only related to positive behaviors

15. You have studied a particular concept and believe that you really know it. When you go to take the exam, you find that there is not a single question concerning this TOPIC that you understand so well. This illustrates

    a. vicarious reinforcement

    b. variable reinforcement

    c. a cognitive map

    d. latent learning

Dr. G's Best Study Tips #5

USING THE PREMACK PRINCIPLE

Now that you are studying learning theory, let's apply what you have learned to your own studying behavior. The Premack principle tells us that we can use a high frequency behavior to reinforce a low frequency one. For many students, studying is a low frequency behavior. They simply do not do it often enough or for sufficient periods of time.

Select a behavior that you really like to do and do often (a high frequency response). You might choose making a phone call to a friend, going out, working out, eating out, or even watching TV. Now comes the difficult part. You must withhold this high frequency response and only do this behavior after you study. Then making the call or getting the pizza becomes a reward for studying.

Using the Premack principle in this way is a good idea because we have learned that for reinforcement to be effective, it should be immediate. The other reinforcers for studying, getting good grades, graduation, and so forth are usually delayed for long periods after we have studied very hard. You may feel as if your study behavior is not reinforced at all if you don't take the reinforcement into your own hands and use the Premack principle to reward yourself.

CHAPTER 6—MEMORY: REMEMBERING... AND FORGETTING TOPIC 6A—THE NATURE OF MEMORY

LEARNING OBJECTIVES TOPIC 6A

Memory is central to our sense of self and to our perception of the world. There appear to be several types of memory that actively process information. Students should be able to:
1. Define memory and compare the two theoretical models of memory.
2. Discuss sensory memory, including its capacity and duration.
3. Describe how material is put into short-term memory and how long it is kept there.
4. Understand how much information can be held in short-term memory and how chunking effects that amount.
5. Discuss the issues of acoustic coding in short-term memory.
6. Discuss the issue of permanence in long-term memory.
7. Explain how elaborative rehearsal and maintenance rehearsal encode information into long-term memory.
8. Describe four possible systems or types of long term memory.
9. List the ways that information may be represented in long-term memory.
10. Describe the role of amnesia in locating memory in the brain and explain the changes that take place in the brain (neurons) when memories are formed.

LEARNING TOPIC 6A VOCABULARY

On your own paper, write the definition for each of the following key terms. Your learning will be facilitated by writing the definition in your own words rather than copying the exact definition from your text.

MEMORY	ENCODING
STORAGE	RETRIEVAL
MULTISTORE MODELS	LEVELS OF PROCESSING MODELS
SENSORY MEMORY	SHORT-TERM MEMORY
MAINTENANCE REHEARSAL	CHUNK
LONG-TERM MEMORY	ELABORATIVE REHEARSAL
PROCEDURAL MEMORY	SEMANTIC MEMORY
EPISODIC MEMORY	METAMEMORY
CATEGORY CLUSTERING	SUBJECTIVE ORGANIZATION
NETWORK MODELS	ACT THEORY

MATCHING

Match the following key terms from your textbook with the appropriate definition.

____ 1. episodic memory   ____ 2. ACT theory

____ 3. retrieval   ____ 4. chunk

____ 5. sensory memory   ____ 6. long-term memory

____ 7. memory   ____ 8. elaborative rehearsal

____ 9. subjective organization   ____10. procedural memory

____11. storage   ____12. maintenance rehearsal

____13. encoding   ____14. semantic memory

____15. network models   ____16. metamemory

____17. levels of processing models   ____18. category clustering

____19. multistore models of memory   ____20. short-term memory

a. The cognitive ability to encode, store, and retrieve information.
b. The active process of representing, or putting of information into memory.
c. The process of holding encoded information in memory.
d. The process of locating, removing, and using information that is stored in memory.
e. Descriptions of memory that propose a number of separate and distinct types (or stores) of memory, each with its own manner of processing information.
f. The view that there is only one memory, but that information can be processed within that memory at different degrees, levels, or depths.
g. The type of memory that holds large amounts of information registered at the senses for very brief periods of time.
h. A type of memory with limited capacity and limited duration.
i. A process of rote repetition to keep information in short-term memory.
j. A somewhat imprecise concept, referring to a meaningful unit of information as represented in memory.
k. A type of memory with virtually unlimited capacity and very long, if not limitless, duration.
l. A mechanism for processing information into long-term memory that involves the meaningful manipulation of the information to be remembered.
m. In long-term memory, where learned S-R associations and skilled patterns of responses are stored.
n. In long-term memory, where vocabulary, facts, simple concepts, rules, and the like are stored.
o. In long-term memory, where life events and experiences are stored.
p. In long-term memory, our stored knowledge of how our own memory systems work.
q. At recall, grouping words together into categories even if they are presented in a random order.
r. The tendency of subjects to impose some order on their recall of randomly presented events or items.
s. Organizational schemes that describe the relationships among meaningful units stored in semantic memory.
t. A network model of long-term memory that suggests that we store meaningful, and related propositions that can be judged as true or false.

TRUE-FALSE PRACTICE TEST

_____ 1. The information processing view of memory comes from an ancient theory held by the Greeks.

_____ 2. All the information in our memories first passes through sensory memory.

_____ 3. There is evidence of sensory memory for all five senses.

_____ 4. Information can be stored in short-term memory for several minutes.

_____ 5. Based on the idea of chunking, our memory can hold between 5 and 9 meaningful bits of information.

_____ 6. Information in our sensory memory is held in the same form in which it was initially presented.

_____ 7. Information is always represented in short-term memory acoustically.

_____ 8. The capacity for long-term memory can be described as virtually limitless.

_____ 9. Eliminating the effects of injury or illness, one could assume that certain information in long-term memory would never be forgotten.

_____ 10. The majority of psychologists agree that once information is transferred to long-term memory, it stays there till we die.

_____ 11. Lashley's research indicated that specific memories are stored in specific locations in the brain.

_____ 12. When information is encoded as a memory, changes actually take place in the nervous system

_____ 13. One theory of memory formation is that more neurons are formed when a new memory is added.

_____ 14. One theory suggests that changes in the brain when memories are formed take place at the synapse.

_____ 15. There are conflicting opinions about the role of neurotransmitters in memory formation.

FILL-IN PRACTICE TEST

1. The process of putting information into memory is called _____.

2. The type of memory with the shortest duration is called _____ memory.

3. Short-term memory is also called _____ memory.

4. In regard to memory, a meaningful unit of information is called a/an _____.

5. The type of rehearsal used to keep material active in short-term memory is called _____ rehearsal.

6. In order to get information into long-term memory, one should use _____ rehearsal.

7. According to Tulving, organisms retain learned connections between stimuli and responses through _____ memory.

8. Vocabulary, rules, and simple concepts are stored in _____ memory.

9. Life events and experiences are stored in _____ memory.

10. Our knowledge of how our memory systems work is called _____.

11. _____ organization refers to clustering information when it does not fit into neat categories.

12. The _____ theory is a network model of semantic memory that suggests that we store information in a series of interrelated propositions.

13. The inability to form new long-term memories is known as _____ amnesia.

14. The inability to remember events that happened in the past is known as _____ amnesia.

15. The two neurotransmitters most often involved in memory studies are acetylcholine and _____.

MULTIPLE CHOICE PRACTICE TEST 1 TOPIC 6A

1. Which of the following represents the correct sequence of events for the process of memory?
   a. encoding-retrieving-storing
   b. storing-retrieving-encoding
   c. retrieving-storing-encoding
   d. encoding-storing-retrieving

2. The levels of processing model of memory supports the idea of
   a. one basic type of memory process
   b. memory stores that are inter-related
   c. separate, distinct memory stores
   d. all of the above

3. The practical problem with sensory memory is that
   a. the capacity is limited
   b. the duration is limited
   c. so much information is not easily categorized
   d. both capacity and duration are limited

4. The type of memory with large capacity, very short duration, and little processing is
   a. sensory memory
   b. short-term memory
   c. long-term memory
   d. metamemory

5. Which type of memory is also referred to as working memory?
   a. sensory memory
   b. short-term memory
   c. long-term memory
   d. metamemory

6. Information is encoded into short-term memory by
   a. elaborative rehearsal
   b. chunking
   c. attention to the stimuli
   d. perception

7. Repeating a phone number over and over while waiting to use a pay phone is an example of
   a. chunking
   b. elaboration
   c. metamemory
   d. maintenance rehearsal

8. When information is stored or represented by sound, it is in our _____ memory.
   a. short-term
   b. long-term
   c. sensory
   d. metamemory

9. In regard to long-term memory, Elizabeth and Geoffrey Loftus believe that
   a. all information in long-term memory can be retrieved at any time
   b. long term memories are largely reconstructions from the original information
   c. people don't remember anything that happened before age three
   d. memory failure involves permanent forgetting, not just retrieval failure

10. To get information into long-term memory, one should use
   a. attention
   b. maintenance rehearsal
   c. elaborative rehearsal
   d. repetition

11. Your memory of how to swim is recorded in
   a. episodic memory
   b. metamemory
   c. semantic memory
   d. procedural memory

12. Research on organization in long-term memory indicates that
   a. organization is neither useful or used much
   b. all information is categorized into similar categories by all people
   c. some people remember information well without organizing it at all
   d. people use some type of organizational structure even when categories are not readily available

13. Which of the following is NOT a correct match?
    a. declarative knowledge - knowing that
    b. procedural knowledge - knowing how
    c. metamemory - knowing memory systems
    d. network models - knowing how to

14. Which of the following is the most accurate statement about our knowledge of long-term memory?
    a. It is categorical.
    b. It is hierarchical.
    c. Psychologists are not quite sure how it is organized.
    d. Psychologists believe that there is no organization in long-term memory.

15. The case of "H.M." who underwent brain surgery as a treatment for epilepsy, illustrated the role of the _____ in memory.
    a. cerebral cortex
    b. cerebellum
    c. thalamus
    d. hippocampus

MULTIPLE CHOICE PRACTICE TEST 2 TOPIC 6A

1. Multistore models of memory support the idea of
    a. one basic type of memory process
    b. memory stores that are inter-related
    c. several separate, distinct memory stores
    d. all of the above

2. Memory is described in the text in terms of
    a. the levels of processing model
    b. the multistore model
    c. a combination of levels of processing and multistore models
    d. none of the above

3. One significant change in the way we think about memory today as opposed to 30 years ago is that we now see memory as
    a. processing much less information than we once believed
    b. a much more active processor of information
    c. being much less likely to fail us
    d. a remarkably accurate recorder of everyday experiences

4. The type of memory with large capacity, very long duration, and a great deal of processing is
    a. sensory memory
    b. short-term memory
    c. long-term memory
    d. metamemory

5. Information can get into short-term memory from
    a. sensory memory
    b. long-term memory
    c. metamemory
    d. both sensory memory and long-term memory

6. What type of memory is employed when you are computing the answer to a multiplication problem in your head, without the use of pencil and paper?
    a. sensory memory and long-term memory
    b. sensory memory, short-term memory, and long term memory
    c. short-term memory and long-term memory
    d. long-term memory, metamemory, and short-term memory

7. The capacity of short-term memory can be increased through
    a. chunking
    b. attention
    c. rehearsal
    d. selective encoding

8. In Baddeley's research, subjects had the most difficulty remembering short word lists composed of words that rhymed. This demonstrates that
    a. the subjects did not use maintenance rehearsal
    b. information in short term memory is represented acoustically
    c. words with similar meanings are difficult to chunk
    d. the subjects were not attending to the rhyming words

9. Which statement concerning storage in LTM would be most readily accepted as TRUE by most psychologists?

   a. Once encoded in LTM, information is safe from any possible distortion.

   b. Simple repetition of information is not, in itself, sufficient to get information into LTM.

   c. At the moment, we know of no experimental procedure to determine just how long information is held in LTM.

   d. It is likely that we distort our memories of the distant past by responding in whatever way we feel at the moment of recall.

10. Research indicates that as processing of information increases, recall

    a. remains the same

    b. decreases

    c. fails

    d. increases

11. A person's memory of their first kiss would be stored in _____ memory.

    a. semantic

    b. episodic

    c. metamemory

    d. procedural

12. A subject in a memory experiment is asked to think about the general category of "buildings." According to a network model of memory storage (such as that of Collins and Quillian) which of the following questions should the subject be able to answer the fastest?

    a. Does a library have books?

    b. Does a library have walls?

    c. Does a library have a roof?

    d. All of the above would be answered equally fast.

13. Lashley concluded from research that specific memories have no specific location in the brain. The most logical exception to this would be

    a. metamemory

    b. procedural memory

    c. memory of sensations

    d. memory of life events

14. Which of the following is the best explanation concerning changes in the brain when memories are formed?

    a. The formation of memories makes some synaptic transmissions easier than they were before.

    b. Neurotransmitters increase at the synapse when memories are formed.

    c. Neurotransmitters decrease at the synapse when memories are formed.

    d. Physical changes take place in the neuronal membranes when memories are formed.

15. You look at a question on your psychology test and clearly know that you do not know the answer because you made a mistake about the reading assignment. This illustrates

    a. episodic memory

    b. metamemory

    c. retrieval failure

    d. forgetting

CHAPTER 6—MEMORY: REMEMBERING. . . AND FORGETTING TOPIC 6B—RETRIEVAL . . . AND RETRIEVAL FAILURE

LEARNING OBJECTIVES TOPIC 6B

When memory fails it is most commonly because retrieval has failed. How we get information into memory is one of the most important factors in how effectively and efficiently we retrieve information from memory. Students should be able to:

1. Explain how measures of recall, recognition, and relearning affect assessment of retrieval.
2. Explain implicit tests of retention and what they tell us about long-term memory.
3. Describe how the situation in which encoding is done affects retrieval.
4. Define meaningfulness and explain how it relates to retrieval.
5. Define mnemonic devices and describe four examples.
6. Define schemas and explain how they affect retrieval.
7. Define overlearning, massed practice, and distributed practice and explain how they affect retrieval.
8. Distinguish between retroactive and proactive interference and explain how each affects retrieval.

LEARNING TOPIC 6B VOCABULARY

On your own paper, write the definition for each of the following key terms. Your learning will be facilitated by writing the definition in your own words rather than copying the exact definition from your text.

RECALL	RECOGNITION
RELEARNING	ENCODING SPECIFICITY PRINCIPLE
STATE-DEPENDENT MEMORY	FLASHBULB MEMORIES
MEANINGFULNESS	MNEMONIC DEVICES
NARRATIVE CHAINING	PEG WORD METHOD
METHOD OF LOCI	SCHEMA
OVERLEARNING	RETROACTIVE INTERFERENCE
PROACTIVE INTERFERENCE	

MATCHING

Match the following key terms from your textbook with the appropriate definition.

____ 1. peg word method	____ 2. proactive interference
____ 3. state-dependent memory	____ 4. mnemonic devices
____ 5. narrative chaining	____ 6. overlearning
____ 7. encoding specificity principle	____ 8. recall
____ 9. retroactive interference	____10. recognition
____11. meaningfulness	____12. schema
____13. flashbulb memories	____14. relearning

_____15. method of loci

a. A measure of retrieval in which an individual is provided with the fewest possible cues to aid retrieval.
b. A measure of retrieval in which an individual is required to identify material previously learned as being familiar.
c. A measure of memory in which one notes the improvement in performance when learning material for a second time.
d. The hypothesis that we can only retrieve what we have stored and that retrieval is enhanced to the extent that retrieval cues match encoding cues.
e. The hypothesis that retrieval can be enhanced by the extent to which one's state of mind at retrieval matches one's state of mind at encoding.
f. Particularly clear, and vivid memories that are easily retrieved, but not necessarily accurate in all detail.
g. The extent to which information evokes associations with information already in memory.
h. Strategies for improving retrieval that take advantage of existing memories in order to make new material more meaningful.
i. The mnemonic device of relating words together in a story, thus organizing them in a meaningful way.
j. The mnemonic device of forming interactive visual images of materials to be learned and items previously associated with numbers.
k. The mnemonic device that mentally places information to be retrieved in a series of familiar locations.
l. A system of organized, general knowledge, stored in long-term memory, that guide the encoding and retrieval of information.
m. The practice or rehearsal of material over and above what is needed to learn it.
n. The inhibition of retrieval of previously learned material caused by material learned later.
o. The inhibition of retrieval of recently learned material caused by material learned earlier.

TRUE-FALSE PRACTICE TEST

_____ 1. Retrieval failure suggests that information is no longer in long-term memory.

_____ 2. Asking subjects to remember a word list in the order it was presented is an example of serial recall.

_____ 3. Retrieval by recognition is always superior to retrieval by recall.

_____ 4. A multiple choice test item and an essay item would both measure retrieval by recall.

_____ 5. Relearning generally takes as many trials or presentations of the material as the first learning.

_____ 6. Some nonsense syllables are more meaningless than others.

_____ 7. In tests of implicit memory, amnesia victims have performed as well as non-amnesia subjects.

_____ 8. The encoding specificity principle applies only to humans.

_____ 9. According to the encoding specificity principle, when cues that were present at encoding are also present at retrieval, retrieval is enhanced.

_____ 10. According to research by Gordon Bower, even the mood a person is in when material is encoded can be an important factor for retrieval.

_____ 11. There is evidence that memories of emotionally arousing events are easier to recall than memories of emotionally neutral events.

_____ 12. Meaningfulness of material to be learned is determined by the nature of the material.

_____ 13. The greatest effect of overlearning appears with longer retention intervals.

_____ 14. Research results clearly indicate that massed practice is superior to distributed practice.

_____ 15. As a general study strategy, cramming is very inefficient.

FILL-IN PRACTICE TEST

1. A memory task where the fewest possible cues are provided to aid retrieval is called _____.

2. A memory task requiring a subject to identify previously learned material is called _____.

3. A fill-in item such as this one measures retrieval by _____.

4. In order to neutralize the effects of previous experience and meaningfulness, Ebbinghaus used _____ _____ in his memory research.

5. Relearning is referred to as a/an _____ test of memory.

6. Recall is an example of a/an _____ test of memory.

7. Knowing how to swim is an example of _____ knowledge.

8. Although amnesia victims seem to have forgotten everything, their _____ memories are actually still in tact.

9. Memories of important events that are especially clear and vivid are called _____ memories.

10. Complex cognitive representations of general knowledge are referred to as _____.

11. Aids to retrieval that help organize material and make it meaningful are called _____ _____.

12. _____ _____ is a technique by which information is organized into a meaningful story.

13. An organized general knowledge structure that is stored in long-term memory is a/an _____.

14. The process of practicing or rehearsing material over and above what is needed to learn it is called _____.

15. When interfering activities follow the material to be learned, the interference is called _____.

MULTIPLE CHOICE PRACTICE TEST 1 TOPIC 6B

1. Which of the following is NOT a correct match?
   a. fill-in test item - recall
   b. multiple choice test item - recognition
   c. essay test item - recognition
   d. true-false test item - recognition

2. Which of the following would be an example of procedural memory?
   a. driving a car home from the airport after a long vacation
   b. spelling a word correctly to win a spelling bee
   c. making the highest grade in the class on a history exam
   d. answering a difficult question in a game of Trivial Pursuit

3. Which of the following statements is true concerning victims of retrograde amnesia?
   a. There is no direct recollection of any long-term memories.
   b. Short-term memory is impaired.
   c. Sensory memory is the only functioning memory.
   d. Procedural memory appears to function normally.

4. All of the following factors may have some influence on our ability to retrieve information from our memory. Which of these is probably the MOST important, or influential?
   a. where in memory the information is stored (i.e. short-term, sensory, or long-term)
   b. the relationship between how (or if) it was encoded and how we are searching for it
   c. the manner in which the information is stored in memory (i.e. the code used: acoustic, semantic, etc.)
   d. the extent to which we are able to overcome the inhibitory influence of repression

5. According to the encoding specificity principle, the best place to study for an exam in this course is
   a. at home where you are in familiar surroundings
   b. in the library where it is quiet
   c. at a friend's house where you can get help
   d. in the classroom where the test will be administered

6. Flashbulb memories are most likely stored in
   a. episodic memory
   b. procedural memory
   c. semantic memory
   d. sensory memory

7. Words like angel, redwood, and vehicle are easier to retrieve than words like political, religious, and betrayal because
    a. they are shorter words
    b. they are more meaningful words
    c. they lend themselves better to the use of mental images
    d. they don't require elaborative rehearsal techniques to transfer to long-term memory

8. According to Bower, the most effective use of mental images will involve images that are
    a. bizarre
    b. very rare
    c. common and interactive
    d. bizarre and interactive

9. Which of the following mnemonic devices does NOT involve the use of mental imagery?
    a. key word method
    b. narrative chaining
    c. peg words
    d. method of loci

10. Geraldine reported that she wasn't nervous on her first night to teach a creative writing class even though she had never taught before. She explained that she knew what a teacher should do because she had taken so many classes herself. Her knowledge of appropriate behavior for a teacher can best be explained by
    a. a schema
    b. rote practice
    c. elaborative rehearsal
    d. mnemonics

11. If you prepare for your next psychology exam by studying for several short periods separated by rest periods or breaks, you are using
    a. massed practice
    b. distributed practice
    c. cramming
    d. elaborative rehearsal

12. Research indicates that in order to protect recently learned information from interference, the best thing to do right after studying would be
    a. get something to eat
    b. reread your notes
    c. go to sleep
    d. watch TV or listen to the radio

13. Which of the following factors influences the impact of interference on learning?
    a. the nature of the material being learned
    b. the organization and meaningfulness of the information learned
    c. the type of activity that follows studying
    d. all of the above

14. A student has studied psychology in high school and then takes sociology in college. Because the two subjects are somewhat similar, she finds that she has trouble remembering the psychology. Her forgetting is best explained by
    a. retroactive inhibition
    b. proactive inhibition
    c. massed practice
    d. failure to practice overlearning

15. Answering the questions in this study guide is an example of
    a. massed practice
    b. distributed practice
    c. retrieval practice
    d. proactive practice

MULTIPLE CHOICE PRACTICE TEST 2 TOPIC 6B

1. The psychologist noted for research on memory using nonsense syllables was
    a. Ebbinghaus
    b. Schacter
    c. Tulving
    d. Smith

2. Ebbinghaus conducted memory experiments using _____ as his subject.
    a. his daughter
    b. himself
    c. a chimpanzee
    d. a graduate student

3. Which of the following would a sufferer of retrograde amnesia be LEAST likely to remember?
    a. How to talk.
    b. The name of someone he has just met.
    c. His home address.
    d. How to drive a car.

4. Students in which of the following classes are likely to do the BEST on their exam, assuming everything else is equal?

    a. A class expects a fill-in-the-blank test, and is given a multiple-choice test.

    b. A class expects a fill-in-the-blank test, and is given a fill-in-the-blank test.

    c. A class expects a multiple-choice test, and is given a fill-in-the-blank test.

    d. A class expects a multiple-choice test, and is given a multiple-choice test.

5. Which of the following statements about state-dependent memory is TRUE?

    a. Retrieval is best when mood at retrieval matches mood at learning.

    b. State-dependent memory applies only to mood and not to other conditions.

    c. Students cannot recall information effectively under the influence of drugs.

    d. Various conditions affecting state dependent memory are the same for both men and women.

6. The most important process in elaborative rehearsal is the learner's attempt to

    a. make the material meaningful

    b. repeat the material as often as possible

    c. organize the material in the way in which it is presented

    d. distribute practice in such a way as to minimize overlearning

7. The best memory strategy for learning foreign language vocabulary is probably

    a. mental imagery

    b. method of loci

    c. key word method

    d. peg word method

8. The mnemonic strategy that is particularly useful for remembering items in order is

    a. mental imagery

    b. method of loci

    c. key word method

    d. peg word method

9. Key words, peg words, and the method of loci all have in common, the use of

    a. schemas

    b. short-term memory

    c. bizarre associations

    d. mental imagery

10. Which of the following statements is TRUE?

    a. A large amount of forgetting takes place immediately after learning.

    b. Overlearning improves retrieval, with the greatest effect on longer retention intervals.

    c. There is a diminishing return on overlearning, especially after 100 percent overlearning.

    d. All of the above.

11. Pace learned to water ski as a child. Now he is in college, he wants to learn to snow ski. He finds that the principles for water skiing get in the way when he tries to learn snow skiing. This can be explained by the phenomenon of

   a. proactive interference

   b. retroactive interference

   c. massed practice

   d. procedural memory

12. Which of the following study situations will least likely be affected by proactive interference?

   a. study psychology then study math

   b. study psychology then study sociology

   c. study biology then study microbiology

   d. study history then study political science

13. The discussion of overlearning and distribution of practice makes it clear that when studying for a final exam in a college-level course, a student is best advised to

   a. study as much as possible, spreading study sessions out over time

   b. get in most preparation in the day or two just before the exam is scheduled

   c. study for that course in a limited number (3-5) reasonably long (1-2 hour) study sessions during the semester

   d. separate study sessions with 3-5 second rest intervals and engage in 100% overlearning

14. Which of the following would be LEAST likely to improve retrieval?

   a. retrieval practice

   b. massed practice

   c. overlearning

   d. distributed practice

15. Constructing your own practice test questions and answering them would be an example of

   a. maintenance rehearsal

   b. retrieval practice

   c. proactive interference

   d. mnemonics

Dr. G's Best Study Tips #6

USING MNEMONIC STRATEGIES AS STUDY METHODS

Some of the concepts presented in Chapter 7 can be directly applied to study methods. For example, the serial position effect tells us that when we study a series, the natural tendency is that the items at the beginning and end of the series will be easiest to learn. Our application should be to study the information in the middle of a chapter or in the middle of our notes a little more thoroughly to offset the serial position effect.

The concepts of state-dependent and context-dependent recall have some application to studying. State-dependent recall tells us that for optimum recall, we should take the test in the same state we were in when we learned the material. Context-dependent recall tells us that the setting actually serves as a cue. I sometimes suggest that my students return to their classroom in the afternoons when they are usually empty, and spend time studying psychology there. After all, it is the context in which they will take their exams.

We can also use other ideas such as the concept of chunking. Many mnemonic strategies employ this technique to create greater memory capacity. For instance, you may have learned this mnemonic to help you remember the order of operations in algebra: "Please excuse my dear Aunt Sally," or PEMDAS. This chunk forms a cue to help us remember to solve algebraic equations by attending to P = parenthesis, E = exponents, M = multiply, D = divide, A = add, and S = subtract in that order. Many of these mnemonics already exist, FACE tells us the notes on the spaces of the music scale and HOMES reminds us of the names of the great lakes, Huron, Ontario, Michigan, Erie, and Superior.

You may use other mnemonics that you have learned, but you can also create your own. If the letters do not conveniently spell a word, such as HOMES or FACE, simply form a chunk by creating a sentence that uses words beginning with the appropriate letters. For example, rehearsal, elaboration, and chunking are ways of extending the length of time that information stays in short-term memory. The first letters of these words are r, e, and c. You might put these into a sentence such as "Rats eat cheese."

You may remember that meaningfulness is an important aspect of long-term memory. Since words and sentences have meaning to us, they are easily stored and retrieved, making great cues. Mnemonic devices work even better when you create your own because you are processing the information while making the mnemonic. Try creating your own using some information from your text.

If you are intrigued by the idea of improving your memory and would like to know more, I recommend a small paperback book by Harry Lorraine and Jerry Lucas called, The Memory Book. I am confident that you can find other excellent sources of information on memory in the library.

CHAPTER 7—HIGHER COGNITIVE PROCESSES
TOPIC 7A—CONCEPTS AND LANGUAGE

LEARNING OBJECTIVES TOPIC 7A

Higher cognitive processes rely on the basic processes of perception, learning, and memory. How we understand things through concept formation and communicate with others through language are two of these higher processes. Students should be able to:
1. Explain how attributes and rules define concepts.
2. Discuss how the concept of prototype helps explain concepts.
3. Explain how concept formation occurs.
4. List the defining characteristics of language.
5. Define phonemes and explain how they are rule-governed.
6. Define semantics.
7. Define morphemes.
8. Define syntax, linguistic intuitions, and pragmatics.
9. Describe the landmark events that occur during language acquisition.
10. Explain the learning-oriented and biology oriented theories of language acquisition.

LEARNING TOPIC 7A VOCABULARY

On your own paper, write the definition for each of the following key terms. Your learning will be facilitated by writing the definition in your own words rather than copying the exact definition from your text.

CONCEPT	FORMAL CONCEPTS
NATURAL CONCEPTS	PROTOTYPE
PSYCHOLINGUISTICS	LANGUAGE
PHONEME	SEMANTICS
MORPHEME	SYNTAX
LINGUISTIC INTUITIONS	PRAGMATICS
BABBLING	HOLOPHRASTIC SPEECH
OVERREGULARIZATION	

MATCHING

Match the following key terms from your textbook with the appropriate definition.

_____ 1. overregularization   _____ 2. holophrastic speech

_____ 3. concept   _____ 4. language

_____ 5. semantics   _____ 6. pragmatics

_____ 7. linguistic intuitions   _____ 8. natural concepts

_____ 9. formal concepts   _____10. babbling

_____11. prototype   _____12. phoneme

_____13. psycholinguistics   _____14. morpheme

_____15. syntax

a. A mental representation of a category or class of events or objects.
b. Concepts with relatively few, well-defined attribute values and clearly defined rules to relate them.
c. The potentially "fuzzy" sorts of concepts that occur in real life, with ill-defined attributes and/or rules.
d. The member of a concept or category that best typifies or represents that concept or category.
e. The science that studies the cognitive processes involved in the use and acquisition of language.
f. A large collection of arbitrary symbols that have significance for a language-using community, and that follow certain rules of combination.
g. The smallest unit of sound in the spoken form of a language.
h. The study of the meaning of words and sentences.
i. The smallest unit of meaning in a language.
j. The rules that govern how the morphemes of a language may be combined to form meaningful utterances.
k. Judgments or decisions about the syntactic acceptability of utterances without the ability to specify why.
l. The study of how social context affects the meaning of linguistic events.
m. Speech sounds produced in rhythmic, repetitive patterns.
n. The use of one word to communicate a number of different meanings.
o. The excessive application of an acquired language rule in a situation where it is not appropriate.

TRUE-FALSE PRACTICE TEST

_____ 1. Concepts can be thought of as building blocks for human thought and behavior.

_____ 2. One problem with the attribute-rule approach to concepts is that not all examples of concept membership are equally good examples.

_____ 3. Most psychologists agree that concepts are acquired through experience.

_____ 4. Research indicates that we sometimes form usable concepts that we cannot describe.

_____ 5. Research indicates that concepts are formed by developing strategies and testing hypotheses.

_____ 6. Speech and language are synonymous terms.

_____ 7. In English, there is only one phoneme for each letter of the alphabet.

_____ 8. In most languages, there are more morphemes than words.

_____ 9. The question of how humans acquire language remains basically unanswered.

_____ 10. A child's babbling contains all the know phonemes of all languages.

_____ 11. Babies of various nationalities have their own way of babbling, according to the phonetic structure of the language their parents speak.

_____ 12. In vocabulary acquisition, comprehension preceded production.

_____ 13. Virtually all babies babble, even those with hearing problems.

_____ 14. Most babies speak in two word phrases by age one.

_____ 15. The best explanation for language acquisition appears to be a combined effect of nature and nurture.

FILL-IN PRACTICE TEST

1. A _____ is the mental representation of a category, or class of events or objects.

2. Defining a concept according to some features that are related according to some rule is using the _____ approach.

3. _____ concepts are those in which the attribute values are relatively few in number, clearly defined, and clearly related by a rule.

4. _____ concepts must have all of the relevant features.

5. _____ concepts may have one feature or another feature.

6. A _____ is a member of a category that best typifies or represents the category to which it belongs.

7. Scientists who study both psychology and linguistics are called _____.

8. The individual speech sounds of a language are called _____.

9. The study of meaning in language is called _____.

10. The smallest unit of meaning in language is a _____.

11. The rules that govern the way sentences are formed in a language are referred to as the _____.

12. _____ is the study of how linguistic events are related to the social context in which they occur.

13. The production of phonemes in rhythmic, repetitive patterns is called _____.

14. The use of just one word to communicate a range of intentions and meanings is referred to as _____ speech.

15. _____ is the continued application of an acquired language rule in situations where it is not appropriate.

MULTIPLE CHOICE PRACTICE TEST 1 TOPIC 7A

1. Which of the following is NOT considered part of one's cognitions?
   a. ideas
   b. thoughts
   c. feelings
   d. images

2. According to the classical view, learning new concepts is a matter of learning
   a. all possible instances
   b. a set of related features
   c. rules for concept formation
   d. creative thinking

3. The description of superman contains _____ concepts.
   a. conjunctive
   b. disjunctive
   c. affirmative
   d. relational

4. Cognitive processes rely on
   a. perception
   b. learning
   c. memory
   d. all of the above

5. Which of the following is NOT a component of the definition of language?
   a. arbitrary symbols
   b. has significance for a language using community
   c. follows rules of combination
   d. is synonymous with speech

6. Native speakers of English would generally recognize that gzlarp is not a proper English word because
   a. they know syntax
   b. the phonemes are wrong for English
   c. the morphemes are wrong for any language
   d. the pragmatics are inappropriately used

7. What is the correct number of morphemes in the word, "uncensored?"
   a. one
   b. two
   c. three
   d. four

8. When we make a decision about what utterances would be acceptable in our language, we are using
   a. linguistic intuition
   b. syntax
   c. pragmatics
   d. psycholinguistics

9. The fact that you probably would not use a swear word in a conversation with your priest or minister illustrates your understanding of

   a. semantics
   b. pragmatics
   c. morphemes
   d. syntax

10. Which of the following is NOT a correct match?

   a. phonemes — sound
   b. morphemes — meanings
   c. pragmatics — grammar
   d. syntax — structure

11. A baby's first words are usually produced at about age

   a. six months
   b. nine months
   c. twelve months
   d. eighteen months

12. Holophrastic speech and telegraphic speech have in common the fact that

   a. both consist primarily of nouns
   b. both carry great meaning in small number of words
   c. both omit articles and prepositions
   d. all of the above

13. Which of the following is the correct order of speech acquisition?

   a. babbling - single words - telegraphic speech
   b. babbling - single words - holophrases
   c. holophrases - single words - telegraphic speech
   d. babbling - telegraphic speech - holophrases

14. The biggest support for the presence of an LAD is the fact that language is

   a. learned in an orderly fashion
   b. learned according to what is reinforced
   c. learned easily at an early age
   d. learned in spite of poor models

15. One fact that fails to support the learning theory explanation of language is that

   a. parents correct content rather than form
   b. parents do not reinforce language learning
   c. parents do not model correct language usage
   d. all of the above

MULTIPLE CHOICE PRACTICE TEST 2 TOPIC 7A

1. Conjunctive concepts are to disjunctive concepts as _____ is to _____.
    a. all; either or
    b. one; many
    c. only; few
    d. some; none

2. In baseball, the concept of a strike is a _____ concept.
    a. conjunctive
    b. disjunctive
    c. affirmative
    d. relational

3. Formal concepts are to the laboratory as _____ concepts are to the real world.
    a. natural
    b. conjunctive
    c. affirmative
    d. relational concepts

4. Which statement concerning the formation of concepts is TRUE?
    a. Concepts can only be formed for objects and events that can be represented by one's language.
    b. Concept formation is typically a random, unsystematic process.
    c. Formal and natural concepts are typically acquired in the same general way.
    d. Once a concept has been acquired, it will not be forgotten.

5. The smallest unit of sound in a language is called a
    a. morpheme
    b. phoneme
    c. syllable
    d. dipthong

6. The study of the meaning of language is called
    a. syntax
    b. grammar
    c. semantics
    d. phonetics

7. Which of the following statements best describes the strings of letters "syntax" and "sin tax?"
    a. they have the same number of morphemes
    b. they have the same number of phonemes
    c. they both have phonemes but no morphemes
    d. they both have morphemes but no phonemes

8. With regard to morphemes, which statement is FALSE?
   a. Morphemes are verbal labels for acquired concepts.
   b. There are many more morphemes in a language than there are words.
   c. Within a language, acceptable morphemes can be combined in virtually any order.
   d. The study of morphemes involves the study of the meaning of utterances in a language.

9. Which of the following questions would a person studying semantics find most interesting?
   a. What are the perceptual differences between the sound of "d" and the sound of "t?"
   b. How do we know that the plural of box is boxes, but the plural of ox is oxen, not oxes?
   c. Why is the statement, "Boys will be boys." not considered to be simply redundant?
   d. Why do people say, "Do you know what time it is?" when they really want to know, "What time is it?"

10. Which of the following statements best captures the essence of what pragmatics is all about?
    a. You often cannot tell what a person means without considering the social context.
    b. The order in which words occur in a spoken sentence determines who did what to whom.
    c. It is no wonder that people have difficulty spelling with a language that uses only 26 letters to represent 45 sounds.
    d. Most language processing is intuitive and automatic.

11. At what age can most children demonstrate large vocabulary and a variety of sentence structures?
    a. 2
    b. 3
    c. 5
    d. 7

12. Telegraphic speech is distinguished by the lack of
    a. nouns
    b. verbs
    c. sentence structure
    d. articles or prepositions

13. A child who says, "I have two foots," is demonstrating
    a. overregularization
    b. holophrastic speech
    c. telegraphic speech
    d. a grammar error

14. If it exists, the LAD or language acquisition device is believed to be responsible for
    a. babbling
    b. rapid language development between ages 1 and 5
    c. a child's comprehension of more words than can be produced
    d. holophrastic and telegraphic speech

15. The best explanation for learning language is
    a. the presence of the language acquisition device
    b. the model provided by parents and the use of reinforcement
    c. a combination or interaction of both nature and nurture
    d. a biologically determined ability to acquire language

CHAPTER 7—HIGHER COGNITIVE PROCESSES
TOPIC 7B—PROBLEM-SOLVING

LEARNING OBJECTIVES TOPIC 7B

The study of problem-solving behaviors is a classic one in psychology. Problem solving is a higher cognitive process which uses perception, learning, and memory. Students should be able to:

1. List three components of a problem and explain how to distinguish problems that are well-defined or ill-defined.
2. Describe problem representation.
3. Discuss how algorithmic and heuristic strategies are used to solve problems.
4. Define mental set and explain how it affects problem-solving.
5. Define functional fixedness and describe its affects on problem-solving.
6. Define the representativeness and availability heuristics and discuss how they affect problem-solving.
7. Contrast divergent thinking and convergent thinking.
8. List the four stages of creative problem solving.
9. Discuss Glaser's position on teaching problem-solving.

LEARNING TOPIC 7B VOCABULARY

PROBLEM	STRATEGY
ALGORITHM	HEURISTIC
MENTAL SET	FUNCTIONAL FIXEDNESS
AVAILABILITY HEURISTIC	REPRESENTATIVENESS HEURISTIC
POSITIVE TEST STRATEGY	DIVERGENT THINKING
CONVERGENT THINKING	

MATCHING

Match the following key terms from your textbook with the appropriate definition.

_____ 1. convergent thinking   _____ 2. problem

_____ 3. mental set   _____ 4. divergent thinking

_____ 5. representativeness heuristic   _____ 6. availability heuristic

_____ 7. positive test strategy   _____ 8. strategy

_____ 9. functional fixedness   _____10. heuristic

_____11. algorithm

a. A situation in which there is a discrepancy between one's current state and one's desired, or goal state, with no clear way of getting from one to the other.
b. In problem-solving, a systematic plan for generating possible solutions that can be tested to see of they are correct.
c. A problem-solving strategy in which all possible solutions are generated and tested an acceptable solution is guaranteed.

d. A problem-solving strategy in which hypotheses about problem solutions are generated and tested in a time-saving and systematic way, but that does not guarantee an acceptable solution.

e. A tendency to perceive or respond to something in a predetermined, set way.

f. The phenomenon in which one is unable to see a new use or function for an object because of experience using the object in some other function.

g. The rule of thumb that suggests that whatever is more available in our memory is also more common or probable.

h. The rule of thumb that suggests that judgments made about a prototypic member of a category will hold for all members of the category.

i. The heuristic of sticking with an acceptable decision or solution, even if a better one might exist.

j. The creation of many ideas or potential problems solutions from one idea.

k. The reduction or focusing of many different ideas into one possible problem solution.

TRUE-FALSE PRACTICE TEST

_____ 1. Effective problem-solving requires perceiving, learning, and remembering.

_____ 2. Psychologists are more likely to study ill-defined problems than well-defined ones.

_____ 3. In order to be an effective problem-solver, one must always start with the goal and work backwards.

_____ 4. Solving really complex problems may require the combined use of several strategies.

_____ 5. Effectively solving problems requires the use of memory, regardless of which strategy is used.

_____ 6. Mental sets always hinder problem-solving.

_____ 7. In general, people are not very good at estimating the frequency of events, but rather tend to be biased by their own experiences.

_____ 8. Creativity and intelligence appear to be highly correlated.

_____ 9. Divergent and convergent thinking are just two different names for the same cognitive process.

_____ 10. The negative effects of mental set and functional fixedness can present a problem in the preparation stage of creative problem-solving.

_____ 11. In general, the American education system seems to be succeeding at teaching creative problem-solving and higher level thinking skills.

_____ 12. Research indicates that little is gained by simply teaching students about problem-solving.

_____ 13. Problem solving is generally enhanced if the learners have a general knowledge base.

_____ 14. A "knowledge-free" approach to problem-solving indicates that no particular expertise is required on the part of the student.

_____ 15. Cognitive psychologist, Robert Glaser believes that problem-solving relies on a sound knowledge base.

FILL-IN PRACTICE TEST

1. Visualizing a problem situation in order to solve the problem is an example of _____.

2. A systematic plan for generating possible problem solutions that can be tested is called a/an _____.

3. A/an _____ is a problem-solving strategy that guarantees that you will eventually arrive at a solution if the strategy is correctly applied.

4. An informal, rule-of-thumb method of generating and testing problem solutions is called a/an _____.

5. Keeping the final goal in mind while working toward subgoals is _____ analysis.

6. A problem-solving strategy that requires that every action we take moves us closer to our goal is called _____.

7. The tendency to perceive or respond to something in a specific way is called _____ _____.

8. The _____ heuristic is the assumption that things which come readily to mind are more common, or occur more frequently, than things that are difficult to recall or think of.

9. The _____ heuristic is the assumption that judgments made about the most prototypic member of a category will hold for all members of the category.

10. _____ thinking involves starting with one idea and generating from it a number of alternative possibilities.

11. _____ thinking involves taking many different ideas and reducing them to just one possible solution.

12. The _____ stage of creative problem-solving is somewhat like a rest period.

13. Testing a proposed solution occurs during the _____ stage of problem-solving.

14. During the _____ stage of problem-solving, the basic elements of the problem are considered and past experience becomes relevant.

15. The stage of problem-solving in which an insight is most likely to occur is the _____ stage.

MULTIPLE CHOICE PRACTICE TEST 1 TOPIC 7B

1. Which of the following is NOT one of the components of a problem-solving situation?
   a. initial state
   b. goal state
   c. possible strategies
   d. solutions state

2. Trying to choose a college major would be an example of a/an
   a. unsolvable problem
   b. ill-defined problem
   c. well-defined problem
   d. common problem

3. A generate-test problem-solving strategy is another name for the use of
   a. heuristics
   b. strategies
   c. goals
   d. algorithms

4. When you solve a problem by starting with the goal, you are probably using the _____ problem-solving strategy.
   a. working backward
   b. algorithmic
   c. hill climbing
   d. heuristic

5. The inability to discover an appropriate new use for an object because of experience using the object in some other way defines
   a. mental set
   b. tunnel vision
   c. functional fixedness
   d. heuristic thinking

6. Which of the following is NOT a barrier to problem-solving?
   a. hill climbing
   b. biased heuristics
   c. mental set
   d. functional fixedness

7. A motorist returning from the grocery store is stuck on an icy patch of roadway. The car will not move in any direction, as the tires spin freely on the ice. A passenger takes a bag of "kitty litter" from a grocery sack and spreads it on the ice under the tires, thus freeing the car. The driver is impressed, and claims that he never would have thought of doing that, thus demonstrating
   a. poor problem representation
   b. functional fixedness
   c. the availability heuristic
   d. divergent thinking

8. The fact that many Americans overestimate the number of plane crashes that occur each year illustrates
   a. means-end analysis
   b. poor math skills
   c. the availability heuristic
   d. a probability bias

9. The fictional detective, Sherlock Holmes, was well-known for his ability to observe many different clues and use them to solve a difficult mystery. His ability demonstrates
   a. divergent thinking
   b. convergent thinking
   c. availability heuristic
   d. means-end analysis

10. In the _____ stage of creative problem-solving, the problem is represented in a number of different ways.
   a. incubation
   b. illumination
   c. preparation
   d. anticipation

11. In problem-solving, a sudden insight is most likely to be part of the _____ stage.
   a. preparation
   b. incubation
   c. illumination
   d. verification

12. One basic difference between good problem-solvers and poor problem-solvers is that the good ones
   a. are more intelligent
   b. have more education
   c. make better use of resources
   d. are more aware of what they do

13. An important criterion for the solution to a problem is that it
   a. is original
   b. is unique
   c. represents correct problem-solving procedures
   d. works

14. An old saying goes,"You can't see the forest for the trees." If a person could put all the trees together to see the forest, he would be demonstrating
   a. mental set
   b. convergent thinking
   c. divergent thinking
   d. means-end analysis

15. Attempting to discover all the uses for a paper towel is an example of
    a. divergent thinking
    b. convergent thinking
    c. creativity
    d. availability heuristic

MULTIPLE CHOICE PRACTICE TEST 2 TOPIC 7B

1. Working a crossword puzzle would be an example of a/an
    a. unsolvable problem
    b. ill-defined problem
    c. well-defined problem
    d. common problem

2. Joe has a problem. He is unemployed. He knows that his goal is to get a job. However, he has no idea how to begin finding employment. We might say that his problem solving skills have broken down at the _____ stage.
    a. initial
    b. goal
    c. possible strategies
    d. solutions

3. Means-ends analysis, working backward, and hill climbing are all examples of
    a. heuristics
    b. algorithms
    c. goals
    d. strategies

4. You have a map to a friend's new house. You plan to find the street first and then look for the house number. The strategy you are using is
    a. an algorithm
    b. means-ends analysis
    c. working backward
    d. hill climbing

5. Lisa has locked her keys in her car. She uses a coat hanger to unlock the door and retrieve the keys. One thing we can say for sure is that she does not suffer from
    a. functional fixedness
    b. lack of strategies
    c. mental set
    d. algorithmic thinking

6. Research indicates that in certain situations labeling items
   a. increases functional fixedness
   b. decreases functional fixedness
   c. has no impact on functional fixedness
   d. increases strategies

7. Wade is playing a game with his two sons, Chad and Coty. In the game, Wade has rolled a "six" on the die four times in succession. Now, Wade would like to roll another six, but he believes that there is no chance that this could happen five times in a row. Wade's thinking illustrates
   a. backward thinking
   b. availability heuristic
   c. representativeness heuristic
   d. mental set

8. The problem-solving strategy most related to the idea, "If it ain't broke don't fix it," would be
   a. mental set
   b. functional fixedness
   c. availability heuristic
   d. positive test

9. Studies have shown that problem-solving skills
   a. cannot be taught effectively
   b. can be taught, but only to more gifted students
   c. can be taught, especially when students have a general background
   d. can be taught, but only to college-level students

10. Which of the following represents the correct order for the stages of creative problem-solving?
    a. incubation, verification, illumination, preparation
    b. preparation, incubation, illumination, verification
    c. verification, illumination, preparation, incubation
    d. illumination, verification, incubation, preparation

11. A study of the performance of American school children seems to indicate that
    a. rote skills are declining
    b. rote skills are increasing, but problem-solving is declining
    c. both rote skills and problem-solving are increasing
    d. only problem-solving skills are increasing

12. The 1978 study by Chi in which ten-year-olds performed better than adults when the memory task related to chess illustrates Glaser's notion that
    a. problem-solving skills are best taught in relation to a specific domain
    b. even very young children can learn problem-solving skills
    c. only bright children such as those who play chess can learn problem-solving skills
    d. there is no relation between age and ability to learn problem-solving skills

13. The relationship between tests of intelligence and tests of creativity can best be described as
    a. high positive correlation
    b. low positive correlation
    c. negative correlation
    d. no relationship

14. A limit on the use of algorithms is the
    a. lack of mathematical models for all problem types
    b. number of possible solutions to be tested
    c. fact that they are applicable only to verbal problems
    d. failure to yield a solution to some problems

15. Convergent thinking is to divergent thinking as _____ is to _____.
    a. success; failure
    b. incubation; illumination
    c. contraction; expansion
    d. algorithm; heuristic

Dr. G's Best Study Tips #7

GETTING ALONG WITH YOUR PROFESSOR

Although your grade may not depend on it, you may enjoy your class more and learn more if you create a positive relationship with the instructor. Research on adult thinking indicates that a college education is a very influential factor in cognitive development and that interacting with professors is one of the key influences. Here are some do's and don'ts that will help you get along and create a positive impression.

DO'S:

1. Learn the instructor's name and appropriate title.

2. Attend every class and be on time.

3. Make an appointment to visit your instructor during office hours. Express an interest in the course and in your grades. Learn about the professor's interests.

4. Prepare for class by reading assignments ahead so that you can answer and ask informed questions.

5. Sit near the front of the room or down the center aisles.

6. Inform the instructor of any special problems or needs you may have. For example, if you are epileptic or have hearing or vision problems, the instructor should be informed.

DON'TS:

1. Don't do anything that will call negative attention to yourself such as talking at inappropriate times or going late to class repeatedly.

2. If you miss class, NEVER ask, "Did we do anything in class today?"

3. Do not confess to the instructor that you have not read the assignments or prepared for class and do not offer excuses.

4. Do not miss an exam unless you are absolutely too ill to walk into the room and in that event, try to let the instructor know ahead of time that you cannot be there.

5. Don't be afraid to approach your instructor with concerns about class — most of us are human.

CHAPTER 8—INTELLIGENCE AND PSYCHOLOGICAL TESTING TOPIC 8A—INTELLIGENCE TESTING

LEARNING OBJECTIVES

A science is only as good as its measurement and much of psychological measurement involves tests. Psychological tests are used for many reasons, but perhaps the most common is to measure intellectual abilities. Students should be able to:

1. Discuss the theories of Spearman, Guilford, Vernon, Thurstone, and Sternberg.
2. Understand the operational definition of intelligence.
3. Define psychological test.
4. Distinguish between test retest reliability and split-half reliability.
5. Differentiate between concurrent validity, predictive validity, and content validity.
6. Define norms and understand their use in psychological testing.
7. Describe the 1986 revision of the Stanford-Binet Intelligence Test.
8. Describe the Wechsler Intelligence Scales.
9. Discuss the advantages and disadvantages of group and individual intelligence tests.

LEARNING TOPIC 8A VOCABULARY

On your own paper, write the definition for each of the following key terms. Your learning will be facilitated by writing the definition in your own words rather than copying the exact definition from your text.

INTELLIGENCE	G-FACTOR
S-FACTORS	PRIMARY MENTAL ABILITIES
PSYCHOLOGICAL TEST	RELIABILITY
TEST-RETEST RELIABILITY	SPLIT-HALF RELIABILITY
VALIDITY	PREDICTIVE VALIDITY
CONCURRENT VALIDITY	CONTENT VALIDITY
NORMS	G-SCORE
STANDARD AGE SCORE (SAS)	

MATCHING

Match the following key terms from your textbook with the appropriate definition.

____ 1. test-retest reliability   ____ 2. standard age score

____ 3. reliability   ____ 4. intelligence

____ 5. s-factors   ____ 6. psychological test

____ 7. split-half reliability   ____ 8. validity

____ 9. norms   ____ 10. g-score

____ 11. content validity   ____ 12. g-factor

____ 13. predictive validity   ____ 14. primary mental abilities

____ 15. concurrent validity

a. The capacity to understand the world and the resourcefulness to cope with its challenges; that which an intelligence test measures.
b. In Spearman's model, a general, overall intellectual skill.
c. In Spearman's model, those specific cognitive abilities that together with "g" constitute intelligence.
d. In Thurstone's model, the 7 unique abilities taken to comprise intelligence.
e. An objective, standardized measure of a sample of behavior.
f. Consistency or dependability; in testing, consistency of test scores.
g. A check of a test's consistency determined by correlating the results of a test taken by the same subjects at two different times.
h. A check on the internal consistency of a test found by correlating one part of a test with another part of the same test.
i. In testing, the extent to which a test measures what it claims to be measuring.
j. The extent to which a test can be used to predict future behaviors.
k. The extent to which the scores on a test are correlated with other assessments made at about the same time.
l. The extent to which a test provides an adequate and fair sample of the behaviors being measured.
m. Results of a test taken by a large group of subjects whose scores can be used to make comparisons or give meaning to new scores.
n. A measure of one's overall, general intellectual abilities, commonly thought of as "IQ".
o. A score on an intelligence test in which one's performance is compared to that of others of the same age; average equals 100.

TRUE-FALSE PRACTICE TEST

_____ 1. Defining intelligence as "that which intelligence tests measure" exemplifies an operational definition.

_____ 2. Charles Spearman used a research technique called naturalistic observation.

_____ 3. Spearman believed that the g-factor was independent of content or knowledge of facts.

_____ 4. Thurstone developed a theory suggesting that intelligence is made up of seven primary mental abilities.

_____ 5. Sternberg's triarchic theory of intelligence is the one that most psychologists favor.

_____ 6. A psychological test should be a standardized objective test.

_____ 7. Predictive validity is one characteristic of a good psychological test that is not established by correlation.

_____ 8. The usefulness of a psychological test often depends on the adequacy of the norms used to make comparisons of scores.

_____ 9. A test can be reliable without being valid, but it cannot be valid without being reliable.

_____ 10. Lewis Terman wrote the first intelligence test.

_____ 11. The Stanford-Binet intelligence test yields a measure similar to Spearman's g-factor.

_____ 12. The average standard age score on the Stanford-Binet test always equals 100.

_____ 13. Unlike the Stanford-Binet, Wechsler's first intelligence test was designed primarily for adults.

_____ 14. Surveys indicate that psychologists agree that intelligence tests are valuable in spite of the controversies surrounding them.

_____ 15. The biggest advantage of individual intelligence tests is that they are economical and save time.

FILL-IN PRACTICE TEST

1. The assignment of numbers to some characteristic of interest according to rules or an agreed upon system defines _____.

2. The concept of general intelligence suggested by Charles Spearman has become known as the _____.

3. The specific abilities of intelligence are called _____.

4. A _____ _____ is an objective, standardized measure of a sample of behavior.

5. Consistency or dependability in a psychological test is referred to as _____.

6. In _____ reliability, a test is administered to the same group on two different occasions.

7. The statistical procedure used to establish test reliability is _____.

8. The extent to which a test actually measures what it claims to measure is called _____.

9. If a psychological test is highly correlated with other tests or measures of the same characteristic, it is said to have _____ validity.

10. The extent to which a test adequately samples the behaviors that it claims to be testing is called _____ validity.

11. Results of a test taken by a large group of subjects whose scores can be used to make comparisons are called _____.

12. The author of the first intelligence test was _____ _____.

13. In terms of content, a major difference between the Stanford-Binet test and the WAIS, is that the WAIS relied less on _____ skills.

14. The most commonly used of all psychological tests is the _____.

15. The first group intelligence test was the _____ _____.

MULTIPLE CHOICE PRACTICE TEST 1 TOPIC 8A

1. In psychology, a great deal of the measurement involves
   a. laboratory experiments
   b. physical measurements
   c. psychological testing
   d. field observation

2. The psychologist who proposed that intelligence consists of three intersecting dimensions was
    a. Thurstone
    b. Vernon
    c. Spearman
    d. Guilford

3. The psychologist who proposed the triarchic model of intelligence was
    a. Vernon
    b. Spearman
    c. Sternberg
    d. Guilford

4. A psychological test measures
    a. behavior
    b. aptitudes
    c. feelings
    d. all of the above

5. If a test is administered in such a way that all who take the test get the same instructions, the same time limits, and virtually the same testing conditions, we say that the test is
    a. objective
    b. standardized
    c. valid
    d. reliable

6. To qualify as a good psychological test, an instrument should have
    a. reliability
    b. validity
    c. adequate norms
    d. all of the above

7. The _____ of a test sets limits on its _____.
    a. reliability; validity
    b. length; norms
    c. validity; reliability
    d. objectivity; standardization

8. The foreman of the Peter Piper Pickle Packing Plant wants to test new trainees to determine which ones will become the best pickle packers. If the company psychologist develops a test that will accurately measure this, we could say the test has
    a. validity generalizability
    b. predictive validity
    c. test-retest reliability
    d. adequate norms

9. Your psychology teacher brings in a pop quiz and as you begin taking the test, you notice that the questions are about history rather than psychology. For this class, the test lacks

   a. test-retest reliability
   b. split-half reliability
   c. concurrent validity
   d. content validity

10. Standard age scores compare an individual's performance on an intelligence test with the performance of:

    a. that same individual when he/she took the test at a younger age
    b. others of different age levels who have taken the same test
    c. others of the same age who have taken other standard tests
    d. others of the same age who have taken the same test

11. Which of the following is NOT true of the Stanford-Binet Test?

    a. There are fifteen different subtests.
    b. The test is both valid and reliable.
    c. The test yields an IQ score calculated by dividing the subject's mental age by chronological age and multiplying by 100.
    d. The test includes measures for crystallized abilities, fluid-analytic abilities, and short-term memory.

12. A psychologist working in a rehabilitation center needs to know the "IQ" of a single adult client. The best test to use would be the

    a. WAIS-R
    b. AFQT
    c. Stanford-Binet
    d. OLSAT

13. Psychological tests used to make predictions about future behaviors are called

    a. group intelligence tests
    b. aptitude tests
    c. tests of mental abilities
    d. achievement tests

14. Angie is a junior in high school. She would like to prepare as much as possible for the college entrance exams she must take next year. The best test for her to take is the

    a. GRE
    b. ACT
    c. WPPSI
    d. PSAT

15. A significant difference between aptitude tests and intelligence tests is the
    a. content of the tests
    b. purpose for which each is used
    c. standardization and objectivity
    d. norms

MULTIPLE CHOICE PRACTICE TEST 2 TOPIC 8A

1. In regard to intelligence, all psychologists agree that
    a. it can be easily defined and measured
    b. it is a reflection of one's cognitive reactions
    c. it is made up of a number of specific factors
    d. intelligence is not always reflected in behavior

2. Which of the following definitions of intelligence can be attributed to David Wechsler?
    a. The capacity of the individual to understand the world about him and his resourcefulness to cope with its challenges.
    b. The sum total of everything you know.
    c. The ability to learn and profit from experience.
    d. One's ability to solve problems and cope with the environment.

3. The psychologist who proposed that intelligence is made up of seven primary mental abilities was
    a. Spearman
    b. Guilford
    c. Vernon
    d. Thurstone

4. Vernon theorized that intelligence consists of
    a. g-factors and s-factors
    b. seven primary mental abilities
    c. a number of skills and abilities arranged in a hierarchy
    d. three intersecting dimensions

5. To require that a test be objective is to require that
    a. different evaluators interpret results in the same way
    b. answers can be given in terms of letters or numbers
    c. there be just one examiner for each person being tested
    d. everyone take the test under the same conditions

6. Many of the so-called psychological tests found in the popular press tend NOT to be good tests because they lack
   a. objectivity
   b. standardization
   c. validity and reliability
   d. none of the above

7. For which of the following would we be LEAST likely to use a correlational statistical method?
   a. test-retest reliability
   b. split-half reliability
   c. concurrent validity
   d. content validity

8. If we wish to measure the internal consistency of a test regardless of whether the test is consistent over time, we would use a measure of
   a. test-retest reliability
   b. split-half reliability
   c. concurrent validity
   d. predictive validity

9. Which of the following is NOT true of the WAIS-R.
   a. It consists of 11 subtests divided into verbal and performance scales.
   b. It is an intelligence tests for adults.
   c. The Wechsler tests are not as valid or reliable as the Stanford-Binet.
   d. A standard score is computed for each of the subtests, in addition to an overall score.

10. Which of the following is NOT one of the controversies that usually surround intelligence tests.
    a. the tests are culturally biased
    b. the tests are age biased
    c. the tests do not truly measure intelligence, only academic success
    d. the tests may be used to further certain political causes

11. The Army Beta test was designed for
    a. female soldiers
    b. deaf soldiers
    c. black soldiers
    d. illiterate soldiers

12. Today, the two largest consumers of group intelligence tests are
    a. industry and education
    b. state and federal employment services
    c. education and the military
    d. military and other government agencies

13. A psychologist wishes to know the "IQ" of a class of third graders. The best test to administer would be the

    a. OLSAT
    b. AGCT
    c. WAIS-R
    d. ACT

14. Which of the following is NOT a key difference between group and individual tests?

    a. Group tests are much less expensive.
    b. Individual tests take less time and expertise to administer.
    c. The administrator of an individual test can get to know the examinee.
    d. Group tests may not provide as much information or be as valid as individual tests.

15. Many educational aptitude tests are pencil and paper tests of general intellectual abilities that are used to make predictions about future academic performance. Which of the following tests does NOT fit this description?

    a. WISC
    b. GRE
    c. PSAT
    d. ACT

CHAPTER 8—INTELLIGENCE AND PSYCHOLOGICAL TESTING TOPIC 8B—DIFFERENCES IN MEASURED INTELLIGENCE

LEARNING OBJECTIVES

One of the most important ways in which people differ is in their intellectual abilities. However, there is less than perfect agreement on what intelligence is and whether it can be measured accurately. Students should be able to:

1. Explain what psychologists have learned about the importance of heredity and the environment in determining intelligence from the study of twins and adopted children.
2. List some of the reasons that might account for group differences in IQ.
3. Discuss sex differences in intelligence.
4. Discuss age related changes in intelligence in light of cross-sectional and longitudinal research.
5. Discuss the racial and ethnic differences in performance on IQ tests.
6. Discuss the possible explanations for racial or ethnic differences on IQ tests.
7. Describe Terman's study of gifted individuals, including selection, problems, and results.
8. List six ways in which individuals can be considered to be gifted.
9. Define mental retardation.
10. Discuss the causes, treatment, and prevention of mental retardation.
11. Describe Down's syndrome.
12. Describe phenylketonuria.

LEARNING TOPIC 8B VOCABULARY

On your own paper, write the definition for each of the following key terms. Your learning will be facilitated by writing the definition in your own words rather than copying the exact definition from your text.

FLUID INTELLIGENCE   CRYSTALLIZED INTELLIGENCE

MENTALLY GIFTED   MENTAL RETARDATION

DOWN'S SYNDROME   PHENYLKETONURIA

MATCHING

Match the following key terms from your textbook with the appropriate definition.

____ 1. phenylketonuria   ____ 2. mentally gifted

____ 3. fluid intelligence   ____ 4. Down's syndrome

____ 5. crystallized intelligence   ____ 6. mental retardation

a. Those cognitive skills dependent on speed, adaptation, flexibility, and abstract reasoning.
b. Those cognitive skills dependent on knowledge, accumulated experience, and general information.
c. Demonstrating outstanding ability or aptitude in a number of possible areas; usually general intelligence where an IQ of 130 is a standard criterion.
d. A condition indicated by an IQ below 70 that began during the developmental period and is associated with impairment in adaptive functioning.

e. A condition of many symptoms including mental retardation, caused by an extra (47th) chromosome.

f. A genetically caused disorder that produces mental retardation and that is now detectable and preventable.

TRUE-FALSE PRACTICE TEST

_____ 1. The best explanation of the relationship of heredity and the environment to intelligence is that both are important.

_____ 2. Inherited traits, including intelligence, are generally unchangeable.

_____ 3. In studies of the effects of genetics and environment on intelligence, as genetic similarities among subjects increase, correlations of IQ scores also increase.

_____ 4. In general, the more extreme the differences in environment that individuals experience, the greater the resulting differences in IQ.

_____ 5. Boy-girl socialization processes provide the best explanation for male/female ability differences in mathematics.

_____ 6. Since IQ scores of children younger than seven are not correlated to adult IQ, it is probably a waste of time to test young children.

_____ 7. It would be correct to say that fluid intelligence is more vulnerable to the effects of aging than crystallized intelligence.

_____ 8. Black children score higher on IQ tests than Asian children.

_____ 9. In general, psychologists agree that environmental factors alone cannot explain racial differences in IQ.

_____ 10. About 95 percent of all IQ scores are between 70 and 130.

_____ 11. Evidence suggests that measures of creativity are unrelated to measures of general intelligence.

_____ 12. A person who has outstanding leadership skills can be considered gifted.

_____ 13. A talented gymnast would NOT be considered a gifted individual.

_____ 14. Terman's study of gifted destroyed most of the stereotypes about bright children.

_____ 15. The IQ cutoff score for mental retardation is 70.

FILL-IN PRACTICE TEST

1. Studies that examine the impact of genetics and environment on intelligence typically use the statistical procedure of _____.

2. IQ scores obtained before the age of _____ do not correlate highly with adult IQ scores.

3. Average IQ for any age is _____.

4. IQ scores gathered using the _____ method seem to indicate that IQ declines with age.

5. IQ scores gathered using the _____ method indicate that IQ continued to rise into the mid-50s and then gradually decline.

6. One specific area of knowledge that shows no decline with age is _____.

7. Intellectual abilities that relate to speed, adaptation, flexibility, and abstract reasoning are referred to as _____ _____.

8. Intellectual abilities that relate to acquired knowledge, accumulated experiences, and general information are referred to as _____ _____.

9. People who use the term "mentally gifted" are most likely referring to people who are gifted _____.

10. To be considered intellectually gifted, one would have to score above _____ on a standardized IQ test.

11. The psychologist who contributed most to our knowledge of gifted individuals was _____.

12. The individuals in Terman's study are sometimes referred to as _____.

13. The term mentally retarded is being replaced with the term _____ _____.

14. A genetic cause of mental retardation characterized by the presence of a 47th chromosome is _____ _____.

15. PKU is the abbreviation for a disorder called _____ which can cause mental retardation if untreated.

MULTIPLE CHOICE PRACTICE TEST 1 TOPIC 8B

1. Identical twins are frequently used in studies of the effects of heredity and environment on IQ because they
   a. have similar environments
   b. have similar genetics
   c. are born about the same time
   d. are easily identified in most cultures

2. Which of the following statements regarding correlations of IQ scores is NOT true?
   a. Correlations for fraternal twins are greater than those for non-twin siblings.
   b. As genetic similarities increase, correlations also increase.
   c. Correlations for identical twins are as high as those for test reliability on IQ tests.
   d. Correlations for subjects raised together are higher than those for subjects raised apart.

3. Studies by Scarr and Weinberg indicated that the factor which may account for the high correlation between the IQs of children and their adoptive parents is
   a. heredity
   b. environment
   c. socioeconomic status
   d. whether the child is a twin

4. From comparisons between Umaloos and Takatees that were described in the text, we can say that as a group, the Takatees have higher IQs than the Umaloos, but it will be difficult to make statements about individuals because

    a. of the overlapping (variability) of the scores of the two groups

    b. the groups were too small

    c. intelligence cannot be compared

    d. the mean differences could be due to change

5. A researcher who wanted to present the most optimistic outlook on age related changes in IQ should report studies using the _____ method.

    a. correlational

    b. cross-sectional

    c. longitudinal

    d. none of the above

6. In the early stages of Alzheimer's disease, a person will have difficulty remembering the name of a new person, but will be able to remember past events in great detail. This indicates that the function which is most impaired is

    a. spatial relations

    b. crystallized intelligence

    c. fluid intelligence

    d. global intelligence

7. According to a review of age related studies by Salthouse, the area of ability where one should expect the greatest decline with age is in

    a. spatial relations

    b. crystallized intelligence

    c. fluid intelligence

    d. global intelligence

8. Which of the following students is likely to make the highest score on an IQ test that contains mathematics problems?

    a. an white American boy

    b. an Asian boy

    c. a Black American girl

    d. a white American boy

9. Intellectually gifted individuals make up only about _____ percent of the population.

    a. 3

    b. 5

    c. 10

    d. 15

10. Lewis Terman's research on gifted individuals was _____ research.
    a. cross-sectional
    b. longitudinal
    c. naturalistic observation
    d. correlation

11. Which of the following is NOT true of the results of Terman's study of giftedness?
    a. Gifted children are taller, faster, and better coordinated.
    b. Gifted children have fewer emotional problems.
    c. Gifted children grow into successful adults with high-paying jobs.
    d. All gifted children grow up to be rich and famous and live happily ever after.

12. The definition of mental retardation suggests that the symptoms must appear by age
    a. 1
    b. 5
    c. 10
    d. 18

13. Which of the following is NOT true of Down's syndrome?
    a. the individuals will never be able to live independently
    b. the risk increases as the age of either parent increases
    c. it is a clear case of a genetic cause of retardation
    d. during childhood, behavioral development is delayed in Down's individuals

14. PKU is detected by
    a. visual examination of a newborn
    b. urine test
    c. blood test
    d. prenatal exam

15. Which of the following is NOT a possible cause of mental retardation?
    a. prenatal hypertension
    b. exposure to X-rays
    c. mother's use of drugs during pregnancy
    d. baby born late or overdue

MULTIPLE CHOICE PRACTICE TEST 2 TOPIC 8B

1. Which of the following pairs would result in the highest correlation of IQ?
    a. fraternal twins
    b. same sex siblings
    c. mother-daughter
    d. identical twins

2. We study the IQ scores of identical twins raised apart when we want to control the heredity and vary the environment. If we want to control the environment and vary the heredity we would study

   a. adopted children

   b. fraternal twins raised together

   c. identical twins raised together

   d. non-twin siblings

3. With regard to male/female differences, which of the following statements is NOT true?

   a. females are usually better at fine motor dexterity

   b. males are usually better at spatial relations

   c. females are usually better at verbal fluency and reading

   d. males are usually better at clerical speed and accuracy

4. Evidence suggests that male/female differences on tests of general mathematics abilities have been

   a. increasing over the past 50 years

   b. decreasing over the past 25 years

   c. seriously overestimated

   d. increased only in elementary school children

5. The best explanation for the fact that males score higher on the mathematics portion of the SAT is that males

   a. are genetically predisposed to understand math

   b. are socialized to be better in math

   c. take more math classes in high school

   d. inherit math genes from their fathers

6. The best explanation for ethnic differences in IQ test scores is

   a. the tests are biased

   b. environmental and motivational factors

   c. genetic factors

   d. all of the above

7. The psychologist who argued against an environmental explanation of racial differences in IQ scores was

   a. Jensen

   b. Mackenzie

   c. Salthouse

   d. Binet

8. According to Arthur Jensen, his research regarding racial differences in IQ was intended to
    a. prove that blacks are inferior to whites
    b. prove that whites are inferior to Asians
    c. illustrate the bias in IQ tests
    d. provoke further scientific study of racial differences in IQ

9. Which of the following is NOT one of the problems associated with Lewis Terman's research on gifted individuals?
    a. failing to control for factors such as socioeconomic level or parent's education level
    b. using too narrow a definition for giftedness
    c. failing to include black children
    d. excluding children who had psychological problems

10. According to the AAMD, the definition of mental retardation should include
    a. only individuals whose IQ is lower than 70
    b. some measure of a person's ability to adapt to the environment
    c. only a deficiency in skills measured by IQ tests
    d. the 5 percent of the population with the lowest IQ scores

11. Which of the following statements best describes extremes in intelligence?
    a. the numbers of gifted individuals and retarded individuals are about equal
    b. there are twice as many gifted individuals as retarded ones
    c. there are twice as many retarded individuals as gifted ones
    d. the relationship between the number of gifted and the number of retarded people is undetermined

12. Of all the cases of mental retardation, what percent develop before, during, or just after birth?
    a. 10
    b. 20
    c. 25
    d. 40

13. Perhaps the greatest hope in dealing with mental retardation is in the area of
    a. increasing the IQ of the profoundly retarded
    b. curing Down's syndrome
    c. preventing retardation by learning more about the prenatal environment
    d. redefining retardation so that fewer individuals are labeled

14. PKU is treated by
    a. drugs
    b. radiation
    c. diet
    d. physical therapy

15. Which of the following statements best summarizes the existing knowledge about intelligence?

    a. We have no idea what causes average intelligence.

    b. We do not know what causes intellectual giftedness.

    c. We know some, but not all of the causes of mental retardation.

    d. All of the above.

Dr. G's Best Study Tips #8

USING 3X5 CARDS

An excellent way to study the extensive vocabulary that psychology presents is to use 3x5 cards. Prepare the cards by writing the term you want to learn on one side and a definition or related fact on the other side. Take the cards with you in your purse or pocket and study them whenever you have a few minutes. You might be stuck in traffic or waiting in the dentist's office, or you might even get out of class a few minutes early. Remember, we have already discussed the benefits of short, frequent study periods.

Tape a few of the cards around your bathroom mirror and study them while you shave, brush your teeth, or comb your hair. You will be surprised how much you gain from these few minutes. Ten minutes a day for six days means one hour that you don't have to spend in the library or sitting at your desk.

When you study the cards, look at the term and say the definition aloud. If you can define the term, place the card in a discard pile. If you cannot, then read the definition three times and place the card on the bottom of the stack. When you have gone through the cards once, shuffle them just as you would playing cards. This prevents you from learning the definitions in some sort of order and becoming dependent on that order as a memory cue. A real benefit of this study method is that you have evidence that it works: just look at the discard pile. That represents the terms you have already learned. In addition, the studying task has been reduced. Each time you study, you are focusing on the information you do not know and you are reducing the learning task as you discard the terms you do know.

CHAPTER 9—DEVELOPMENTAL PSYCHOLOGY
TOPIC 9A—THE DEVELOPMENT OF CHILDREN

LEARNING OBJECTIVES

There are common patterns and ways in which the continuous, slow, and gradual process of development proceeds. Each of the three domains of development (physical-motor, sensory-perceptual, and cognitive-social) is continually interacting with and influencing the others as the human organism develops from conception through childhood. Students should be able to:

1. Explain the epigenetic model and relate it to the nature-nurture controversy.
2. List the three stages of prenatal development.
3. Discuss the impact of diet, drugs, and stress on prenatal development.
4. List the reflexes that neonates possess and discuss their importance.
5. Describe the landmarks of early motor development.
6. Describe the basic sensory capacities of the neonate.
7. Describe the cognitive skills that develop during the sensorimotor stage.
8. Define egocentrism and understand how it affects cognition in preoperational children.
9. Discuss the cognitive skills present in the concrete operations stage.
10. Discuss the cognitive skills of the formal operations stage.
11. Discuss the criticisms of Piaget's theory.
12. Describe Erikson's four crisis stages of childhood development.
13. Explain Kohlberg's theory of moral development.
14. Discuss the importance of attachment.

LEARNING TOPIC 9A VOCABULARY

On your own paper, write the definition for each of the following key terms. Your learning will be facilitated by writing the definition in your own words rather than just copying the exact definition from your text.

NATURE-NURTURE CONTROVERSY	EPIGENETIC MODEL
PLASTICITY	ZYGOTE
PRENATAL PERIOD	STAGE OF THE ZYGOTE
STAGE OF THE EMBRYO	STAGE OF THE FETUS
VIABILITY	FETAL ALCOHOL SYNDROME
NEONATE	SCHEMA

MATCHING

Match the following key terms from your textbook with the appropriate definition.

____ 1. zygote	____ 2. neonate
____ 3. plasticity	____ 4. viability
____ 5. fetal alcohol syndrome	____ 6. epigenetic model
____ 7. nature-nurture controversy	____ 8. stage of the zygote
____ 9. schema	____ 10. prenatal period
____ 11. stage of the embryo	____ 12. stage of the fetus

a. The debate over which is more important in development, one's genetic, inherited nature, or one's nurture, one's experience through interaction with the environment.

b. An interactionist view of development that claims that development emerges, based on one's genetic programming and one's experiences.

c. A demonstration of flexibility, or a capacity to be molded and shaped in a wide range of ways.

d. The one-cell product of the union of sperm and ovum at conception.

e. That period of development from conception to birth.

f. Developmental period from conception to the age of 2 weeks.

g. Developmental period from 2 to 8 weeks.

h. Developomental period from week 8 until birth.

i. The ability to survive without interference or intervention.

j. A cluster of symptoms associated with a child born to a mother who was a heavy drinker of alcohol during pregnancy.

k. The newborn, from birth to age of 2 weeks.

l. One's organized, mental representations of the world.

TRUE-FALSE PRACTICE TEST

_____ 1. Growth and development mean essentially the same thing.

_____ 2. The embryonic stage typically lasts from week 2 to week 8 of the prenatal period.

_____ 3. During the embryonic stage, both the number and type of cells increases.

_____ 4. The central nervous system is the one part of the body that is at risk during the entire period of prenatal development.

_____ 5. The fetus is generally unaffected by the nutrition of the mother.

_____ 6. When a nutritional deficiency exists in a pregnant woman, she may suffer because the available nutrients go first to the fetus.

_____ 7. Although research clearly establishes the harmful effects of smoking on the smoker, there is no evidence that smoking affects a fetus.

_____ 8. Babies born to mothers who abused psychoactive drugs during pregnancy are likely to experience withdrawal after birth.

_____ 9. The best advice to pregnant women concerning the use of drugs, is to consult a doctor and use extreme caution.

_____ 10. Reflexive behaviors can often be used to diagnose the quality of a neonate's development.

_____ 11. A pregnant woman under stress may be unknowingly depriving her baby of oxygen.

_____ 12. Relatively little of a neonates behavior is reflexive.

_____ 13. In general, the rate of development of motor skills in infancy predicts adult characteristics such as intelligence and coordination.

_____ 14. Although the rate of development may vary, the sequence of motor development is usually the same.

_____ 15. There is no significant sex difference with regard to motor development.

FILL-IN PRACTICE TEST

1. Developing organisms demonstrate a capacity to be molded and shaped by their experiences. This is known as _____.

2. The single cell organism created by the union of the sperm cell and the ovum is called a/an _____.

3. The time from conception to birth is called the _____ period.

4. The stage of the zygote ends when _____ occurs.

5. The developing organism is at greatest risk during the _____ stage.

6. The bodily organs actually begin to function during the stage of the _____.

7. The time when the fetus is capable of sustaining life outside the uterus is referred to as the point of _____.

8. Consuming 3 ounces or more of alcohol per day during pregnancy results in _____ _____ _____.

9. During the first two weeks after birth, the infant is referred to as a _____.

10. Although all senses are functioning to some degree at birth, the last sense to develop is _____.

11. The apparatus used to test depth perception in children is called a _____ _____.

12. An organized mental representation of the world is called a/an _____.

13. When children take new information and fit it into an existing schema, they are practicing _____.

14. When children change or revise existing schema, they are practicing _____.

15. When a child understands that changing the form or the appearance of something does not really change what the thing is, he/she has mastered _____.

MULTIPLE CHOICE PRACTICE TEST 1 TOPIC 9A

1. According to the epigenetic model, the role of nature and nurture in development can best be described as
   a. interaction
   b. more heavily influenced by environment
   c. more heavily influenced by heredity
   d. neither is as important as was once believed

2. Which of the following is NOT a stage of prenatal development?

    a. stage of the zygote

    b. stage of the embryo

    c. stage of defferentiation

    d. stage of the fetus

3. Birth defects are most likely to develop during the stage of the

    a. zygote

    b. embryo

    c. fetus

    d. birth process

4. Which of the following is NOT true of smoking mothers?

    a. They have more miscarriages than nonsmoking mothers.

    b. They experience more stillbirths than nonsmoking mothers.

    c. Their babies have increased risk of dying soon after birth.

    d. Their babies are only affected if they smoke two packs of cigarettes a day.

5. In one study of the effects of alcohol on the unborn fetus, when women were given a single drink in the 37th to 39th weeks of pregnancy, the fetus was

    a. essentially unaffected

    b. observed to stop breathing movements

    c. observed to stop all movement

    d. observed to show signs of distress in all vital functions

6. The fact that one of the first motor skills an infant masters is control over his head is evidence for

    a. the cephalocaudal sequence of motor development

    b. the proximodistal sequence of motor development

    c. the presence of reflexive responses

    d. a regular rate of development

7. Research conducted by Robert Fantz indicates that even young infants

    a. prefer to look at patterns resembling a human face

    b. have great difficulty sustaining attention to any visual stimuli

    c. do not experience the phenomenon of habituation

    d. are unable to focus on patterns with small details

8. A child's adaptation from feeding from a bottle to eating more solid, chunkier food, would be described by Piaget as

    a. forming a schema

    b. assimilation

    c. accommodation

    d. just part of normal development

9. During which of the Piagetian stages does object permanence develop?

    a. sensorimotor

    b. preoperational

    c. concrete operational

    d. formal operations

10. Which of the following is NOT a correct match?

    a. formal operations — abstract concepts

    b. concrete operations — drawing a map

    c. preoperational — egocentrism

    d. sensorimotor — schema

11. Your eight year-old brother is upset because you have two pieces of gum and he has only one. You break his one in half and say, "There, now you have as many as I do." Your brother would probably

    a. be satisfied that he too now had two pieces of gum

    b. still be upset because he knows that you still have more gum than he does

    c. forget about the whole incident and act as though it never happened

    d. not understand any of your efforts

12. A major strength of Erikson's theory is that it

    a. gives an opposing view of cognitive development

    b. offers a better explanation of childhood cognitive processes

    c. deals with social development instead of cognition

    d. covers the entire lifespan, dealing with issues of adult development

13. The goal of the _____ stage in Erikson's developmental theory is for the child to develop a strong sense of joy at trying new things.

    a. trust vs. mistrust

    b. initiative vs. guilt

    c. industry vs. inferiority

    d. autonomy vs. shame and doubt

14. Which of the following statements about Kohlberg's theory of moral development is NOT true?

    a. Research supports the basic theory and suggests that it has crosscultural applications.

    b. There is little evidence that many people operate at the higher levels.

    c. Children may be capable of operating at much higher levels than Kohlberg suggested.

    d. A child's answers to the Kohlberg dilemmas can predict criminal behavior later in life.

15. Carol Gilligan (1982) has argued that the moral reasoning of females is _____ when compared to that of males.

    a. slower to develop

    b. faster to develop

    c. less complex

    d. different in nature

MULTIPLE CHOICE PRACTICE TEST 2 TOPIC 9A

1. The major impact of heredity occurs

    a. at conception

    b. during the prenatal period

    c. when the cells of the zygote divide

    d. right after birth

2. The first differentiation of cells takes place during the

    a. stage of differentiation

    b. period of the fetus

    c. period of the embryo

    d. period of the zygote

3. Developmental psychologists tend to be interested in:

    a. those stages in one's development that are different from those of any one else

    b. those patterns of development that we all have in common and that make each of us unique

    c. developmental stages that make humans different from nonhumans

    d. genetic and biological factors affecting growth and development to the exclusion of concern over environmental factors

4. Which of the following is NOT a characteristic of fetal alcohol syndrome?

    a. retarded physical growth

    b. poor coordination and muscle tone

    c. heart defects

    d. intellectual retardation

5. At present, the best advice for a pregnant woman is

    a. limit the intake of alcohol

    b. smoking or drinking alone is ok in moderation, but don't do both

    c. totally abstain from both smoking and drinking

    d. do not smoke or drink during the period of the fetus

6. Danny is a newborn. His mother has placed a mobile over the crib. According to the proximodistal sequence of development, Danny will probably

   a. be able to wave his arm and move the mobile, but not actually grasp it

   b. grasp the mobile, but not be able to let it go

   c. be unable to direct his arm movements in such a way as to hit the mobile

   d. be totally uninterested in the mobile until visual development improves

7. Which of the following statements most accurately describes the development of depth perception in children?

   a. Neonates appear to have no sense of depth perception.

   b. Depth perception develops as a product of increased visual acuity and experience.

   c. Depth perception develops after the fear of heights.

   d. Few children can make an appropriate response to depth perception before they can walk.

8. Which of the following is not an appropriate match?

   a. object permanence — sensorimotor stage

   b. causality — preoperational stage

   c. egocentrism — preoperational stage

   d. conservation — concrete operational stage

9. The abilities to manipulate concepts and to organize things into categories appear during the _____ stage of cognitive development.

   a. sensorimotor

   b. preoperational

   c. concrete operational

   d. formal operational

10. The ability to reason about hypothetical situations appears during the _____ stage.

    a. sensorimotor

    b. preoperational

    c. concrete operational

    d. formal operational

11. Which of the following is NOT a criticism of Piaget's theory?

    a. Little attention is given to the impact of language development.

    b. The borderlines between the stages are much less clearly defined than Piaget indicated.

    c. Piaget overestimated the ability of children in the stages of preoperational and concrete operational development.

    d. Piaget underestimated the cognitive ability of preschool children.

12. Erik Erikson's work was heavily influenced by the theories of

    a. Jean Piaget

    b. Lawrence Kohlberg

    c. John Watson

    d. Sigmund Freud

13. Mark is considering taking a cookie even though his father has told him not to. He thinks to himself, "I better not, because if I do, I'll be punished." This child is showing thinking characteristic of _____ morality.

    a. utilitarian

    b. preconventional

    c. conventional

    d. postconventional

14. During Erikson's stage of _____ the focus moves away from interaction with the family and focuses on the world beyond.

    a. trust vs. mistrust

    b. initiative vs. guilt

    c. industry vs. inferiority

    d. autonomy vs. shame and doubt

15. Which of the following statements about attachment is NOT true?

    a. Attachment is considered to be the root of social development.

    b. Attachment is believed to be a product of evolution, having a strong survival purpose.

    c. Attachment is associated with more freedom to explore the environment, greater curiosity, and more adaptive problem solving in the child.

    d. Children with unhealthy or abnormal attachment to their parents tend to be more competent in interacting with peers.

CHAPTER 9—DEVELOPMENTAL PSYCHOLOGY —TOPIC 9B DEVELOPMENT IN ADOLESCENCE AND ADULTHOOD

LEARNING OBJECTIVES

We continue to develop throughout our lives. The changes that reflect our development after childhood may be more gradual and difficult to observe but are no less significant. Students should be able to:

1. Define adolescence from a physical, social and psychological point of view.
2. Describe the physical changes that accompany adolescence.
3. Compare and contrast how Erikson and Marcia describe the adolescent's search for identity.
4. Describe adolescent egocentrism.
5. Discuss drug use and abuse in adolescence.
6. Describe sexuality in adolescence and the associated problem of teenage pregnancy.
7. Describe the characteristic developments of early adulthood.
8. Discuss the issues that are typically faced during middle adulthood.
9. Describe the elderly population in the United States.

LEARNING TOPIC 9B VOCABULARY

On your own paper, write the definition for each of the following key terms. Your learning will be facilitated by writing the definition in your own words rather than just copying the exact definition from your text.

ADOLESCENCE	GROWTH SPURT
PUBERTY	MENARCHE
IDENTITY CRISIS	IDENTITY STATUS
ADOLESCENT EGOCENTRISM	AGEISM

MATCHING

Match the following key terms from your textbook with the appropriate definition.

____ 1. ageism   ____ 2. growth spurt

____ 3. menarche   ____ 4. adolescent egocentrism

____ 5. adolescence   ____ 6. identity status

____ 7. puberty   ____ 8. identity crisis

a. The developmental period between childhood and adulthood, often begun at puberty and ending with full physical growth—generally between the ages of 12 and 20.
b. A marked increase in both height and weight that accompanies the onset of adolescence.
c. The stage of physical development at which one becomes capable of sexual reproduction.
d. A female's first menstrual period, often taken as a sure sign of the beginning of adolescence.
e. The struggle to define and integrate one's sense of self and what one's attitudes, beliefs, and values should be.
f. One of four states in identity formation, reflecting both a sense of conflict and/or a sense of commitment.

g. Self-centered cognitions, plus the belief that one is the center of other's attention.

h. Discrimination or negative stereotypes about someone formed solely on the basis of age.

TRUE-FALSE PRACTICE TEST

_____ 1. The biological definition for adolescence suggests that it begins with the onset of puberty and ends with the end of physical growth.

_____ 2. Over the past 25 years, the view of adolescence has changed from a picture of turmoil to a view of adjustments that are generally made in healthy ways.

_____ 3. Boys usually begin the growth spurt earlier than girls and end it with greater strength and size.

_____ 4. Some changes during adolescence such as the change in voice pitch are more noticeable in boys.

_____ 5. Whereas girls are very much aware of the onset of puberty, boys may not know when it occurs.

_____ 6. In general, late maturation is preferable to early maturation.

_____ 7. In general, both drug use and positive attitudes about drugs are on the decline.

_____ 8. Drug use among adolescents is greater than for any other segment of the population.

_____ 9. In general, sexual activity is increasing among males but not among females.

_____ 10. Teenage pregnancy is less of a problem in the United States than in other developed countries.

_____ 11. Adult development may not follow orderly transitions and may be significantly different for men and women.

_____ 12. The old saying "opposites attract" still proves true for marriage partners.

_____ 13. The decision not to have children is being made more often even though it results in a decline in satisfaction later in life.

_____ 14. The notion of a mid-life crisis is mostly myth.

_____ 15. One misconception about the elderly is that they live in misery.

FILL-IN PRACTICE TEST

1. The two physical signs of adolescence are sexual maturation and the _____ _____.

2. The onset of _____ marks a significant increase in the production of sex hormones.

3. An adolescent is in Piaget's stage of _____ _____ in terms of cognitive development.

4. When one struggles to define and integrate the sense of who one is, what one is to do in life, and what one's attitudes, beliefs, and values should be, one is having a/an _____ _____.

5. A pattern of self-centered thinking in which the individual believes that everyone else is thinking about him/her too is _____ _____.

167

6. Stories that teenagers generate about themselves on the basis of irrational beliefs are called
_____ _____.

7. According to Turner and Helms, one is in the _____ stage of career development when one gives up part of the self to the job.

8. In the career stage of _____, the career decision is actually implemented.

9. The period of _____ _____ is marked by transition.

10. Adults who are caring for both children and aging parents have been referred to as the
_____ _____.

11. According to Erikson, one who does not experience generativity in middle adulthood will experience _____.

12. The psychologist who described seven tasks that must be accomplished in middle adulthood was _____.

13. Discrimination on the basis of age is referred to as _____.

14. The fact that experience can compensate for loss of speed in mental abilities can be thought of as an example of _____.

15. The elderly are sometimes categorized according to health and social factors as young-old and _____.

MULTIPLE CHOICE PRACTICE TEST 1 TOPIC 9B

1. Which of the following is NOT a correct definition of adolescence as discussed in your text?
   a. the period beginning with puberty and ending with the end of physical growth
   b. a psychological process occurring within the individual that includes an increase in problem-solving skills and abstract thinking
   c. the period during which a person is not yet an adult, but no longer a child
   d. the period from age 10 to 20 during which it is abnormal to be normal

2. Which of the following is NOT true of early maturing girls?
   a. They are likely to approached more for dates and have more sexual encounters.
   b. They may have problems with self image.
   c. They may fall behind in intellectual functioning.
   d. They are rated below average in leadership skills and popularity.

3. The concept of the identity crisis faced by adolescents is part of the social development theory of
   a. Anna Freud
   b. G. Stanley Hall
   c. Lawrence Kohlberg
   d. Erik Erikson

4. Natalie's father is an attorney. He has encouraged her to go to law school since she was a child. Now that Natalie is in high school, she is taking courses and looking at colleges that would most likely get her into a good law school in a few years. She is in Marcia's identity state of

    a. identity diffusion
    b. foreclosure
    c. moratorium
    d. identity achieved

5. One characteristic of adolescent egocentrism is

    a. the construction of an imaginary audience
    b. the inability to take another's point of view
    c. the belief that one is always right
    d. an increase in bragging about one's accomplishments

6. According to a major study of adolescent drug use, the group who were better adjusted and more psychologically healthy were the

    a. abstainers
    b. experimenters
    c. frequent users
    d. ones who could not be categorized

7. A reasonable estimate for the number of teenage pregnancies in the United States each year is

    a. 250,000
    b. 400,000
    c. 1,000,000
    d. 1,500,000

8. According to Erikson, early adulthood revolves around the choice of

    a. intimacy vs. isolation
    b. identity vs. role confusion
    c. career vs. family
    d. getting married vs. staying single

9. Which of the following would be the best predictor of a successful marriage?

    a. the partners are opposites but really attracted to each other
    b. the partners both have a history of close effective relationships to other people
    c. both partners have a good sense of humor, are attractive, and have good jobs
    d. both partners have important goals but they are not shared goals

10. Which of Erikson's social development tasks would most likely be satisfied by having a child?

    a. identity

    b. intimacy

    c. generativity

    d. integrity

11. Which of the following is NOT true of middle adulthood?

    a. most of the sensory capacities begin t diminish

    b. the evidence of physical decline such as graying hair and wrinkles is present

    c. most people experience a mid-life crisis

    d. people become more aware of their own mortality

12. The period of development in which individuals turn their attention to social concerns and civic responsibilities is

    a. adolescence

    b. early adulthood

    c. middle adulthood

    d. late adulthood

13. By the year 2020, Americans over age 65 will make up ____ percent of the population.

    a. 20

    b. 15

    c. 10

    d. 5

14. According to Kubler-Ross, the first stage that individuals go through as they attempt to come to terms with the fact that they are dying is called:

    a. bargaining

    b. denial

    c. who me?

    d. depression

15. In the stages of death and dying, the final stage is marked by

    a. resentment and envy of others

    b. dealing with God

    c. a sense of hopelessness

    d. a rather quiet acceptance, facing the final reality of death

1. In adolescence, puberty is marked by
   a. the beginning of the growth spurt for both boys and girls
   b. voice changes in boys
   c. the menarche in girls
   d. the end of physical growth for both boys and girls

2. Which of the following is NOT true of the early maturing boy?
   a. He will have more dating experience.
   b. He will have a poorer body image and lower self-esteem.
   c. He will have more sexual encounters.
   d. He will have higher status among his peers.

3. Which of the following individuals would benefit most from being a little off schedule in terms of maturation?
   a. a girl who is an early-bloomer
   b. a boy who is an early bloomer
   c. a girl who is a late bloomer
   d. a boy who is a late bloomer

4. Jessica is in her second year of college and she is still an undecided major. She has been to the career counseling center and has tried to sample a number of different options through her selection of classes. But, she often feels anxious and worried because she has no clear goal. She is most likely in Marcia's identity stage of
   a. identity diffusion
   b. foreclosure
   c. moratorium
   d. identity achieved

5. One characteristic that increases in the presence of adolescent egocentrism is
   a. self-consciousness
   b. self-esteem
   c. self-confidence
   d. self-denial

6. In terms of sexual activity, the greatest increase has been in
   a. boys age 17
   b. boys younger than 17
   c. girls older than 16
   d. girls age 15

7. Most people say that happiness in adulthood depends on
   a. a satisfying career
   b. good health
   c. a successful marriage
   d. quality friendships

8. Which of the following is NOT a factor in choosing a marriage partner?
   a. availability
   b. eligibility
   c. attractiveness
   d. proximity

9. In passing through Turner and Helms' stages of career development, a mistake is most likely to be made at the stage of
   a. exploration
   b. choice
   c. career clarification
   d. reformation

10. Which of the following psychologists was NOT concerned with development in middle adulthood?
    a. Hall
    b. Havighurst
    c. Levinson
    d. Erikson

11. Which of the following is true of mental abilities in late adulthood?
    a. there is a general decline in all mental abilities
    b. accumulated experience cannot offset the losses that occur in mental ability
    c. one real loss is in the speed of mental processing
    d. memory loss occurs in all areas of knowledge

12. One problem faced by the elderly is death of a spouse. In the over 65 age group, _____ percent of women are likely to be widows.
    a. 30
    b. 40
    c. 50
    d. 60

13. One frequently held misconception about the elderly is that many live in nursing homes. In fact, only about ____ percent actually live in nursing homes.
    a. 5
    b. 8
    c. 12
    d. 15

172

14. Which of the following is NOT one of the major controllable factors which contribute to the decline in old age ?

    a. smoking

    b. alcohol consumption

    c. lack of social support

    d. financial status

15. The psychologist who contributed a great deal to our understanding of how individuals deal with their own death is

    a. Levinson

    b. Kubler-Ross

    c. Havighurst

    d. Erikson

Dr. G's Best Study Tips #9

BE A STAR IN CLASS

Prepare for class by reading assignments ahead of time. As you read, make notes about topics that are particularly interesting to you. Also note any material you do not understand. Becoming familiar with the text information will invariably help you in taking notes as you will more readily understand the lecture material. You will not be struggling for spelling of key terms.

Pose potential questions that you can ask in class. Write them down. If there is something you don't understand, you can be sure there are others who are also finding the information puzzling. Asking a question is a very good way to get involved and turn yourself on to a class that might otherwise be of less interest (although with the subject matter of psychology, I cannot imagine such a situation).

CHAPTER 10—PERSONALITY TOPIC 10A— THEORIES OF PERSONALITY

LEARNING OBJECTIVES

Personality theories may be organized into four basic types, or approaches. They help describe individuals in ways that allow us to recognize all those differences that we know exist among people. Students should be able to:
1. Discuss the three levels of consciousness proposed by Freud.
2. List Freud's three structures of personality and the principles by which they operate.
3. Explain the contributions of Adler, Jung, and Horney to the psychoanalytic approach.
4. Describe the personality theories of Watson, Skinner, Dollard and Miller, and Bandura.
5. Discuss the humanistic approach of Rogers and Maslow to personality.
6. Define personality trait.
7. List the "Big Five" personality dimensions.
8. Discuss the strengths and weaknesses of the psychoanalytic, humanistic, trait, and behaviorist approaches to personality.
9. Discuss the issues and outcome of the situation vs. personality debate started by Mischel.
10. List the goals of personality assessment.
11. Describe how behavioral observations are used for assessing personality.
12. Discuss the advantages and disadvantages of the interview as a personality assessment technique.
13. Describe the MMPI and define multiphasic.
14. Describe the Rorschach and the TAT and describe the characteristics of projective techniques.

LEARNING TOPIC 10A VOCABULARY

On your own paper, write the definition for each of the following key terms. Your learning will be facilitated by writing the definition in your own words rather than just copying the exact definition from your text.

PSYCHOANALYTIC	NEW-FREUDIANS
LIFE INSTINCTS (EROS)	LIBIDO
DEATH INSTINCTS (THANATOS)	ID
PLEASURE PRINCIPLE	EGO
REALITY PRINCIPLE	DEFENSE MECHANISMS
SUPEREGO	IDEALISTIC PRINCIPLE
INFERIORITY COMPLEX	LOCUS OF CONTROL
PHENOMENOLOGICAL	TRAITS
BEHAVIORAL OBSERVATION	INTERVIEW
MMPI	PROJECTIVE TECHNIQUE
RORSCHACH INK BLOT TEST	THEMATIC APPERCEPTION TEST (TAT)

MATCHING

Match the following key terms from your textbook with the appropriate definition.

____ 1. MMPI		____ 2. psychoanalytic	
____ 3. inferiority complex		____ 4. neo-Freudians	
____ 5. death instincts		____ 6. libido	
____ 7. projective technique		____ 8. superego	
____ 9. behavioral observation		____10. traits	
____11. Thematic Apperception Test		____12. locus of control	
____13. life instincts		____14. ego	
____15. interview		____16. Rorschach ink blot test	
____17. idealistic principle		____18. phenomenological	
____19. id		____20. reality principle	
____21. pleasure principle		____22. defense mechanisms	

a. The approach to personality associated with Freud and his followers that relies on instincts and the unconscious as explanatory concepts.

b. Personality theorists (including Adler, Jung, and Horney) that kept many basic psychoanalytic principles, but differed from a strict Freudian view, adding new concepts of their own.

c. Those inborn impulses proposed by Freud that compel one toward survival, including hunger, thirst, and sex.

d. The energy that activates the life (sexual) instincts (largely of the id).

e. Those inborn impulses proposed by Freud that compel one toward destruction, including aggression.

f. That instinctive aspect of personality that seeks immediate gratification of impulses; operates on the pleasure principle.

g. The impulse of the id to seek immediate gratification to reduce tensions.

h. That aspect of personality that encompasses the sense of "self"; in contact with the real world; operates on the reality principle.

i. Governs the ego; arbitrating between the demands of the id, the superego, and the real world.

j. Unconsciously applied techniques that protect the self (ego) from feelings of anxiety.

k. That aspect of personality that refers to ethical or moral considerations; operates on the idealistic principle.

l. Governs the superego; opposed to the id, seeks adherence to standards of ethics and morality.

m. The Adlerian notion that as children we develop a sense of inferiority in dealing with our environment, needs to be overcome to reach maturity.

n. A general belief that what happens is either under our control or a matter of chance and environmental factors.

o. An approach that emphasizes one's perception and awareness of events as being more important than the events themselves.

p. Distinguishable, relatively enduring ways in which individuals may differ.

q. The personality assessment technique of drawing conclusions about one's personality on the basis of observations of his or her behaviors.

r. The personality assessment technique involving a conversational interchange between the interviewer and subject to gain information about the subject.

s. A paper-and-pencil inventory of 567 true-false questions used to assess a number of personality dimensions, some of which may indicate the presence of a psychological disorder.

t. A personality assessment technique requiring subjects to respond to ambiguous stimuli, thus projecting their "self" into their responses.

u. A projective technique in which the subject is asked to say what is seen in a series of ink blots.

v. A projective technique in which subjects are asked to tell a story about each of a set of ambiguous pictures.

TRUE-FALSE PRACTICE TEST

_____ 1. Freud's personality theory rests on the two basic premises of innate drives and the power of the unconscious.

_____ 2. Freud referred to the sexual instincts as eros.

_____ 3. The basic structure of personality that operates on the pleasure principle is the ego.

_____ 4. John Watson and B.F. Skinner were neo-Freudians.

_____ 5. The behaviorists disagreed with the principles of psychoanalytic theory on the basis that the study of the unconscious was not observable or verifiable.

_____ 6. Albert Bandura is a neo-Freudian who suggested that personality is learned by observing the behaviors of others and noting which of those behaviors are reinforced.

_____ 7. The phenomenological approach to personality suggests that what matters most is how a person views himself and other people.

_____ 8. Abraham Maslow criticized most of the current psychological theory of his time as being too negative and pessimistic.

_____ 9. Allport, Eysenck, and Cattell all have in common the fact that they are trait theorists.

_____ 10. One important aspect of psychoanalytic theory is that it helped us focus on the importance of adolescence.

_____ 11. At present, there is no single theory that adequately explains personality without shortcomings.

_____ 12. Interactionism refers to the fact that personality may best be explained as an interaction between stable personality traits and the individual's perception of a particular situation.

_____ 13. The MMPI is the most researched test in all of psychology.

_____ 14. The MMPI and the Rorschach are the same type of personality tests.

_____ 15. In a projective test, subjects are asked to respond to ambiguous stimuli.

FILL-IN PRACTICE TEST

1. An organized collection of testable ideas used to explain a particular subject matter is a/an _____.

2. The affects, behaviors and cognitions of people that can characterize them in a number of situations over time is referred to as _____.

3. Freud's technique of therapy that was derived from his personality theory is known as _____.

4. Ideas, feelings, and motives of which we are aware are said to be _____.

5. According to Freud, our behaviors, thoughts, and feelings are governed by _____ _____.

6. The impulses for survival are called life instincts or _____.

7. The impulses of destruction are referred to as death instincts or _____.

8. According to Freud, people deal with anxiety by using _____ _____.

9. The psychologist chosen by Freud to be his successor, and the man who developed the idea of the collective unconscious was _____ _____.

10. Carl Jung believed that the unconscious contained universal patterns and forms called _____.

11. Dollard and Miller argued that personality is determined by one's _____ which are formed in response to environmental cues.

12. A distinguishable, relatively enduring way in which one individual differs from another is a/an _____.

13. Gordon Allport described characteristics that are shared by almost everyone as _____ _____.

14. Using a technique called _____, a psychologist may have a client act out a given life situation in order to learn more about the client's personality.

15. The most important instrument of clinical assessment is the _____.

MULTIPLE CHOICE PRACTICE TEST 1 TOPIC 10A

1. Which of the following is NOT included in the textbook definition of personality?
   a. affects
   b. behaviors
   c. preferences
   d. cognitions

2. Awareness is to consciousness as availability is to _____.
   a. preconsciousness
   b. unconsciousness
   c. psychoanalysis
   d. affect

3. John is an alcoholic who at times feels suicidal. Which of the following terms would best describe in Freudian terms what motivates those thoughts?

    a. basic instincts

    b. the preconscious

    c. eros

    d. thanatos

4. The Freudian personality structure that keeps us in touch with reality is the

    a. id

    b. ego

    c. superego

    d. libido

5. Alfred Adler developed the idea of the

    a. inferiority complex

    b. defense mechanism

    c. collective unconscious

    d. phenomenological approach

6. Which of the following is NOT a correct match?

    a. Adler—inferiority complex

    b. Jung—archetypes

    c. Freud—defense mechanism

    d. Karen Horney—collective unconscious

7. The neo-Freudian who theorized that people have three ways of interacting, moving away, moving toward, and moving against other people was

    a. Alfred Adler

    b. Carl Jung

    c. Karen Horney

    d. Anna Freud

8. Which of the following is NOT a correct match?

    a. Cattell—source trait

    b. Eysenck—extroversion

    c. Allport—common trait

    d. Maslow—factor analysis

9. Which of the following is NOT one of the "Big Five" dimensions of personality in the recently developed "Five-Factor Model"?

    a. extroversion-introversion

    b. psychoticism

    c. conscientiousness

    d. stability-instability

10. Of the following, which would NOT be considered to be a lasting contribution of Freud's psychoanalytic approach to personality?

    a. focusing on aggression as a central concern

    b. stressing the role of early experience and childhood

    c. introducing the notion of the unconscious

    d. attending to the impact of sexuality on personality

11. Which of the following personality theories was criticized for relying too heavily on the notion of biological drives and for concepts that are untestable?

    a. psychoanalytic approach

    b. trait theory

    c. behaviorist approach

    d. humanism

12. Which of the following would be the LEAST valid reason for personality assessment?

    a. theory construction

    b. genetic planning

    c. predicting other behaviors

    d. clinical diagnosis

13. When analyzing responses to the TAT, what does a psychologist look for?

    a. emerging themes or stories that provide insights about the subject

    b. the extent to which the subject attended to or ignored the colors in the stimulus card

    c. the average number of items correct for each subtest

    d. attention to detail and descriptions of animals

14. In what way is the MMPI a "criterion referenced" test?

   a. Items were included only if they differentiated among diagnosed groups.

   b. The standardization groups, used to establish test norms, were very large.

   c. The test includes items that determine the extent to which the subject is taking the test seriously.

   d. The authors had a full and complete theory of personality traits in mind before they began writing test items.

15. If you meet someone new at a party, what personality assessment technique are you likely to use to evaluate that person?

   a. interview

   b. paper and pencil test

   c. projective

   d. behavioral observation

MULTIPLE CHOICE PRACTICE TEST 2 TOPIC 10A

1. Which of the following is NOT one of the sources upon which Freud drew to form his theory of personality?

   a. great works of philosophy

   b. observations of his patients

   c. self-examination

   d. observation of his children

2. One of the goals of psychoanalysis is to help a person get in touch with his/her

   a. conscious

   b. preconscious

   c. unconscious

   d. conscience

3. Which of the following is NOT a correct match?

   a. id—pleasure principle

   b. ego   reality principle

   c. conscience—morality principle

   d. superego—idealistic principle

4. Alfred Adler, Carl Jung, and Karen Horney all have in common the fact that they

   a. had their beginnings in the psychoanalytic theory

   b. were neo-Freudians

   c. offered alternate ideas to psychoanalytic theory

   d. all of the above

5. One of the first psychologists to accuse Freud of male chauvinism was
   a. Horney
   b. Jung
   c. Skinner
   d. Adler

6. The psychologist who believed that people strive to become fully functioning was
   a. Karen Horney
   b. Carl Rogers
   c. Carl Jung
   d. Neil Miller

7. Which of the following may be viewed as the major advantage of the so-called behavioral-learning approach to personality?
   a. Most of the psychologists who support this approach were already famous for other contributions.
   b. It focuses entirely on external forces, such as the environment and other people.
   c. It relies on concepts that are observable and measurable.
   d. It has given rise to the fullest, most comprehensive of theories.

8. What one thing most separates humanistic approaches to personality from behavioral and psychoanalytic approaches?
   a. The humanistic view is non-deterministic.
   b. The humanist position is based on research data.
   c. Humanism relies most heavily on cognitions.
   d. Humanism focuses on early childhood learning.

9. The psychologist who used factor analysis to examine traits was
   a. Eysenck
   b. Cattell
   c. Allport
   d. Dollard

10. The psychologist who proposed that personality can be divided into just two and later three dimensions was
    a. Eysenck
    b. Cattell
    c. Allport
    d. Dollard

11. Which of the personality theories was criticized for being deterministic and dehumanizing?
    a. psychoanalytic approach
    b. trait theory
    c. behaviorist approach
    d. humanism

12. Humanism and psychoanalytic have in common the fact that both
    a. emphasize early childhood experiences
    b. have been criticized as being untestable
    c. focus on biological drives
    d. support the notion that man is basically good

13. Which of the following pencil and paper personality tests is NOT multiphasic?
    a. MMPI
    b. 16 PF
    c. CPI
    d. TMAS

14. Which of the following is NOT a projective technique?
    a. Rorschach Ink blot Test
    b. Thematic Apperception Test
    c. word association tests
    d. MMPI

15. Projective techniques all have in common the fact that
    a. they rely on pictures to stimulate the subject's responses
    b. they are given as group tests
    c. they do not require any special skill on the part of the test administrator
    d. they are scored subjectively and present the subject with ambiguous stimuli

CHAPTER 10—PERSONALITY TOPIC 10B—HUMAN SEXUALITY AND GENDER

LEARNING OBJECTIVES

Human sexual behavior is influenced by many external factors. It also varies in its expression. An important, related aspect of personality is gender. Students should be able to:
1. Describe how sex is genetically determined.
2. Discuss the role of hormones in the determination of sex.
3. Discuss the changes that occur during the human sexual response.
4. Define homosexuality and discuss the possible causes.
5. List and describe six sexual dysfunctions.
6. Describe five sexually transmitted diseases.
7. Distinguish between gender identity and gender roles.
8. Discuss the male/female differences that can be attributed to gender.
9. Define androgyny.

LEARNING TOPIC 10B VOCABULARY

On your own paper, write the definition for each of the following key terms. Your learning will be facilitated by writing the definition in your own words rather than just copying the exact definition from your text.

X AND Y CHROMOSOMES	GONADS
ANDROGENS	TESTOSTERONE
PROGESTERONE	EROGENOUS ZONES
APHRODISIAC	REFRACTORY PERIOD
HOMOSEXUALS	SEXUAL DYSFUNCTION
SEXUALLY TRANSMITTED DISEASES	CHLAMYDIA
GONORRHEA	SYPHILIS
GENITAL HERPES	ACQUIRED IMMUNE DEFICIENCY SYNDROME
GENDER IDENTITY	GENDER ROLE
ANDROGYNY	

MATCHING

Match the following key terms from your textbook with the appropriate definition.

____ 1. androgyny   ____ 2. AIDS

____ 3. chlamydia   ____ 4. X and Y chromosomes

____ 5. erogenous zones   ____ 6. sexual dysfunction

____ 7. gonads   ____ 8. sexually transmitted disease

____ 9. genital herpes   ____10. progesterone

____11. homosexuals   ____12. androgens

_____13. refractory period   _____14. gonorrhea

_____15. gender role   _____16. gender identity

_____17. testosterone   _____18. aphrodisiac

_____19. syphilis   _____20. estrogens

a. The chromosomes that determine one's genetic sex; XX for females, XY for males.
b. The sex glands—testes in males, ovaries in females.
c. The male sex hormones produced by the testes.
d. The most important of the male androgens, or sex hormones.
e. The female sex hormones produced by the ovaries.
f. One of the most important of the female estrogens, or sex hormones.
g. Areas of the body that, when they are stroked, lead to sexual arousal.
h. A substance that, when drunk or eaten, increases sexual arousal; none are known to exist.
i. During the process of the human sexual response, that period following orgasm during which arousal in the male is not possible.
j. Those persons who are sexually attracted to and aroused by members of their own sex.
k. Any of a number of chronic difficulties or problems with sexual functioning; usually caused by psychological factors.
l. Contagious diseases that are usually transmitted through sexual contact.
m. A very common STD; a bacterial infection of the genital area.
n. An STD caused by a bacterial infection of moist tissue in the genital area.
o. An STD caused by a bacterial infection, which may pass through four stages, ultimately resulting in death.
p. The most common STD; a skin infection in the form of a rash or blisters in the genital area.
q. A deadly disease caused by a virus (the HIV) that destroys the body's natural immune system, and which can be transmitted by sexual behaviors.
r. A basic sense or self-awareness of one's maleness or femaleness.
s. Attitudes and expectations about how a person should act, think, and/or feel solely on the basis of being a female or a male.
t. A balanced combination of traits that are both masculine and feminine.

TRUE-FALSE PRACTICE TEST

_____ 1. An individual's sex is determined at conception.

_____ 2. The relationship between XYY chromosome patterns and violent criminal behavior has recently been proven to be weak or nonexistent.

_____ 3. For up to six weeks after conception, there is no differentiation between male and female zygotes.

_____ 4. The presence of a Y chromosome causes the ovaries to develop in the undifferentiated zygote.

_____ 5. Both males and females produce both male and females hormones, and the really critical issue is balance.

_____ 6. Sexual arousal brought about by visual stimuli is more common in men than women.

_____ 7. Unlike animals, humans appear to produce no pheromones which might stimulate sexual arousal.

_____ 8. Masters and Johnson contradicted the old Freudian notion that women experience two types of orgasm.

_____ 9. Contrary to popular opinion, most homosexuals are indistinguishable from heterosexuals in their appearance and mannerisms.

_____ 10. In general, sex therapy as a treatment for sexual dysfunction is not very successful.

_____ 11. There appears to be movement away from such rigid gender roles, even though the change is slow.

_____ 12. Research indicates that there are many more similarities between males and females than there are differences.

_____ 13. AIDS is now considered to be at epidemic proportions in the United States.

_____ 14. In terms of sex differences, on any given trait, the variability between the two sexes is often greater than the variability within the same sex.

_____ 15. There are no sex differences in general intelligence as indicated by IQ scores.

FILL-IN PRACTICE TEST

1. _____ _____ is a condition in which an individual has sex chromosomes in the XXY pattern, resulting in male genitals that are smaller than normal and possible sterility.

2. Collectively, the hormones produced by the gonads are called _____.

3. In a male, the gonads produce _____, the most important of which is testosterone.

4. In the female, the gonads produce _____, the most important of which is progesterone.

5. Areas of the body that lead to sexual arousal when touched are called _____ _____.

6. A substance that leads to sexual arousal when consumed is called a/an _____.

7. Persons who are sexually attracted to and aroused by members of their own sex are called _____.

8. Erectile dysfunction is the preferred term for what is more commonly known as _____.

9. Female sexual unresponsiveness is the preferred term for what is more commonly called _____.

10. A basic sense of one's maleness or femaleness is referred to as _____ _____.

11. Attitudes about how a person should think, feel, or act based solely on whether the person is male or female are _____ _____.

12. A combination of traits usually associated with either males or females is called _____.

13. The oldest of the STDs is _____.

14. The most deadly of the STDs is _____.

15. In general, females may earn superior scores on tests of _____ skills.

MULTIPLE CHOICE PRACTICE TEST 1 TOPIC 10B

1. One's genetic sex:
   a. cannot be determined until at least six or seven weeks following conception
   b. is determined by the zygote's gonads
   c. depends on whether one gets and X or Y chromosome from one's father
   d. depends on whether one is influenced by testosterone or estrogen before birth

2. Klinefelter's syndrome would best be treated with
   a. male hormones
   b. female hormones
   c. psychotherapy
   d. sex therapy

3. According to the Masters and Johnson model, which of the following represents the correct sequence of the human sexual response?
   a. excitement, resolution, orgasm, plateau
   b. plateau, orgasm, excitement, resolution
   c. plateau, excitement, resolution, orgasm
   d. excitement, plateau, orgasm, resolution

4. In terms of sexual response, men and women differ most in the _____ phase.
   a. excitement
   b. orgasm
   c. plateau
   d. resolution

5. Which of the following is the best explanation for homosexuality?
   a. It is the result of environmental influences.
   b. It may be the result of environmental or genetic influences but no one really knows for sure.
   c. It appears to run in families so it must be genetically determined.
   d. It is caused by a hormonal imbalance during prenatal development.

6. Most sexual dysfunctions are caused by
   a. reduced hormone levels
   b. reduced sensory functioning
   c. psychological factors such as anxiety
   d. lack of practice

7. Which is the most common sexual dysfunction among men?
   a. erectile dysfunction
   b. premature ejaculation
   c. retarded ejaculation
   d. male unresponsiveness

8. Which of the following STDs cannot be cured with penicillin or antibiotics?
   a. syphilis
   b. herpes
   c. gonorrhea
   d. chlamydia

9. The transmission of the AIDS virus from one person to another requires
   a. only casual contact
   b. direct physical contact such as kissing
   c. exchange of bodily fluids such as blood or semen
   d. intimate sexual contact such as mutual masturbation

10. Scott tells Ricky that he can't play with their sister's dolls because dolls are for girls. Clearly, Scott has developed
    a. gender identity
    b. gender role
    c. both gender identity and gender role concepts
    d. androgyny

11. Which of the following people is most likely to be considered androgynous?
    a. a man with many feminine characteristics and few masculine ones
    b. a woman with only feminine characteristics
    c. a man with both feminine and masculine traits
    d. a woman with masculine characteristics and not many feminine ones

12. Whereas women tend to make superior scores on tests of verbal abilities, men tend to score higher on tests of
    a. historical facts
    b. sports trivia
    c. automobiles
    d. spatial relations

13. Males have been found to be more aggressive than females
    a. only at preschool age
    b. all through the lifespan
    c. only in adulthood
    d. only in business situations

MULTIPLE CHOICE PRACTICE TEST 2 TOPIC 10B

1. The ovaries are to estrogen as the _____ are to _____.
   a. gonads; androgens
   b. ovaries; testes
   c. testes; testosterone
   d. steroids; progesterone

2. Which of the following is NOT involved in the biological process of producing hormones?
   a. pituitary gland
   b. hypothalamus
   c. adrenal gland
   d. pancreas

3. Although commonly discussed, there really is no known substance such as
   a. steroids
   b. aphrodisiacs
   c. hormones
   d. pheromones

4. Which of the following stages of sexual response is the briefest?
   a. excitement
   b. plateau
   c. orgasm
   d. resolution

5. In their studies of human sexuality, William Masters and Virginia Johnson focused their attention on:
   a. analyzing survey data from a wide variety of sources and cultures
   b. the behavior of prostitutes and homosexuals
   c. physiological changes that occur during sexual behaviors
   d. the sexual practices and attitudes of adolescents

6. Female sexual unresponsiveness is often related to feelings of
   a. shame and guilt
   b. anger and dismay
   c. fear and dread
   d. disgust

7. Which of the following STDs is least contagious?
   a. chlamydia
   b. gonorrhea
   c. herpes
   d. AIDS

8. The incidence of sexual dysfunctions is probably
   a. lower than people think
   b. more common in men than people think
   c. higher in women than people think
   d. much higher in both men and women than people think

9. The psychologist who developed an instrument to measure sex roles was
   a. Eleanor Macoby
   b. Virginia Johnson
   c. Sandra Ben
   d. Karen Horney

10. One striking aspect of research on gender differences is that
    a. males are frequently found to be superior in many ways
    b. the research fails to find male/female differences
    c. females are frequently found to be superior in many ways
    d. findings relate to innate biological differences, for instance males are stronger and faster

11. The two social behaviors that show gender differences are
    a. aggression and communication
    b. friendliness and competitiveness
    c. aggression and cooperativeness
    d. introversion and communication

12. At the moment, our best prediction is that of those persons with AIDS, about _____ percent will die within four years.
    a. 25
    b. 50
    c. 75
    d. 100

Dr. G's Best Study Tips #10

SUGGESTIONS FOR TAKING NOTES

1. At the start of class, date your notes and give them a title that corresponds with the TOPIC to be presented in lecture. Be sure to number the pages as you go and date each page.

2. Don't try to write every word the professor says, just get the important facts and details. Listen for key words that alert you to what's coming. Numerical terms signal a list, e.g., "three" reasons for taking good notes are. Other possible key words and phrases are "if", "then", "when", "next", "as a result", "leading up to", "because of." I am sure you get the idea.

3. If the professor writes something on the board or an overhead projector, write it down.

4. Write your notes in your own words. It is important that you understand what you write and not just memorize words that have no real meaning for you.

5. Try to write in complete thoughts or sentences as much as possible.

6. Ask your instructor to clarify any points you don't understand.

7. Review your notes as soon after class as possible, definitely the same day. The longer you wait, the more difficult it will be to add any ideas, clarify, or rewrite.

8. Use your textbook or handouts to add or clarify points you don't understand.

9. Use abbreviations only to the extent that you can understand or remember the symbols and short forms you are using and interpret them later.

10. Do not rely solely on your notes for studying. You must also read your text and other assigned material.

CHAPTER 11—MOTIVATION, EMOTION, STRESS TOPIC 11A— MOTIVATIONAL ISSUES

LEARNING OBJECTIVES

The study of motivation deals with the origin, the direction, the maintenance, and the cessation of behaviors. There are two types of motives—those related to survival and those learned or social in nature. Students should be able to:
1. Discuss how instinct, drive, and incentive have been used to explain motivated behaviors.
2. Discuss cognitive dissonance theory.
3. Explain how the concept of balance or equilibrium can be used to explain motivated behaviors.
4. Describe how homeostasis relates to temperature regulation as a physiologically based drive.
5. List the factors that may influence drinking behavior.
6. Describe the ways in which the sex drive is a unique physiologically based drive.
7. Discuss the internal and external factors that influence the drive to eat.
8. Describe the symptoms of anorexia nervosa and bulimia, their causes and treatment.
9. Discuss achievement motivation and explain how it is measured.
10. Discuss the needs for power, affiliation, and competence and explain what is meant by intrinsic and extrinsic control of behavior.

LEARNING TOPIC 11A VOCABULARY

On your own paper, write the definition for each of the following key terms. Your learning will be facilitated by writing the definition in your own words rather than copying the exact definition from your text.

MOTIVATION	AROUSAL
INSTINCTS	NEED
DRIVE	INCENTIVES
HOMEOSTASIS	SET POINT
COGNITIVE DISSONANCE	HYPOTHALAMUS
ANOREXIA NERVOSA	BULIMIA
PROGNOSIS	NEED TO ACHIEVE
THEMATIC APPERCEPTION TEST	NEED FOR POWER
NEED FOR AFFILIATION	NEED FOR COMPETENCE

MATCHING

Match the following key terms from your textbook with the appropriate definition.

____ 1. cognitive dissonance	____ 2. need for affiliation
____ 3. motivation	____ 4. anorexia nervosa
____ 5. need for competence	____ 6. arousal
____ 7. bulimia	____ 8. incentives

_____ 9. prognosis   _____10. thematic apperception test

_____11. drive   _____12. instincts

_____13. hypothalamus   _____14. need to achieve

_____15. set point   _____16. homeostasis

_____17. need for power   _____18. need

a. The process of arousing, maintaining, and directing behavior.
b. One's level of activation or excitement; indicative of a motivational state.
c. Unlearned, complex patterns of behavior that occur in the presence of particular stimuli.
d. A lack or shortage of some biological essential resulting from deprivation.
e. A state of tension resulting from a need that arouses and directs an organism's behavior.
f. External stimuli that an organism may be motivated to approach or avoid.
g. A state of balance or equilibrium among internal, physiological conditions.
h. A normal, optimum level of equilibrium or balance among physiological or psychological reactions.
i. A motivating discomfort or tension caused by a lack of balance or consonance among one's cognitions.
j. A small brain structure involved in many drives, including thirst, hunger, sex, and temperature regulation.
k. An eating disorder characterized by the reduction of body weight through self-starvation and/or increased activity levels.
l. An eating disorder characterized by recurrent episodes of binge eating and then purging to remove the just-eaten food.
m. The prediction of the outlook, or likely course for an illness or a disorder.
n. The learned need to meet or exceed some standard of excellence in performance.
o. A projective personality test requiring a subject to tell a series of short stories about a set of ambiguous pictures.
p. The learned need to be in control of events or persons, usually at another's expense.
q. The need to be with others and to form relationships and associations.
r. The need to meet the challenges provided by one's environment.

TRUE-FALSE PRACTICE TEST

_____ 1. According to Clark Hull's theory, when an organism is in a drive state, it is motivated.

_____ 2. When the strength of a need increases, the strength of the accompanying drive always increases as well.

_____ 3. Drive reduction theory appears to be a good explanation for all human behavior.

_____ 4. One important aspect about incentive theory is that it offers an alternative to the biological concepts previously offered as explanations for behavior.

_____ 5. Arousal is probably lowest when a person is in the deepest stages of sleep.

_____ 6. There appears to be an optimum arousal level for most tasks which if exceeded will detract from the performance of the task.

_____ 7. Shivering when you are too cold is a behavior that demonstrates arousal theory.

_____ 8. The hypothalamus is involved in maintaining equilibrium in terms of body temperature.

_____ 9. Involuntary actions that help the body maintain equilibrium can be supplemented by voluntary actions.

_____ 10. In general, in the male of any species, sexual behavior is entirely controlled by the presence of the male hormones.

_____ 11. As the complexity of the organism increases, from rats to dogs to humans, the role of internal cues in the sex drive becomes less important.

_____ 12. One interesting thing about anorexia nervosa is its predominance among females.

_____ 13. With treatment, the prognosis for patients with eating disorders is very good.

_____ 14. Both power needs and the need for achievement are measured by the TAT.

_____ 15. Conflict may arise if a person is high in both need for achievement and need for affiliation.

FILL-IN PRACTICE TEST

1. A person's level of activation or excitement is called _____.

2. Unlearned, complex patterns of behavior that occur in the presence of certain stimuli are _____.

3. The psychologist who suggested that human behavior is motivated by eleven basic instincts was _____.

4. Drives based on learned responses are called _____ drives.

5. Drives based on physiological, unlearned needs are called _____ drives.

6. According to Maslow, the needs that motivate human behavior are limited in number and arranged in a/an _____.

7. According to Maslow, once a person's basic needs for food, water, and shelter are met, the person will be motivated by need for _____.

8. External events that act to pull our behavior are called _____.

9. A person's most suitable or normal level of activity for certain functions is called _____ _____.

10. A person who needs very high levels of arousal is referred to by Zuckerman as a _____ _____.

11. A state of tension or discomfort that exists when we hold inconsistent, dissonant cognitions is called _____ _____.

12. _____ is an eating disorder characterized by repeated episodes of binge eating and purging.

13. The usual means for measuring the need for achievement is by administering the _____ _____ _____.

14. Women who were said to back off from competition for fear of winning and thus losing popularity and femininity were said to be suffering from _____ ____ _____.

15. The need to form friendships and associations is known as the need for _____.

MULTIPLE CHOICE PRACTICE TEST 1 TOPIC 11A

1. The biggest problem with using instincts to explain human behavior is that
   a. humans don't have instincts
   b. this approach simply renames the behaviors and didn't really explain anything
   c. the list of instincts becomes unmanageable
   d. it makes human behavior seem too much like animal behavior

2. Which of the following is an example of a secondary drive?
   a. A baby is crying because it is hungry.
   b. A toddler goes to the refrigerator and asks for "drink".
   c. An adolescent girl tells her mother she needs a new pair of shoes.
   d. A ten year old has a fever and asks his mother for aspirin.

3. Which of the following is the correct order for Maslow's hierarchy of needs?
   a. safety-physiological-esteem-belonging-self-actualization
   b. physiological-safety-esteem-belonging-self-actualization
   c. physiological-safety-belonging-esteem-self-actualization
   d. belonging-esteem-physiological-safety-self-actualization

4. Climbing a mountain because it is there is an example of motivation best explained by
   a. incentives
   b. need for affiliation
   c. Maslow's safety needs
   d. need for power

5. Explaining motivated behavior based on incentives seems quite similar to the theory of
   a. Maslow's hierarchy
   b. operant conditioning
   c. drive reduction
   d. homeostasis

6. Which of the following situations is best explained by set point theory?
   a. A person feels bored and so he goes and takes a nap.
   b. A person climbs a mountain because it is there.
   c. A person does a job so he will get paid.
   d. A person loses weight while ill and then quickly gains it back.

7. Which of the following is NOT a correct match?
   a. Cannon — homeostasis
   b. Zuckerman — sensation seekers
   c. Maslow — needs hierarchy
   d. Festinger — arousal

8. The observation that some people will drink only Pepsi, while others drink Coke and still others prefer some other brand supports the notion that:

    a. drives like the thirst drive are exclusively physiological in nature

    b. in blind taste tests those same people could not tell the difference between their favorite brand and the others

    c. learning and past experience can have a strong influence on how physiological drives are expressed

    d. in the long run, our bodies "know" what is best for us, a concept called the "wisdom of the body" by W. Cannon

9. Our most important physiological cues for eating come from

    a. the liver and the hypothalamus

    b. stomach contractions

    c. the sight sight food

    d. the smell of food

10. The prognosis for anorexia nervosa is particularly poor with almost _____ percent relapsing within a year of the end of treatment.

    a. 20

    b. 35

    c. 50

    d. 60

11. The need to achieve

    a. is innate

    b. develops in childhood

    c. appears in adulthood

    d. does not exist

12. Research by David McClelland on his concept of "need to achieve" would predict that someone with a high nAch, if given a choice, would choose a job:

    a. in which he or she was almost bound to be successful

    b. that was challenging, but could be done well with effort

    c. that was so difficult that it almost certainly could not be done well

    d. in which he or she could succeed, but only at the expense of others

13. In Houston, Texas, the mayor and police chief are both women. The state of Texas has a woman governor as well. One might say that the women in Texas appear to differ from women in general in that they have

    a. an unusually high need for power

    b. a high fear of failure

    c. an imbalance between innate and learned needs

    d. a high need for affiliation

14. If we differentiate approaches to motivation on the basis of being either intrinsic (internal) or extrinsic (external), the approach that is most clearly extrinsic is an approach based on

    a. incentives

    b. balance or equilibrium

    c. cognitive dissonance

    d. drives

15. Beth wants to be a teacher because she believes it is important for the future of the world to help children become literate. She is motivated by

    a. need for power

    b. need for competence

    c. need for affiliation

    d. need for achievement

MULTIPLE CHOICE PRACTICE TEST 2 TOPIC 11A

1. One thing we learned from early attempts to explain human behavior based on instincts is that

    a. none of human behavior is instinctive

    b. some behaviors are purely physiologically based

    c. all human behavior stems from a psychological basis

    d. the concept of instincts is too simple to explain complex human behavior

2. The psychologist who converted drive reduction theory into a motivational theory based on a needs hierarchy was

    a. Maslow

    b. McDougall

    c. Hull

    d. Rogers

3. One problem with Maslow's theory is that

    a. people are not motivated by physiological needs

    b. there appear to be exceptions to the hierarchical structure or ordering of needs

    c. research seems to refute the theory

    d. drive reduction theory offers a better explanation of motivation

4. A prison inmate goes on a hunger strike to impress on prison authorities the need for certain reforms. His behavior demonstrates that

    a. he is at the physiological needs level on Maslow's hierarchy

    b. he is self-actualizing

    c. not all behavior can be explained by Maslow's hierarchy

    d. Maslow's theory can explain all behavior in terms of motivation

5. A person who has a disturbance in the noradrenergic system is likely to prefer
   a. reading
   b. a night at the symphony
   c. a long nap
   d. skydiving

6. A smoker justifies his smoking by coming to believe that although smoking is bad in general, it isn't really bad for him/her as an individual. This thinking is best explained by _____ theory.
   a. cognitive dissonance
   b. drive reduction
   c. set point
   d. incentive

7. Which of the following is NOT a way that the sex drive differs from other physiological drives?
   a. The survival of the individual does not depend on it.
   b. The satisfaction of the sex drive depletes bodily energy whereas the satisfaction of other drives maintains bodily energy.
   c. It is not present at birth.
   d. It is motivated only by internal cues such as hormones.

8. Which of the following is LEAST likely to be a factor in the presence of an eating disorder?
   a. parenting and family style
   b. a strong need for achievement and approval
   c. being from a lower socioeconomic status
   d. cultural influences suggesting that "thin is in"

9. The most successful treatment for anorexia is one that
   a. involves behavior modification
   b. involves the patient's family
   c. combines hospitalization with behavior modification
   d. treats the psychological symptoms

10. People who are high in need to achieve would like be _____ risk takers.
    a. high
    b. moderate
    c. low
    d. none

11. The need to achieve and excel is one thing, but Robert White claims that there is a more general, common need, the need:
    a. for power — to control and be in charge
    b. for competency — to cope and get by
    c. for affiliation — to be social and form interpersonal relationships
    d. for the avoidance of failure — to work in order not to be punished

12. Which of the following is not a CORRECT match?

    a. McClelland — nAch
    b. White — need for competency
    c. Murray — need for power
    d. Horner — fear of success

13. Which of the following pairs of needs is most likely to result in conflict?

    a. power and affiliation
    b. achievement and power
    c. affiliation and achievement
    d. power and achievement

14. Which of the following needs may be at least partially biologically based?

    a. need for power
    b. need for affiliation
    c. need for competency
    d. need for achievement

15. Katie is struggling to put her shoes on and her mother offers to help. Katie responds, "I can do it myself." Katie's response indicates that as a three year old, she is high in need for

    a. affiliation
    b. arousal
    c. competence
    d. power

CHAPTER 11—MOTIVATION, EMOTION, STRESS TOPIC 11B— EMOTION AND STRESS

LEARNING OBJECTIVES

Defining and classifying emotions have proven to be difficult tasks. Pressure to adapt causes stress which acts both like emotions and motivators. Students should be able to:
1. Explain why emotional responses are particularly difficult to study scientifically.
2. List four components that define emotional experience.
3. Name four theories of emotion and briefly describe each.
4. Explain how emotions can be classified.
5. Describe the activities of the sympathetic division of the autonomic nervous system during states of emotionality.
6. Describe the various brain centers that are involved in emotionality.
7. Discuss the relationship between facial expressions and emotion.
8. Define environmental and personal frustration, and give and example of each.
9. Name four types of motivational conflict and give an example of each.
10. Discuss the SRRS as a measure of the stress of everyday life.
11. Discuss some adaptive ways of dealing with stress.
12. Explain the frustration-aggression hypothesis.

LEARNING TOPIC 11B VOCABULARY

On your own paper, write the definition for each of the following key terms. Your learning will be facilitated by writing the definition in your own words rather than copying the exact definition from your text.

EMOTION	STRESS
STRESSORS	FRUSTRATION
CONFLICT	COGNITIVE REAPPRAISAL
FRUSTRATION-AGGRESSION HYPOTHESIS	

MATCHING

Match the following key terms from your textbook with the appropriate definition.

_____ 1. frustration-aggression hypothesis   _____ 2. frustration

_____ 3. emotion   _____ 4. stress

_____ 5. conflict   _____ 6. stressors

_____ 7. cognitive reappraisal

a. A reaction involving subjective feelings, physiological responses, cognitive interpretation, and behavioral expression.
b. A complex pattern of reactions to real or perceived threats to one's sense of well-being that motivates adjustment.
c. Real or perceived threats to one's sense of well-being; sources of stress.
d. A stressor; the blocking or thwarting of goal-directed behavior.
e. A stressor in which some goals can be satisfied only at the expense of others.

f. A re-thinking of a stressful situation to consider it in a more positive light, e.g. determining if a stressor is real or imagined.

g. The view that all aggression stems from frustration.

True-False Practice Test

_____   1. Stress is like an emotion in that it involves physiological responses and feelings.

_____   2. One of the problems with studying emotion is that it is difficult, if not impossible to conduct experiments dealing with human emotion.

_____   3. The concerns about experiments dealing with humans are mostly technical rather than ethical.

_____   4. Among psychologists, there is no consensus as to the definition of emotion.

_____   5. According to the opponent-process theory, the emotional response to the stimulus decreases with subsequent exposures, but the opposing emotion increases when the stimulus is removed.

_____   6. Psychologists seem to agree on the fact that emotions are valenced.

_____   7. One thing about stress is that everyone experiences it.

_____   8. It may be possible to make one's self happy just by smiling.

_____   9. Stress that results from frustration is somewhat pathological.

_____ 10. Environmental frustration implies that goal-directed behavior is being blocked by something or someone in the environment.

_____ 11. As difficulty in decision making increases, stress level will also increase.

_____ 12. The approach-approach conflict creates the greatest amount of stress.

_____ 13. The positive correlation between scores on the SRRS and physical illness indicate that stress causes illness.

_____ 14. Both stressors and reactions to stress vary considerably from person to person.

_____ 15. One positive result of stress is that we may actually learn new ways to attain our goals.

Fill-In Practice Test

1. The drug that mimics the activity of the sympathetic nervous system is
    _____.

2. According to the _____ theory, when a fear producing stimulus is removed, the opposite feeling, relief, will replace the fear.

3. The psychologist who believes that cognition is not a necessary component of emotion is
    _____.

4. The _____ division of the autonomic nervous system is involved in maintaining a relaxed state.

5. The _____ division of the autonomic nervous system is involved in arousal.

6. The stimuli for stress are called _____.

7. The blocking of goal-directed behavior results in _____.

8. A choice between two equally desirable goals is called a/an _____ conflict.

9. The most stressful type of conflict is the _____.

10. The Social Rating Readjustment Scale measures stress brought about by _____.

11. Richard Lazarus argued that stress doesn't result from the big life changes, but more from the everyday little events or _____.

12. The SRRS was developed by _____ and Rahe.

13. In the context of stress reduction, _____ _____ refers to a re-thinking of the nature of the situation so as to cast it in the best possible light.

14. A general feeling of tension, apprehension, and dread, that involves predictable physiological changes refers to _____.

15. At one time, _____ was believed to be the only cause of aggression.

MULTIPLE CHOICE PRACTICE TEST 1 TOPIC 11B

1. Which of the following is NOT one of the components of emotional reaction?
   a. objective feeling
   b. cognitive reaction
   c. physiological reaction
   d. behavior

2. The James-Lange theory of emotion differs from the common sense interpretation of emotion in that
   a. James and Lange believe that the experience of emotion follows the behavioral response, whereas the common sense approach suggests that the behavior follows the emotional experience
   b. James and Lange suggest a limited number of stimuli that produce particular emotions, whereas common sense denies a limit
   c. the common sense approach omits the cognitive component
   d. James and Lange have proven their theory through research, and no such research exists to confirm the common sense theory

3. Which of the following is the correct sequence for the James-Lange Theory of emotion?
   a. stimulus, emotion, response
   b. response, emotion, consequence
   c. stimulus, response, emotion
   d. response, experience, emotion

4. The emotional theory that most emphasizes cognition is the _____ theory.
   a. Schacter-Singer
   b. common sense
   c. Cannon -Bard
   d. James-Lange

5. One problem with Schacter and Singer's research is that
   a. it was unethical
   b. it could not be replicated
   c. they used deceptive techniques
   d. the data were misinterpreted

6. The major issue involved in attempts to classify emotion (such as those of Wundt, Izard, and Plutchik) is
   a. how to distinguish "good" pleasant emotions from "bad" unpleasant ones
   b. just how many prime, basic and distinct types of affect are experienced
   c. how one's affect or feeling is related to actual, real-life situations
   d. whether or not emotional reactions can occur in varying degrees or strengths

7. Which of the following actions would NOT result from being in an emotional situation?
   a. the pupils dilate
   b. blood is transported from the periphery to the center of the body
   c. blood sugar levels increase
   d. respiration increases, making breathing deeper and more rapid

8. The part of the brain involved in the cognitive aspect of emotion is the
   a. hypothalamus
   b. amygdala
   c. limbic system
   d. cerebral cortex

9. Which of the following is NOT considered one of the sources of stress?
   a. life events
   b. frustration
   c. aggression
   d. conflict

10. The relationship between environmental frustration and personal frustration may also be characterized as
    a. stimulus vs. response
    b. need vs. drive
    c. social vs. nonsocial
    d. external vs. internal

11. Ashley wants an ice cream cone, but she does not want to make the long walk to the store to buy one. She will probably experience the frustration of a/an _____ conflict.
    a. approach-approach
    b. avoidance-avoidance
    c. approach-avoidance
    d. multiple approach-avoidance

12. According to Richard Lazarus, which of the following events would be more stressful?
    a. retirement
    b. divorce
    c. moving to another city
    d. a series of small breakdowns that put your car in the shop

13. Which of the following theories of emotion is most related to the notion of making a cognitive reappraisal as a means of stress reduction?
    a. Schacter-Singer
    b. Cannon-Bard
    c. James-Lange
    d. common-sense approach

14. Which of the following is NOT likely to reduce stress?
    a. relaxation
    b. exercise
    c. cognitive reappraisal
    d. focusing on a smaller hassle

15. According to Dollard's frustration-aggression hypothesis,
    a. frustration and aggression always go together
    b. both frustration and aggression can be reduced by exercise
    c. aggression may produce many different types of frustration
    d. frustration always causes aggression

MULTIPLE CHOICE PRACTICE TEST 2 TOPIC 11B
1. Fara was feeling angry, but instead of yelling, she cried. Which component of emotion does crying exemplify?
    a. subjective feeling
    b. cognitive reaction
    c. physiological reaction
    d. behavior

2. We can see that emotion and motivation are most related by examining the _____ component of emotion.

   a. subjective feeling

   b. cognitive reaction

   c. physiological reaction

   d. behavior

3. The theorist who suggested that we are sad because we cry and happy because we run was

   a. Cannon

   b. James

   c. Schacter

   d. Singer

4. Cannon based his entire criticism of the James-Lange theory on the premise that

   a. James' research was conducted unethically

   b. people feel a wide variety of emotions in response to the same stimuli

   c. people cannot differentiate between psychological feelings and physiological responses

   d. people cannot differentiate between physiological changes that accompany different emotions

5. The emotional theory of Schacter and Singer differs from the others in that it focuses more on the _____ component of emotion.

   a. subjective feeling

   b. cognitive reaction

   c. physiological reaction

   d. behavior

6. Zajonc believed that the _____ component of emotion is not necessary to our experience.

   a. subjective feeling

   b. cognitive reaction

   c. physiological reaction

   d. behavior

7. Which of the following pairs of psychologists represents the two individuals who disagree most in their theories of emotion?

   a. Lazarus and Zajonc

   b. Schacter and Singer

   c. Cannon and Bard

   d. Izard and Plutchik

8. Which reaction to an emotion-producing stimulus seems to be innate?

   a. whether the stimulus is approached or avoided

   b. whether the stimulus makes the organism happy or sad

   c. the facial expression produced in response to the stimulus

   d. the cognitive interpretation produced in response to the stimulus

9. The type of conflict which creates the most stress is

   a. avoidance-avoidance

   b. approach-approach

   c. multiple approach-avoidance

   d. approach-avoidance

10. Jordan wants to play basketball for the UNLV "Running Rebels" when he grows up. However, current predictions of his height indicate that he will be only about five feet eight inches tall. This situation is an example of

    a. environmental frustration

    b. personal frustration

    c. approach-avoidance conflict

    d. approach-approach conflict

11. "Out of the frying pan and into the fire", is a cliche` which refers to a _____ conflict.

    a. avoidance-avoidance

    b. approach-approach

    c. multiple approach-avoidance

    d. approach-avoidance

12. According to the SRRS, the single most stressful life event is

    a. divorce

    b. marriage

    c. death of a spouse

    d. death of a parent

13. In coping with stress, the opposite of change is

    a. stagnation

    b. fixation

    c. frustration

    d. adaptation

14. Procrastination can be interpreted as a form of

    a. stagnation

    b. fixation

    c. frustration

    d. adaptation

15. Which of the following reactions or responses to stress would be considered maladaptive?
    a. relaxation
    b. cognitive reappraisal
    c. aggression
    d. exercise

Dr. G's Best Study Tips #11

TAKING OBJECTIVE TESTS

1. Read instructions carefully and follow them.

2. Reading through the test, answer the questions you know immediately because this will give you a sense of confidence.

3. Once you have answered a question, NEVER change your answer unless you have a sudden insight and know another answer to be correct. Do not change just because you have begun to feel doubtful about your first response.

4. Use other questions to answer or at least give you hints about the questions you don't know.

5. On multiple choice exams, a good approach is to read only the statement and treat it as a fill in the blank question, generating your own response. Then try to find the alternative that best matches your own answer.

6. Read all multiple choice options carefully before you mark an answer.

7. Pay close attention to words such as not, never, true, false, except, always, and only.

8. On true/false exams, guess true if you have no idea at all. It is more difficult to construct false statements, and studies show that the probability of true statements is higher than that for false statements.

9. Always answer every question, even if you just make a wild guess. You will surely get no credit if you leave an answer blank.

10. The absolute best test-taking skill is preparation. Studying will do more for your exam grades than any other suggestion or tip that you can employ.

CHAPTER 12—ABNORMAL PSYCHOLOGY TOPIC 12 A— ANXIETY-BASED AND PERSONALITY DISORDERS

LEARNING OBJECTIVES

Psychological or mental disorders are much more common than most people believe. Because about 19% of the adult population have a psychological disorder, nearly all of us will be in close contact with someone suffering from at least one to them. Students should be able to:

1. Explain how psychological abnormality is defined.
2. Describe the DSM-III-R and discuss the advantages and disadvantages.
3. Characterize phobic disorders.
4. Define panic disorder.
5. Compare and contrast generalized anxiety disorder and panic disorder.
6. Distinguish between obsessions and compulsions.
7. Distinguish between hypochondriasis and conversion disorder.
8. Characterize dissociative disorders.
9. Characterize personality disorders.
10. Distinguish between psychogenic amnesia and psychogenic fugue.
11. Discuss the use of the term "insanity".

LEARNING TOPIC 12A VOCABULARY

On your own paper, write the definition for each of the following key terms. Your learning will be facilitated by writing the definition in your own words rather than copying the exact definition from your text.

ABNORMAL	DIAGNOSIS
ETIOLOGY	INSANITY
ANXIETY	PHOBIC DISORDER
PROGNOSIS	AGORAPHOBIA
PANIC DISORDER	GENERALIZED ANXIETY DISORDER
OBSESSIONS	COMPULSIONS
SOMATOFORM	HYPOCHONDRIASIS
CONVERSION DISORDER	DISSOCIATIVE DISORDER
PSYCHOGENIC AMNESIA	PSYCHOGENIC FUGUE
MULTIPLE PERSONALITY	PERSONALITY DISORDERS

MATCHING

Match the following key terms from your textbook with the appropriate definition.

____ 1. compulsions   ____ 2. prognosis

____ 3. psychogenic fugue   ____ 4. somatoform disorders

____ 5. diagnosis   ____ 6. hypochondriasis

____ 7. dissociative disorder   ____ 8. personality disorders

____ 9. psychogenic amnesia   ____ 10. multiple personality

____ 11. conversion disorder   ____ 12. abnormal

____ 13. obsessions   ____ 14. insanity

____ 15. panic disorder   ____ 16. agoraphobia

____ 17. etiology   ____ 18. generalized anxiety disorder

____ 19. phobic disorder   ____ 20. anxiety

a. Statistically uncommon, maladaptive cognitions, affect, and/or behaviors that are at odds with social expectations and that result in distress or discomfort.
b. The act of recognizing a disorder on the basis of the presence of particular symptoms.
c. The cause or predisposing factors of a disturbance or disorder.
d. A legal term for diminished capacity and inability to tell right from wrong.
e. A general feeling of apprehension or dread accompanied by predictable physiological changes.
f. An intense, irrational fear that leads a person to avoid the feared object, activity, or situation.
g. The prediction of the future course of an illness or disorder.
h. A phobic fear of open places, of being alone, or of being in public places from which escape might be difficult.
i. A disorder in which anxiety attacks suddenly and unpredictably incapacitate; there may be periods free from anxiety.
j. Persistent, chronic, and distressingly high levels of unattributable anxiety.
k. Ideas or thoughts that involuntarily and persistently intrude into awareness.
l. Constantly intruding, stereotyped, and essentially involuntary acts or behaviors.
m. Psychological disorders that reflect imagined physical or bodily symptoms or complaints.
n. A mental disorder involving the fear of developing some serious disease or illness.
o. The display of a severe physical disorder for which there is no medical explanation; often accompanied by an apparent lack of concern on the part of the patient.
p. A disorder in which one separates from or dissociates from aspects of one's personality.
q. A psychologically-caused inability to recall important personal information.
r. A condition of amnesia accompanied by unexplained travel or change of location.
s. The existence within one individual of two or more distinct personalities, each of which is dominant at a particular time.
t. Enduring patterns of perceiving, relating to, and thinking about the environment and one's self that are inflexible and maladaptive.

TRUE-FALSE PRACTICE TEST

_____   1. The question of abnormality should be considered in a cultural context.

_____   2. Mental illness is so pervasive in the U.S. that all of us will experience it either in ourselves or someone we know.

_____   3. In psychology, it is appropriate to consider normal and abnormal as two distinct categories.

_____   4. Most abnormal behavior is dangerous.

_____   5. It is most accurate to say that there are both advantages and disadvantages to classifying mental disorders.

_____   6. The DSM-III-R attempts to overcome the disadvantages of classifying mental disorders by offering suggestions for treatment.

_____ 7. Anxiety based disorders are more common in men than in women.

_____ 8. Healthy individuals may exhibit some of the same behaviors as a person with obsessive-compulsive disorder, with less intensity or frequency.

_____ 9. Conversion disorder is quite rare among the anxiety-based disorders.

_____ 10. Paralysis, deafness, and blindness are classic examples of hypochondriasis.

_____ 11. Conversion disorder was the most commonly diagnosed psychological disorder among military personnel during World War I.

_____ 12. One difference between hypochondriasis and conversion disorder is that in conversion disorder, there is a real medical problem.

_____ 13. In psychogenic amnesia, the person usually forgets the trauma that leads up to the amnesia.

_____ 14. Multiple personality is commonly confused with schizophrenia by the popular press.

_____ 15. Multiple personality is a psychotic disorder.

FILL-IN PRACTICE TEST

1. Recognizing a disorder on the basis of the presence of a set of symptoms is referred to as _____.

2. The _____ is the most widely used classification system in all of mental health.

3. One thing the DSM-III-R avoids is reference to _____, or causes, of disorders.

4. The legal term for mental disorders which is not used in psychology is _____.

5. _____ is a general feeling of apprehension or dread accompanied by predictable physiological changes such as increased muscle tension, shallow rapid breathing, and drying of the mouth.

6. Anxiety based disorders were formerly called _____.

7. _____ disorders are the most common of all the psychological disorders.

8. Phobic disorders are characterized by persistent _____.

9. Unrealistic, excessive, and persistent worry or anxiety characterizes _____ _____ disorder.

10. Hand washing, grooming, counting and checking behaviors are common _____.

11. Victims of kidnapping or rape are likely to suffer from _____ _____ disorder.

12. The _____ disorders involve physical or bodily complaints and symptoms.

13. A person preoccupied with the fear of developing or having some serious disease is suffering from _____.

14. _____ disorder occurs when an individual experiences a loss or alteration of physical functioning that appears to be an expression of psychological conflict or need.

15. When a person suffering from amnesia finds himself in a different location, it is referred to as _____ _____.

MULTIPLE CHOICE PRACTICE TEST 1 TOPIC 12A

1. Statistically speaking, if there are 100 students in your psychology class, how many are likely to suffer from a psychological disorder sometime in their lives?
    a. 10
    b. 15
    c. 20
    d. 30

2. A person's behavior that is strange or bizarre, must also be _____ in order to be considered abnormal.
    a. infrequent
    b. maladaptive
    c. creative
    d. destructive

3. When Kraepelin published the first classification scheme for mental disturbances, the cause of mental illness was thought to be
    a. biological
    b. sociological
    c. environmental
    d. hereditary

4. Which of the following is NOT one of the disadvantages or problems associated with classifying mental disorders?
    a. Classification explains the disorders, but does not offer treatment suggestions.
    b. Labeling people is dehumanizing.
    c. All the attention is focused on the individual and none on the family or society.
    d. Labels create lasting stigmas and negative attitudes about people.

5. For which of the following phobias is a person most likely to seek treatment?
    a. fear of cats
    b. fear of bees
    c. fear of heights
    d. fear of open places

6. Christie has sudden, unpredictable, unprovoked attacks of intense anxiety. She is most likely suffering from

    a. panic disorder

    b. agorophobia

    c. hypochondriasis

    d. generalized anxiety disorder

7. Which of the following disorders is commonly first diagnosed in childhood or adolescence?

    a. panic disorder

    b. obsessive-compulsive disorder

    c. hypochondriasis

    d. generalized anxiety disorder

8. The difference between compulsive behavior such as gambling or eating, and the compulsions associated with OCD is in the

    a. anxiety associated with the compulsive behavior

    b. individual's ability to control or decrease the behavior

    c. pleasure associated with the compulsive behavior

    d. intensity of the person's guilt about the behavior

9. In posttraumatic stress disorder, the likelihood of recovery is related to

    a. the extent to which there are complicating factors such as alcoholism

    b. the extent to which the patient experience psychological problems before the event

    c. the extent to which social support is available

    d. all of the above

10. It is quite possible, of course, for an individual to experience two (or more) psychological disorders at the same time. Which of the following pairs of disorders is MOST LIKELY to occur together?

    a. generalized anxiety disorder — conversion disorder

    b. psychogenic amnesia — compulsive disorder

    c. agoraphobia — panic disorder

    d. hypochondriasis — multiple personality

11. Freud developed the treatment technique of psychoanalysis in order to deal with

    a. conversion disorder

    b. phobias

    c. hypochondriasis

    d. obsessive-compulsive disorder

12. One plausible explanation for psychogenic fugue and psychogenic amnesia is that they are

    a. an attempt to avoid stress

    b. an attempt to get attention

    c. a way of dealing with anxiety

    d. a means of avoiding responsibility

13. Unusually high incidences of child abuse, sexual abuse and drug abuse are related to

    a. schizophrenia

    b. obsessive-compulsive disorder

    c. multiple personality

    d. psychogenic fugue

14. Personality disorders can be distinguished from other disorders on many grounds, but which of the following enables us to differentiate personality disorders from anxiety-based disorders? As opposed to anxiety-based disorders, personality disorders

    a. are more commonly a reaction to frustration and stress

    b. involve a long-standing history of symptoms

    c. are usually found more in children and adolescents

    d. involve some degree of loss of contact with reality

15. Danny seems to overreact to everything and constantly seeks attention and approval. At a party, he is the first to put a lampshade on his head. He describes all his experiences as "peak, the best" and all his troubles as "the worst". He is most likely suffering from _____ personality disorder.

    a. passive-aggressive

    b. schizoid

    c. histrionic

    d. antisocial

MULTIPLE CHOICE PRACTICE TEST 2 TOPIC 12A

1. Abnormality may manifest itself in the manner of bizarre

    a. affect

    b. behavior

    c. cognitions

    d. any combination of the above

2. Which of the following is NOT part of the definition of abnormal behavior?

    a. It is illegal.

    b. It causes personal discomfort.

    c. It is statistically rare.

    d. It is in conflict with social norms.

3. An important aspect of Kraepelin's early description of disorders and their symptoms is that it

    a. was useful to the judicial system in prosecuting criminals

    b. demonstrated the importance of a classification system for mental illness

    c. created admission criteria for mental institutions

    d. could be used by physicians to determine when to make psychiatric referrals

4. The anxiety disorder characterized by persistent fear of some object, activity, or situation is
    a. generalized anxiety disorder
    b. posttraumatic stress disorder
    c. panic disorder
    d. phobic disorder

5. One reason why individuals suffering from phobias do not seek treatment is that
    a. no treatment is available
    b. they are embarrassed to admit their fears
    c. they are successful at avoiding the object of their fears
    d. they are also phobic of therapy

6. The initial attack in panic disorder may be brought about by
    a. exposure to the feared object
    b. stress from the loss of an important relationship
    c. feelings of guilt
    d. physical symptoms of ill health

7. Which of the following individuals may be most in danger of committing suicide?
    a. a person suffering from generalized anxiety disorder
    b. a person suffering from depression
    c. a person suffering from panic disorder with intermittent depression
    d. a person suffering from insanity

8. Which of the following disorders responds well to anti-depressant medication?
    a. generalized anxiety disorder
    b. obsessive-compulsive disorder
    c. panic disorder
    d. phobic disorder

9. Obsessions are to compulsions as _____ are to _____.
    a. feelings; thoughts
    b. thoughts; behaviors
    c. behaviors; feelings
    d. dreams; anxiety

10. Chad complains of chest pains, indigestion, poor circulation, weak muscles, abdominal cramps, insomnia, and headaches, but his doctor can find no medical problems. He is suffering from a
    a. somatoform disorder
    b. fugue state
    c. dissociative disorder
    d. multiple personality disorder

11. More than anything else, what differentiates the anxiety of the anxiety-based disorders from the anxiety that you and I are likely to experience?

    a. Our anxiety is not going to interfere with whatever we are doing.

    b. We're more likely to know why we are anxious.

    c. Our anxiety is less likely to lead to physical symptoms.

    d. We're less likely to experience distress or discomfort with anxiety.

12. Scott is struggling with the decision of whether to join the Peace Corps or get married and find a job in his old home town. Suddenly he disappears without a word to anyone and is found several days later by authorities in a neighboring city. He does not recognize his family and is unable to give his name or address. He is suffering from

    a. psychogenic amnesia

    b. multiple personality

    c. posttraumatic stress disorder

    d. psychogenic fugue

13. Multiple personality disorder is most often confused with

    a. psychogenic fugue

    b. obsessive-compulsive disorder

    c. insanity

    d. schizophrenia

14. Which of the following psychological disorders has the poorest prognosis?

    a. OCD

    b. PSTD

    c. phobic disorder

    d. personality disorders

15. An extreme sensitivity, suspiciousness, envy, and mistrust of others marks the _____ personality disorder.

    a. paranoid

    b. schizoid

    c. antisocial

    d. avoidant

CHAPTER 12—ABNORMAL PSYCHOLOGY—TOPIC 12 B
ORGANIC, MOOD, AND SCHIZOPHRENIC DISORDERS

LEARNING OBJECTIVES

Any psychological disorder can seem severe and debilitating, but psychotic disorders tend to be the most disruptive and discomforting. Persons with these disorders frequently require hospitalization. Students should be able to:

1. List the criteria for classification as psychotic.
2. Describe the syndromes associated with organic mental disorders.
3. Describe Alzheimer's disease and its cause.
4. Define mood disorders.
5. Discuss the prevalence and causes of mood disorders.
6. Discuss the major symptoms of schizophrenia.
7. Distinguish between process and reactive schizophrenia.
8. Distinguish between positive and negative schizophrenia.
9. Describe the distinguishing characteristics of catatonic, disorganized, paranoid, undifferentiated, and residual schizophrenia.
10. Describe the factors suspected as causes of schizophrenia.

LEARNING TOPIC 12B VOCABULARY

On your own paper, write the definition for each of the following key terms. Your learning will be facilitated by writing the definition in your own words rather than copying the exact definition from your text.

PSYCHOTIC DISORDERS

ORGANIC MENTAL DISORDERS

SYNDROME

DEGENERATIVE DEMENTIA

MOOD DISORDERS

SCHIZOPHRENIA

PROCESS SCHIZOPHRENIA

REACTIVE SCHIZOPHRENIA

MATCHING

Match the following key terms from your textbook with the appropriate definitions.

_____ 1. reactive schizophrenia   _____ 2. process schizophrenia

_____ 3. schizophrenia   _____ 4. mood disorders

_____ 5. degenerative dementia   _____ 6. syndrome

_____ 7. organic mental disorders   _____ 8. psychotic disorders

a. Psychological disorders that involve gross impairment in functioning and a loss of contact with reality.
b. Disorders characterized by any of the organic mental syndromes and a known organic cause of the syndrome.
c. A collection of psychological symptoms used to describe a disorder.
d. A marked loss of intellectual and cognitive abilities that worsens with age.
e. Disorders of affect or feeling; usually depression; less frequently mania and depression occurring in cycles.

f. Complex psychotic disorders characterized by impairment of cognitive functioning, delusions and hallucinations, social withdrawal, and inappropriate affect.
g. Schizophrenia in which the onset of the symptoms is comparatively slow and gradual.
h. Schizophrenia in which the onset of the symptoms is comparatively sudden.

TRUE-FALSE PRACTICE TEST

_____ 1. In general, psychotic disorders are more severe and debilitating than anxiety-based disorders.

_____ 2. A person suffering from a psychotic disorder may require hospitalization.

_____ 3. Psychotic disorders are different from anxiety-based disorders in that they impair affect, cognition, and behavior.

_____ 4. Substance-induced mental disorders are typically named after the abused substance and the symptoms it produces.

_____ 5. The symptoms associated with Alzheimer's disease are a normal part of growing old that everyone will eventually experience if he/she lives long enough.

_____ 6. The "early onset" form of Alzheimer's disease tends to run in families.

_____ 7. In mood disorders, it is equally likely that a person will suffer from depression alone, mania alone, or both depression and mania.

_____ 8. According to the DSM-III-R, depression is twice as likely in women as in men.

_____ 9. Recurrences are common in both mania and depression.

_____ 10. Schizophrenic individuals rarely suffer from both delusions and hallucinations.

_____ 11. Although schizophrenics usually lose touch with reality, their affect is generally appropriate.

_____ 12. Actually, schizophrenia is a label that refers to many different disorders.

_____ 13. The prognosis is better for process schizophrenia than for reactive type schizophrenia.

_____ 14. Although process-reactive and positive-negative are descriptors of schizophrenia which provide useful information, neither is actually a dimension or type of diagnosed schizophrenia.

_____ 15. An adopted person who is diagnosed schizophrenic is more likely to have adoptive parents who are schizophrenic than biological parents who are.

FILL-IN PRACTICE TEST

1. _____ disorders are those that involve a gross impairment of functioning and a loss of contact with reality.

2. The most common organic mental disorder caused by abnormal aging is _____ _____.

3. Symptoms that gradually worsen over time are referred to as _____.

4. What were once described as affective disorders, are now referred to as _____ disorders.

5. The opposite of depression is _____.

6. People who swing back and forth between depression and mania, with interspersed periods of normal affect are said to have _____ _____.

7. A disorder called _____ consists of both depression and anxiety.

8. The most devastating, puzzling, and frustrating of all mental illnesses is _____.

9. A person who suffers only from depression and does not also have periods of mania is said to have _____ disorder.

10. Schizophrenics often make up meaningless words called _____.

11. Schizophrenic symptoms that have developed gradually over a period of years are referred to as _____ schizophrenia.

12. _____ schizophrenia refers to the sudden onset of schizophrenic symptoms.

13. One hypothesis about the cause of schizophrenia has to do with the presence of an abundance of the neurotransmitter , _____, in the brain.

14. The type of schizophrenia characterized by periods of extreme withdrawal and a tendency to remain motionless for hours is _____ type.

15. The type of schizophrenia which occurs at the earliest age is the _____ type.

MULTIPLE CHOICE PRACTICE TEST 1 TOPIC 12B

1. Which of the following statements about psychotic disorders is TRUE?
   a. People who suffer from psychotic disorders rarely require hospitalization.
   b. Psychoses and neuroses are the same thing.
   c. Psychotic disorders are not discussed in the DSM-III-R.
   d. Psychotic disorders are characterized by a loss of contact with reality.

2. Which of the following categories of organic mental disorders describes Alzheimer's disease?
   a. substance-induced organic mental disorders
   b. a category of organic disorders with no specific known cause
   c. organic mental disorders caused by trauma to the brain
   d. organic mental disorders caused by abnormal aging

3. Which of the following is NOT a symptom of substance-induced mental disorders?
   a. paranoia
   b. hallucinations
   c. lack of control over the abused substance
   d. intoxication

4. The best explanation for the tremendous increase in the incidence of Alzheimer's disease in recent years is
   a. environmental changes that promote the disease
   b. an increase in the number of people that live to more advanced ages
   c. better diagnostic techniques
   d. the establishment of a hereditary component in the disease

5. Which of the following is NOT one of the seven models that attempt to explain the etiology of Alzheimer's disease?
   a. a genetic basis
   b. a decrease in the presence of the neurotransmitter dopamine
   c. low-level infection
   d. the effect of an environmental poison or toxin

6. Biogenic amines which include the neurotransmitters, serotonin, dopamine, and norepinephrine, have been considered as possible causes for
   a. Alzheimer's disease
   b. depression
   c. mood disorders
   d. substance-induced mental disorders

7. Psychiatrist Aaron Beck offers an explanation for mood disorders that is largely
   a. behaviorist
   b. cognitive
   c. biological
   d. situational

8. Which of the following statements concerning schizophrenic patients is TRUE?
   a. They are usually colorless, socially withdrawn, and not at all dangerous.
   b. They usually exhibit wild, crazed behavior, and may be violent.
   c. Even though they may be having delusions, they are usually able to communicate clearly.
   d. The most common affect is extreme moods, either mania or depression.

9. Factors such as an excess of dopamine, normal brain configuration, severe disruptions early in family life and a relatively good response to treatment are correlated to _____ schizophrenia.
   a. reactive
   b. process
   c. positive
   d. negative

10. Everything else being equal, which person will have the greatest chance of being diagnosed with schizophrenia?

    a. someone who knows and interacts with many schizophrenics on a regular basis

    b. someone who has an identical twin diagnosed as having the disorder

    c. someone with abnormally large ventricles in their cerebral cortex

    d. someone whose mother is generally cold, aloof, and unaffectionate

11. Which of the following statements best describes the prognosis for schizophrenia?

    a. over half of schizophrenics will be symptom free for at least five years

    b. about one-third of schizophrenics will have to be on medication for the rest of their lives

    c. only a small portion of schizophrenics remain constantly symptomatic for more than three years

    d. about one-third of schizophrenics will have to remain institutionalized indefinitely

12. A person in remission following a schizophrenic episode would most likely be diagnosed as _____ type schizophrenic.

    a. residual

    b. disorganized

    c. undifferentiated

    d. paranoid

13. Which of the following can only be diagnosed by autopsy?

    a. catatonic schizophrenia

    b. bipolar disorder

    c. Alzheimer's disease

    d. substance-induced organic mental disorder

14. Dementia refers to

    a. disturbed moods

    b. presence of false beliefs

    c. maladaptive behaviors

    d. loss of cognitive abilities

15. Mr. Streetman, aged 69, is still living at home and can still cook and clean for himself. However, even though he can remember well the events of his childhood, he has difficulty remembering new information such as the names of new people he meets. He is also becoming somewhat apathetic and withdrawn. Mr Streetman is most likely

    a. feeling the onset of disorganized schizophrenia

    b. suffering from a substance-induced mental disorder such as alcohol hallucinosis

    c. in the early stages of Alzheimer's disease

    d. in the depressed period of a bipolar disorder

MULTIPLE CHOICE PRACTICE TEST 2 TOPIC 12B

1. Which of the following statements describes what psychotic disorders and anxiety based disorders have in common?
   a. Both types of disorders involve a loss of contact with reality.
   b. Both disorders may involve impairment of affect, cognition, and behavior.
   c. The prognosis is similar in both types of disorders.
   d. Both types of disorders are equally prevalent.

2. Which of the following is NOT a category of organic mental disorders?
   a. substance-induced organic mental disorders
   b. a category of organic disorders with no specific known cause
   c. organic mental disorders caused by trauma to the brain
   d. organic mental disorders caused by abnormal aging

3. Since the 1970s, the incidence of Alzheimer's disease has increased _____ percent.
   a. 50
   b. 100
   c. 500
   d. 1000

4. Which of the following is NOT one of the brain conditions used to identify Alzheimer's disease during an autopsy?
   a. the presence of tangles in the brain tissue
   b. the presence of plaque in the brain tissue
   c. the presence of small cavities filled with fluid and debris
   d. the enlargement of certain areas in the brain

5. In a mood disorder, which of the following is the criteria that distinguishes a problem from a normal period of moodiness?
   a. intensity
   b. frequency
   c. duration
   d. type of mood

6. Which of the following is NOT a characteristic symptom of depression?
   a. decreased appetite
   b. feelings of worthlessness
   c. persistent unpleasant mood
   d. increased sleep

7. At present, which of the following statements offers the best explanation of the cause of mood disorders?

    a. Depression is a learned reaction to stressors in the environment.

    b. Depression is caused by an overabundance of the neurotransmitter dopamine which blocks more positive moods.

    c. Although depression seems to result from environmental factors, biological factors produce mania.

    d. The disorders tend to run in families and involve some form of genetic predisposition.

8. The term "split of the mind" used by Swiss psychiatrist, Eugen Bleuler, referred to

    a. the altering moods of mania and depression

    b. the schizophrenic's split between withdrawal and crazed behavior

    c. a split or multiple personality

    d. the schizophrenic's split from the real world and its social relationships

9. Around the world, approximately _____ percent of the population is affected by schizophrenia.

    a. 1

    b. 3

    c. 5

    d. 8

10. Which of the following people is most likely to become schizophrenic?

    a. a person whose mother is schizophrenic

    b. a person whose brother is schizophrenic

    c. a person whose mother and father are schizophrenic

    d. a person who abuses amphetamines but has no relatives diagnosed as schizophrenic

11. Schizophrenia is most likely to be treated with

    a. medication

    b. behavior modification

    c. psychotherapy

    d. all of the above

12. A delusion is to a hallucination as a _____ is to a _____.

    a. false affect; true perception

    b. false cognition; break with reality

    c. true perception; imagined event

    d. false belief; false perception

13. The type of schizophrenia characterized by alternating periods of extreme withdrawal and extreme excitement, as well as loss of animation and a tendency to remain motionless for long periods of time is _____ schizophrenia.

    a. undifferentiated

    b. paranoid

    c. catatonic

    d. disorganized

14. An adolescent has begun to exhibit bizarre behavior that includes silliness, peculiar mannerisms, and obscenity. One would suspect the onset of _____ schizophrenia.

    a. undifferentiated

    b. paranoid

    c. catatonic

    d. disorganized

15. The idea of a degenerative dementia implies that the symptoms

    a. are untreatable

    b. gradually worsen over time

    c. gradually improve over time

    d. are associated with inadequate amounts of neurotransmitters

Dr. G's Best Study Tips #12

TAKING ESSAY EXAMS

1. Read through the instructions to make sure you know how many questions to answer and what the scoring system will be. Plan which questions you will answer and in what order and budget your time for each question.

2. Organize and outline your answers to make sure you don't leave out any important information.

3. Read each question carefully and answer only what is asked. Look for key words: describe, define, list, explain, compare and contrast, illustrate.

4. Answer the questions that you know first. This will build your confidence.

5. Start your essay with a TOPIC sentence, present the facts, and follow with a conclusion.

6. Use the vocabulary covered in class and in your text. Give specifics when possible.

7. Use examples to back up your judgments and opinions.

8. Leave space after each answer so you can go back and add details if you have extra time or remember additional facts.

9. Go back and reread each answer to be sure you didn't omit anything. Proofread for spelling and grammatical errors and correct them.

10. Prepare for the test by constructing your own essay questions and writing practice answers. The learning objectives in this study guide will be very helpful in anticipating essay questions.

****

Below are several essay questions that cover abnormal psychology. Use them to practice your essay writing techniques.

1. Discuss the advantages and disadvantages of diagnosis in abnormal psychology.

2. Trace the progression of Alzheimer's disease from onset to death.

3. List and describe five subclassifications of schizophrenia.

CHAPTER 13 — TREATMENT AND THERAPY TOPIC 13A — BACKGROUND AND BIOMEDICAL TREATMENT

LEARNING OBJECTIVES

The idea that people suffering from psychological disorders should be treated to improve the quality of their lives is a relatively new one. The treatments discussed in this TOPIC are medical or physical treatments - not psychological. Students should be able to:
1. Trace the history of the treatment of people with psychological disorders.
2. Define prefrontal lobotomy and discuss its use both past and present.
3. Describe ECT and its current use.
4. Discuss treatment with antipsychotic drugs, listing the various drugs and their effects.
5. Discuss treatment with antidepressant drugs.
6. Discuss treatment with antianxiety drugs and the dangers of their use.
7. Describe deinstitutionalization and its success or failure.

LEARNING TOPIC 13A VOCABULARY

On your own paper, write the definition for each of the following key terms. Your learning will be facilitated by writing the definition in your own words rather than copying the exact definition from your text.

PSYCHOSURGERY   PREFRONTAL LOBOTOMY

ELECTROCONVULSIVE THERAPY   ANTIPSYCHOTIC DRUGS

ANTIDEPRESSANT DRUGS   ANTIANXIETY DRUGS

DEINSTITUTIONALIZATION

MATCHING

Match the following key terms from your textbook with the appropriate definitions.

____ 1. prefrontal lobotomy   ____ 2 deinstitutionalization

____ 3. electroconvulsive therapy   ____ 4. psychosurgery

____ 5. antianxiety drugs   ____ 6. antidepressant drugs

____ 7. antipsychotic drugs

a. A surgical procedure designed to affect one's psychological or behavioral reactions.
b. A psychosurgical technique in which the prefrontal lobes of the cerebral cortex are severed from lower brain centers.
c. A treatment (usually for the symptoms of depression) in which an electric current passed through a patient's head causes a seizure and loss of consciousness.
d. Chemicals, such as chlorpromazine, that are effective in reducing psychotic symptoms.
e. Chemicals, such as MAO inhibitors and tricyclics, that reduce and/or eliminate the symptoms of depression.
f. Chemicals, such as the meprobamates and benzodiazepines, that alleviate the symptoms of anxiety.
g. The practice, begun in the mid-1950s, of releasing patients from mental institutions and returning them to their home communities.

TRUE-FALSE PRACTICE TEST

_____ 1. The systematic, humane treatment of people with psychological problems is a twentieth century phenomenon.

_____ 2. A study of the history of the treatment of people with psychological disorders can help us understand why these problems are viewed with such strong negative attitudes today.

_____ 3. The ancient Greeks and Romans believed that psychological disorders were the results of being possessed by evil spirits or angering the gods.

_____ 4. In the early history of psychological disorders, many people either died as a result of treatment or were killed outright if treatment failed.

_____ 5. In Greek and Roman times, the treatment for psychological disorders was done by shepherds.

_____ 6. Unfortunately, even the enlightened scientists like Hippocrates had little lasting impact on the manner of treatment for individuals with psychological problems.

_____ 7. For hundreds of years, the treatment for mental illness was torture for those who would not confess.

_____ 8. The distinction between the mentally ill and the mentally retarded is a fairly recent one (since the 1800s).

_____ 9. Bedlam was really an exceptionally bad institution, and most of the other asylums were really quite good in their treatment of the insane.

_____ 10. Although the work of Dorothea Dix lead to actual legislative reform, the impact of it was fairly short-lived.

_____ 11. Today, the attitudes toward the mentally ill are radically different and free of prejudice.

_____ 12. At the present time, lobotomies are illegal.

_____ 13. One of the problems with ECT is that the beneficial effects are very short-lived.

_____ 14. The use of drugs to treat mental illness has been hailed as one of the most significant scientific achievements of the last half of the twentieth century.

_____ 15. Most of the antipsychotic drugs work through some effect on neurotransmitters.

FILL-IN PRACTICE TEST

1. The ancient Greeks and Romans might have attempted to treat a psychological disorder by _____.

2. Perhaps the first person to suggest that psychological disorders had physical causes was _____, around 400 B.C.

3. The persecution and oppression of the mentally ill peaked during the _____ _____.

4. The idea that mentally ill people were in league with the devil or possessed by evil spirits continued well into the _____ century.

5. The first insane asylum became known as _____.

6. The man known for unchaining the people at an asylum in France is _____ .

7. The man considered to be the founder of American psychiatry is _____ _____ .

8. _____ _____ , a nurse, was another pioneer in the reform of treatment of the mentally ill in the United States.

9. The person most responsible for the reform now referred to as the mental health movement was _____ _____ .

10. The reform identified as the mental health movement began in the early _____ century.

11. Surgical procedures designed to affect psychological reactions are called _____ .

12. The _____ is a surgical procedure which severs the connections between the prefrontal lobes and the lower brain centers.

13. Electroconvulsive therapy is the more formal term for what are commonly called _____ _____ .

14. Chemicals that have their effect on the person's affect or behavior are collectively referred to as _____ _____ .

15. Most antipsychotic drugs are prescribed for patients suffering from _____ .

MULTIPLE CHOICE PRACTICE TEST 1 TOPIC 13A

1. The first insane asylum was in
   a. London
   b. Rome
   c. Paris
   d. Athens

2. The turning point in the history of the treatment of the mentally ill which marked the beginning of enlightenment and better treatment was
   a. Hippocrates declaration that mental illness has physical causes
   b. the burning of the last witches early in the 17th century
   c. an exorcism performed by Johann Sprenger
   d. the unchaining of inmates in a French asylum

3. Of the well-known individuals who influenced the reform of the treatment of the mentally ill, the one who experienced the atrocities firsthand was
   a. Pinel
   b. Beers
   c. Dix
   d. Rush

4. The first person to perform a lobotomy was
   a. Pinel
   b. Dix
   c. Moniz
   d. Freeman

5. Which of the following results or side effects of lobotomy was not considered to be a problem?
   a. the fact that it was irreversible
   b. the fact that 1 to 4 percent of the patients died
   c. the fact that patients suffered memory loss and seizures
   d. the fact that patients suffered a loss of affect

6. The best explanation for the fact that lobotomies have become so rare is that
   a. they are illegal
   b. doctor's malpractice insurance became too costly
   c. better treatments have replaced them
   d. the AMA declared them immoral

7. The patients best suited for ECT (that is, those who seem to benefit most from this form of treatment) are those suffering from
   a. depression
   b. depression and other psychotic symptoms such as hallucinations
   c. anxiety-based disorders
   d. schizophrenia

8. In terms of the frequency of use of ECT, it is most accurate to say that use is
   a. continuing to decline after peaking in the 1970s
   b. beginning to increase again after a decline in the 1970s
   c. continuing to increase as it has done since its beginning
   d. continuing to decline as it has done since its peak of popularity in the 1950s

9 An alternate form of ECT that appears to be quite successful involves applying the shock to the
   a. hypothalamus
   b. prefrontal lobes
   c. left hemisphere only
   d. right hemisphere only

10. Most antipsychotic drugs are used to treat
   a. anxiety-based disorders
   b. depression
   c. schizophrenia
   d. suicidal patients

11. Which of the following is NOT a problem regarding the use of antipsychotic drugs?
    a. there are certain patients for whom the drugs have no effect
    b. the antipsychotic drugs can produce unpleasant and dangerous side effects
    c. the symptoms are likely to return if the drugs are discontinued
    d. in many cases the drugs actually cause symptoms to worsen

12. Lithium is to _____ as clozapine is to schizophrenia.
    a. bipolar mood disorder
    b. depression
    c. anxiety-based disorders
    d. unipolar mood disorder

13. One difference between antipsychotic drugs and antidepressants is that
    a. antidepressants have no side-effects
    b. antidepressants are more likely to bring about long-term cures
    c. antidepressants have a shorter duration of effect
    d. antidepressants can be bought over the counter without a prescription

14. One real problem associated with antianxiety drugs is that they
    a. just aren't very effective
    b. have tremendous negative side-effects
    c. can only be used with the mildest disorders
    d. are so effective that the patient isn't motivated to deal with the source of the anxiety

15. Which of the following is the LEAST likely reason for deinstitutionalization?
    a. a concern for patient rights
    b. an increasing ability and willingness of family members to care for the mentally ill
    c. the ability to manage symptoms through drugs without hospitalization
    d. the establishment of community mental health centers

MULTIPLE CHOICE PRACTICE TEST 2 TOPIC 13A

1. The man who unchained the insane individuals in the asylum he was assigned to manage was
    a. Hippocrates
    b. an unknown priest
    c. Phillipe Pinel
    d. Johann Sprenger

2. Although Benjamin Rush was a pioneer in the reform of treatment of the mentally ill, he still believed in the barbaric practice of
    a. keeping the inmates chained
    b. mildly torturing those who exhibited violent behavior
    c. bleeding
    d. exorcism

3. What contribution did Clifford Beers make to the improvement of treatment for persons with psychological disorders?

  a. He began the practice of psychiatry in the United States and published the first text in psychiatry.

  b. He managed to get many state governments to open humane asylums for the mentally ill.

  c. He wrote a book about his own recovery from mental illness, demonstrating that it could be done.

  d. He became Freud's strongest supporter in the United States, and translated much of Freud's work into English.

4. The time when lobotomies were performed by the tens of thousands was during the

  a. 1890s

  b. 1900s to 1920

  c. 1930s and 1940s

  d. 1940s and 1950s

5. Lobotomy was generally used to treat patients suffering from

  a. severe disturbances, depression, and schizophrenia

  b. only depression

  c. only schizophrenia

  d. any of the anxiety-based disorders

6. Which of the following is NOT an advantage of the lobotomy?

  a. it appeared to be successful

  b. it could be done in ten minutes

  c. it could be done with local anesthesia

  d. it was irreversible

7. The most frequent side effect of ECT is

  a. hemorrhaging in the brain

  b. loss of memory

  c. loss of affect

  d. insomnia

8. One possible explanation for the effects of ECT is that it

  a. shocks the depressed person into another mood

  b. increases the production of certain neurotransmitters

  c. stimulates pleasure centers in the brain

  d. blocks the production of certain neurotransmitters

9. It appears that one key to successful ECT treatment is

  a. limiting the number of treatments to about 12

  b. using it in conjunction with drugs

  c. applying at least 50 or more treatments

  d. doing many treatments in a very short time period

10. Which of the following patients is the least likely candidate for ECT?
    a. a patient for whom drug therapy has not worked
    b. a patient with acute suicidal tendencies
    c. a patient with bipolar mood disorder
    d. a depressed person who also has delusions

11. One reason for the decline in the use of ECT is that it
    a. has been declared illegal
    b. has been replaced by drug therapy in many cases
    c. proved to be of little benefit
    d. is too costly

12. Which of the following is NOT a side effect generally associated with the use of antipsychotic drugs?
    a. dry mouth and throat
    b. cardiovascular damage
    c. seizures
    d. loss of memory

13. Which of the following pairs of drugs and disorders is NOT correct?
    a. tricyclics - uncomplicated depression
    b. iproniazid - phobias
    c. MAO inhibitors - depression with anxiety
    d. lithium - bipolar mood disorder

14. There are a number of problems associated with the use of antidepressant medications. Of the following, which is of LEAST concern?
    a. Mood elevating drugs have a high street value and need to be carefully guarded.
    b. A drug that is very useful for one person may have very serious side-effects for another.
    c. It takes time (perhaps as long as six weeks) to know if a drug is going to be at all effective.
    d. Both major types of antidepressants have numerous side-effects even when they work.

15. The number of persons hospitalized in county or state supported mental hospitals
    a. has fallen steadily since the mid-1950s
    b. has remained remarkably constant since records were first made in the late 1800s
    c. is higher today than at any other time in our history
    d. goes up and down depending upon a number of factors, including general stress levels

CHAPTER 13 — TREATMENT AND THERAPY TOPIC 13B — THE PSYCHOTHERAPIES

LEARNING OBJECTIVES

There are many different types of psychotherapy with different goals and approaches to dealing with disorders. Because about 30 percent of people will receive psychotherapy at some time it is important to know what is available, how it is done, who does it, and whether it works. Students should be able to:

1. Discuss who may offer psychotherapy and how a person might choose an effective psychotherapist.
2. Describe Freudian psychoanalysis and define its major features.
3. Explain how psychoanalysis is different today from how it was practiced by Freud.
4. Discuss the essential characteristics of client-centered therapy.
5. Describe the techniques used in behavior therapy, including systematic desensitization, flooding, implosive therapy, aversion therapy, contingency management, and contracting, and modeling.
6. Describe rational-emotive therapy and cognitive restructuring therapy.
7. Discuss the advantages of group therapy.
8. List the two assumptions underlying family therapy.
9. Discuss the effectiveness of psychotherapy in general and whether any one type is more effective than others.

LEARNING TOPIC 13B VOCABULARY

On your own paper, write the definition for each of the following key terms. Your learning will be facilitated by writing the definition in your own words rather than copying the exact definition from your text.

PSYCHOTHERAPY	PSYCHOANALYSIS
FREE ASSOCIATION	RESISTANCE
TRANSFERENCE	CLIENT-CENTERED THERAPY
EMPHATIC	BEHAVIOR THERAPY
SYSTEMATIC DESENSITIZATION	FLOODING
IMPLOSIVE THERAPY	AVERSION THERAPY
CONTINGENCY MANAGEMENT	CONTINGENCY CONTRACTING
MODELING	RATIONAL-EMOTIVE THERAPY
FAMILY THERAPY	COGNITIVE RESTRUCTURING THERAPY

MATCHING

Match the following key terms from your textbook with the appropriate definitions.

_____ 1. rational-emotive therapy   _____ 2. family therapy

_____ 3. flooding   _____ 4. modeling

_____ 5. aversion therapy   _____ 6. systematic desensitization

____ 7. free association	____ 8. client-centered therapy
____ 9. psychoanalysis	____ 10. behavior therapy
____ 11. psychotherapy	____ 12. implosive therapy
____ 13. cognitive restructuring therapy	____ 14. contingency management
____ 15. transference	____ 16. contingency contracting
____ 17. resistance	____ 18. emphatic

a. The treatment of mental disorders through psychological means, effecting change in cognitions, affect and/or behavior.

b. The form of psychotherapy associated with Freud, aimed at helping the patient gain insight into unconscious conflicts.

c. The procedure in psychoanalysis in which the patient is to express whatever comes to mind without editing responses.

d. In psychoanalysis, the inability or unwillingness to freely discuss some aspect of one's life.

e. In psychoanalysis, the situation in which the patient comes to feel about the analyst in the same way he or she once felt about some other important person.

f. The humanistic psychotherapy associated with Rogers, aimed at helping the client grow and change from within.

g. Able to understand and share the essence of another's feelings; to view from another's perspective.

h. Techniques of psychotherapy founded on principles of learning established in the psychological laboratory.

i. The application of classical conditioning procedures to alleviate extreme anxiety in which anxiety-producing stimuli are presented while the subject is in a relaxed state.

j. A technique of behavior therapy in which a subject is confronted with the object of his or her phobic fear while accompanied by the therapist.

k. A behavior therapy in which one imagines one's worst fears, experiencing extreme anxiety in the safe surroundings of the therapist's office.

l. A technique of behavior therapy in which an aversive stimulus, such as a shock, is paired with an undesired behavior.

m. Bringing about changes in one's behaviors by controlling rewards or punishers.

n. Establishing a token economy of secondary reinforcers to reward appropriate behaviors.

o. The acquisition of new responses through the imitation of another who responds appropriately.

p. A form of cognitive therapy associated with Ellis, aimed at changing the subject's irrational beliefs or maladaptive cognitions.

q. A form of cognitive therapy, associated with Beck, in which patients are led to overcome negative self-images and pessimistic views of the future.

r. A variety of group therapy focusing on the roles, interdependence, and communication skills of family members.

TRUE-FALSE PRACTICE TEST

____ 1. In all, there are only a few different types of psychotherapies.

____ 2. In the past 30 years, psychotherapy has become more common.

____ 3. Freud referred to a patient's unwillingness to discuss certain aspects of life as resistance.

____ 4. The humanistic and existentialist therapies share a concern for self-examination, personal growth, and development.

_____ 5. Aversion therapy is most effective when used in conjunction with another form of therapy.

_____ 6. The contingency contracting technique is most effective with older adults in an open environment.

_____ 7. Cognitive therapists believe that a change in how a person thinks can bring about a change in the way the person acts.

_____ 8. Aaron Beck would be likely to describe his clients as optimists.

_____ 9. Beck's theory was most similar to Albert Ellis' cognitive theory.

_____ 10. Depression is a problem which responds well to cognitive restructuring therapy.

_____ 11. Only a trained psychoanalyst should conduct group therapy sessions.

_____ 12. About the only benefit to group therapy is saving a little money.

_____ 13. The applications of family therapy are usually limited to working with cases of alcoholism.

_____ 14. According to family therapists, it is very difficult for a therapist to bring about change in a child whose parents will not take part in therapy.

_____ 15. In general, there is some indication that family therapy is a better approach for many problems than individual therapy.

FILL-IN PRACTICE TEST

1. The difference between a Ph.D. and a Psy.D. is generally that a Psy.D. program emphasizes clinical work more and _____ less.

2. The difference between a psychologist and a psychiatrist is that the psychiatrist is trained in _____ as well as in psychology.

3. Freud referred to the symbolic representation of the contents of the unconscious in dreams as _____ content.

4. According to Freud, _____ occurs when the patient unconsciously begins to feels about the analyst the same way he or she feels about some other important person, usually a parent.

5. A therapist who lets his or her feelings and past experiences interfere with their neutral and objective interactions with a patient is experiencing _____.

6. Carl Rogers founded _____ therapy.

7. _____ therapy could be described as methods of psychotherapeutic change founded on principles of learning established in the psychological laboratory.

8. In _____ _____ therapy the therapist controls rewards and punishments in an attempt to modify the patient's behavior.

9. A behavioral technique based on a token economy is called _____ _____.

10. The client's thoughts, perceptions, attitudes, and beliefs about himself are key factors in _____ therapies.

11. Aaron Beck's _____ _____ therapy is similar to RET, but less direct and confrontational.

12. Beck's cognitive approach has proven very effective in the treatment of _____.

13. When a number of people are involved in a therapeutic setting at one time, it is referred to as _____ therapy.

14. According to family therapists, problems are either in the family system or they lie in the family _____.

15. _____ is the statistical technique or research method that was used by Smith, Glass, and Miller to test the effectiveness of therapy.

MULTIPLE CHOICE PRACTICE TEST 1 TOPIC 13B

1. Which psychologist characterized a good therapist as being well-adjusted, warm, empathic, and supportive?
   a. Freud
   b. Beck
   c. Rogers
   d. Beutler

2. When a client relates to the therapist in the way he would relate to other important individuals in his life, it is called _____.
   a. transference
   b. resistance
   c. countertransference
   d. helping alliance

3. Which of the therapies employs the techniques of free association, dream interpretation, and analysis of transference?
   a. psychoanalysis
   b. client-centered therapy
   c. rational-emotive therapy
   d. cognitive therapy

4. Which of the following therapies is associated with unconditional positive regard and a nondirective approach by the therapist?
   a. psychoanalysis
   b. client-centered therapy
   c. rational-emotive therapy
   d. cognitive therapy

5. Which of the following therapies was made popular by Albert Ellis?

    a. psychoanalysis

    b. client-centered therapy

    c. rational-emotive therapy

    d. cognitive therapy

6. Which of the following behavior modification techniques involves the person relaxing and imagining the feared object or situation?

    a. systematic desensitization

    b. flooding

    c. aversion therapy

    d. parent training

7. Joseph's father wants to help him get over his fear of the water, so he takes him to the local pool and gets into the water with him and will not let him out. This is an example of

    a. systematic desensitization

    b. flooding

    c. aversion therapy

    d. parent training

8. Ben went to a smoking cessation clinic where they had him chain smoke until he became ill. This would be an example of

    a. systematic desensitization

    b. flooding

    c. aversion therapy

    d. parent training

9. For therapists Albert Ellis and Aaron Beck, what matters most during the course of psychotherapy?

    a. the pattern of cognitions the person has formed about his or her self and the environment

    b. the formation of healthy, supportive interpersonal networks

    c. getting people to change their behaviors so that their feelings and thoughts will change also

    d. transforming the content of the person's unconscious mind into conscious content that can be openly discussed

10. According to Beck's cognitive restructuring theory, which of the following is NOT considered characteristic of people with disorders?

    a. they tend to have negative self-images

    b. they tend to anticipate a bright future

    c. they overgeneralize

    d. they seek experiences that reinforce their negative expectations

11. Albert Bandura is associated with the behavioral therapy approach known as
    a. contingency management
    b. flooding
    c. implosive therapy
    d. modeling

12. Two related assumptions guide the course of much family therapy. One assumption views each family member as a part of a s system, while the other assumption stresses:
    a. an even distribution of power and control
    b. mutual attempts at reinforcing appropriate behaviors
    c. the extent to which one's happiness depends on the other members of the family group
    d. a concern for improved, open, and honest communication among family members

13. Different forms of psychotherapy have different intermediate goals, but when all is said and done, the "bottom line" final goal of all psychotherapy is to:
    a. help the individual appreciate one's self and enhance one's self esteem
    b. bring about a relatively permanent change in affect, behavior, and/or cognition
    c. provide insight about the nature of whatever problem underlies the disorder being treated
    d. see to it that each patient receives proper medication

14. One advantage of group therapy is saving
    a. money
    b. time
    c. energy
    d. research

15. Which of the following therapists would most likely conduct a group therapy session?
    a. counseling psychologist
    b. licensed professional counselor
    c. social worker
    d. all of the above

Multiple Choice Practice Test 2 Topic 13B

1. The goal of psychotherapy is to
    a. persuade a patient to think differently
    b. persuade a patient to act differently
    c. persuade a patient to feel differently
    d. all of the above

2. Psychotherapies attempt to influence a patient's behavior by _____ means.
   a. medical
   b. surgical
   c. psychological
   d. chemical

3. Your mother has been showing signs of depression and you think that she might benefit from an antidepressant drug. You would want her to make an appointment with a
   a. clinical psychologist
   b. psychiatrist
   c. counseling psychologist
   d. psychoanalyst

4. You have some problems that you think could be helped by psychotherapy and decide to visit the university counseling center. Which of the following professionals are you most likely to see there?
   a. clinical psychologist
   b. psychiatrist
   c. counseling psychologist
   d. psychoanalyst

5. Which of the following is NOT true of the modern version of psychoanalytic therapy?
   a. more time is spent on the present
   b. the therapy is generally of shorter duration
   c. the therapist takes a more passive role
   d. the patient may no longer lie on a couch

6. Which of the following pairs represents the two types of therapy that are most similar?
   a. psychoanalysis - behaviorist
   b. humanistic - existential
   c. behaviorist - humanist
   d. existential - psychoanalysis

7. Which of the following therapies is more focused on the patient's feelings and the present situation, and involves an empathic response from the therapist?
   a. existentialist
   b. client-centered
   c. systematic desensitization
   d. implosive therapy

8. Which of the following therapeutic techniques are most similar?
   a. flooding - implosive therapy
   b. psychoanalysis - systematic desensitization
   c. aversion - client-centered
   d. modeling - contingency management

9. The general public often reacts negatively to behavior therapy, equating it with cruel and unusual punishment and mind control. Which of the following therapies contributed most to this bad reputation?

    a. implosive therapy

    b. systematic desensitization

    c. contingency management

    d. aversion

10. Which of the following therapies is somewhat limited to use in institutional settings or with small children?

    a. psychoanalysis

    b. contingency contracting

    c. client-centered

    d. systematic desensitization

11. In which of the following therapies would the therapist take the MOST active role?

    a. rational-emotive therapy

    b. psychoanalysis

    c. client-centered

    d. existential

12. Which of the following therapists would object most to a technique which focused on changing the client's feelings, but did not give the client any skills or strategies for getting better?

    a. Freud

    b. Rogers

    c. Wolpe

    d. Ellis

13. When comparing different methods of psychotherapy, research indicates that

    a. there is no difference among the major therapies

    b. psychoanalysis is the most effective but also the most time consuming

    c. rational-emotive therapy and cognitive restructuring therapy produce similar results

    d. none of the therapies are really very effective

14. Which of the following is NOT a problem associated with evaluating the effectiveness of therapy?

    a. there isn't much data about the recovery of people who do not seek treatment

    b. there is no agreed upon definition of recovery

    c. it is difficult to assess therapeutic outcomes

    d. each theorist maintains that his own therapeutic techniques are the most effective

15. At present, most of the research concerning the effectiveness of psychotherapy deals with
    a. determining which therapy is best for which disorder
    b. determining if any of the therapy techniques produce long term results
    c. finding the best treatment for phobias
    d. developing a new therapeutic technique that can be used with any disorder

Dr. G's Best Study Tips #13

STRESSED ABOUT THE TEST

Some people suffer from test anxiety so severe that it produces psychosomatic symptoms. Others experience poor performance along with anxiety. Whatever form it takes, test anxiety is unpleasant, but something can be done about it.

Research indicates that an overwhelming majority of test anxiety is related to poor preparation. The other study tips in this guide should help you to overcome this source of anxiety. If you are sure that you are preparing as well as possible and still experience test anxiety, try the following suggestions.

1. Get control of your breathing by focusing on it and counting as you inhale. Then exhale to the same slow count. You should feel much more in control and more relaxed.

2. Close your eyes and visualize a quiet, relaxing place, maybe a beach or a mountain scene. Think about how quiet and soothing the place is and how wonderful it is to be there in your mind. Repeat this as often as needed.

3. Spend some time thinking about why the exam is making you so anxious. What is it that you fear? Failure? Success? Being the last one finished? Disappointing someone? Disappointing yourself?

4. Listen to your self-talk. Is it negative? Do you say things to yourself like, "I'll never pass this test." or "I've always done poorly on essay exams." If so, stop this negative self-talk and replace it with positive messages such as "I am well prepared and know my material." "It doesn't matter if I finish last." "I know I can get this even if it takes a second try."

5. Finally, seek help for the test anxiety. Talk with your instructor or visit the student counseling center. Our counseling center runs free seminars every semester on test anxiety. Perhaps there is similar help available on your campus.

CHAPTER 14 — SOCIAL PSYCHOLOGY TOPIC 14A — SOCIAL COGNITION

LEARNING OBJECTIVES

Social psychology deals with how people interact with, influence, and are influenced by others. The major content area of social psychology known as social cognition deals with how people's cognitive structures and processes influence and shape their interpretation of the world. Students should be able to:

1. Define stereotypes and norms and describe how they are cognitive.
2. Define attitude and list the three components of an attitude.
3. Discuss the functions of attitudes.
4. Explain how attitudes are acquired.
5. Define cognitive dissonance and explain how it relates to attitude change.
6. Discuss the factors associated with cognitive response theory and persuasion.
7. List the two basic types of attribution and explain how attribution becomes distorted or biased.
8. Describe the four theoretical models of interpersonal attraction.
9. Know the four determinants of interpersonal attraction and their effects.

LEARNING TOPIC 14A VOCABULARY

On your own paper, write the definition for each of the following key terms. Your learning will be facilitated by writing the definition in your own words rather than copying the exact definition from your text.

STEREOTYPE	NORMS
ATTITUDE	SOCIAL IDENTIFICATION FUNCTION
PERSUASION	COGNITIVE DISSONANCE
ATTRIBUTION THEORY	INTERNAL ATTRIBUTION
EXTERNAL ATTRIBUTION	FUNDAMENTAL ATTRIBUTION ERROR
JUST WORLD HYPOTHESIS	SELF-SERVING BIAS
ACTOR-OBSERVER BIAS	MERE EXPOSURE PHENOMENON
MATCHING PHENOMENON	IMPRESSION MANAGEMENT FUNCTION

MATCHING

Match the following key terms from your textbook with the appropriate definitions.

____ 1. attribution theory	____ 2. internal attribution
____ 3. matching phenomenon	____ 4. mere exposure phenomenon
____ 5. persuasion	____ 6. stereotype
____ 7. social identification function	____ 8. cognitive dissonance
____ 9. just world hypothesis	____10. attitude
____11. fundamental attribution error	____12. self-serving bias

____13. norms   ____14. impression management function

____15. external attribution   ____16. actor-observer bias

a. A generalized mental representation of someone that minimizes individual differences and is based on limited experience.

b. Rules or expectations that guide our behavior in certain social situations by prescribing how we ought to behave.

c. A relatively stable and general evaluative disposition directed toward some object, consisting of feelings, behaviors, and beliefs.

d. The observation that attitudes communicate information useful in social evaluation.

e. The selective presentation or misrepresentation of one's attitudes in an attempt to present one's self in a particular way.

f. The process of intentionally attempting to change an attitude.

g. The state of tension or discomfort that exists when we hold inconsistent cognitions; we are motivated to reduce dissonance.

h. The cognitions we generate when we attempt to explain the sources of behavior.

i. An explanation of behavior in terms of something within the person; a dispositional attribution.

j. An explanation of behavior in terms of something outside the person; a situational attribution.

k. The tendency to overuse internal attributions when explaining behavior.

l. The belief that the world is just and that people get what they deserve.

m. The tendency to attribute successes to our own effort and abilities, and our failures to situational, external sources.

n. Overusing internal attributions to explain the behaviors of others and external attributions to explain our own behaviors.

o. the tendency to increase our liking of people and things the more we see of them.

p. The tendency to select partners whose level of physical attractiveness matches our own.

TRUE-FALSE PRACTICE TEST

_____ 1. Social psychologists are the only psychologists interested in reactions or behaviors that are social in nature.

_____ 2. Social cognition involves the perception and evaluation of one's self and other people in social situations.

_____ 3. Stereotypes can be helpful in that they help us to simplify and deal more efficiently with a complex world.

_____ 4. Stereotypes and norms are the same thing.

_____ 5. An attitude can be defined by the presence of any two of the three components of beliefs, behaviors, or cognitions.

_____ 6. According to cognitive response theory, people are passive receivers of information which causes them to easily and willingly change their attitudes.

_____ 7. According to Festinger's theory of cognitive dissonance, beliefs follow behaviors.

_____ 8. When a person experiences cognitive dissonance, it is likely that he will change either his behavior or his attitude in order to reduce the dissonance.

_____ 9. When trying to create an attitude change, if the message is rather weak, one would be concerned with the peripheral route of persuasive communication.

_____ 10. In persuasive communication, both the credibility of the source depends largely on expertise and trustworthiness.

_____ 11. Research subjects from eastern cultures are more likely to explain behavior in terms of external attributions than are people from western cultures.

_____ 12. According to attachment theory, one's style of relating to others is very stable throughout the lifespan.

_____ 13. According to the principle of reciprocity, we are most attracted to the people who like us now but did not like us originally.

_____ 14. No harm comes from the fact that physically attractive people are judged more favorably.

_____ 15. The old adage that opposites attract is probably not true.

FILL-IN PRACTICE TEST

1. Social psychologists focus on the _____, whereas sociologists would focus on the group.

2. _____ _____ involves the study of how other people affect the psychological reactions of the individual.

3. A _____ is a generalized set of cognitions about members of a group that is based on limited experience and that does not allow for individual differences.

4. Shared expectations about how the members of a group ought to behave are called social _____.

5. A relatively stable and general evaluative disposition toward some object consisting of beliefs, feelings, and behaviors defines a/ an _____.

6. Conscious, planned attempts to change someone's attitude are referred to as _____.

7. According to cognitive response theory, the power of a persuasive message can be reduced by the presence of _____.

8. In attempting to change a person's attitude, the nature and quality of the persuasive message itself is referred to as the _____ _____.

9. In attempting to change attitudes, the issues above and beyond the actual content of the message are referred to as the _____ _____.

10. In attribution theory, _____ attributions explain the source of behavior in terms of some characteristic of the person.

11. _____ attributions explain the sources of behavior in terms of the situation or social context.

12. The _____ _____ error is the tendency to disregard dispositional factors when we make judgments about behavior.

13. According to the _____ model of interpersonal attraction, we are attracted to people that we associate with rewards.

14. _____ theory suggests that interpersonal relationships can be classified into one of three types depending on the attitudes one has about such relationships.

15. Liking and valuing people who like and value us is referred to as _____.

MULTIPLE CHOICE PRACTICE TEST 1 TOPIC 14A

1. Social psychology can be defined as the study of
   a. how people influence the thoughts, feelings, and behaviors of an individual
   b. how people interact in groups
   c. a person's behavior in social situations
   d. why people form institutions and join groups or associations

2. A relatively stable and general evaluative disposition toward some object consisting of beliefs, feelings, and behaviors defines a/ an
   a. norm
   b. stereotype
   c. attitude
   d. opinion

3. Your beliefs that imported foreign products are a threat to American jobs, priced too low for American goods to compete, and so on, illustrates the _____ component of attitudes.
   a. affective
   b. cognitive
   c. intentional
   d. behavioral

4. Which of the following is NOT one of the three components of attitudes?
   a. affective
   b. cognitive
   c. intentional
   d. behavioral

5. Advertising that relies on testimonials from satisfied customers is relying on forming attitudes through
   a. operant conditioning
   b. classical conditioning
   c. observational learning
   d. persuasion

6. The use of loud music, humor, and novelty in advertising can best be explained by
   a. cognitive dissonance theory
   b. impression management function
   c. social identification function
   d. cognitive response theory

7. Which of the following individuals is likely to be the most persuasive?

   a. a celebrity selling a product related to his fame

   b. a celebrity selling a product unrelated to his fame

   c. an unknown expert, such as a doctor selling a related product

   d. an unknown expert with a very persuasive message

8. Elizabeth was happy with her allowance of two dollars per week until she learned that the other children in the family were all getting five dollars per week. This illustrates the _____ component of attribution theory.

   a. consistency

   b. consensus

   c. distinctiveness

   d. similarity

9. Rachel left her door unlocked and her house was subsequently burglarized. Some of the neighbors said, "she got what she deserved." The neighbors' attitudes exemplify the

   a. self-serving bias

   b. actor-observer bias

   c. fundamental attribution error

   d. just world hypothesis

10. A student who attributes his good grades to his own brilliance and hard work, and his bad grades to poor teachers illustrates the

    a. self-serving bias

    b. actor-observer bias

    c. fundamental attribution error

    d. just world hypothesis

11. Ben was interested in agriculture and wanted to become a rancher. While in high school, he dated a girl that he nicknamed, "five hundred acres" because her father owned a lot of land. One explanation for his attraction to her would be the _____ model.

    a. social exchange

    b. reinforcement

    c. equity

    d. attachment

12. The matching phenomenon suggests that when rejection is a real possibility, people choose partners who are similar to themselves in

    a. ethnicity

    b. socioeconomic status

    c. physical attractiveness

    d. age

13. Which of the following is NOT one of the four determinants of interpersonal attraction?

    a. proximity

    b. similarity

    c. reciprocity

    d. generosity

MULTIPLE CHOICE PRACTICE TEST 2 TOPIC 14A

1. Mark is for legalized gambling in the state of Texas. This illustrates the _____ component of attitudes.

    a. intentional

    b. cognitive

    c. behavioral

    d. evaluative

2. Stephanie and Courtney have been participating in a food drive to help feed the hungry in their community because they believe so strongly that no one should go without food. This illustrates the _____ component of attitudes.

    a. intentional

    b. cognitive

    c. behavioral

    d. evaluative

3. The component of attitude which is questioned by some psychologists is the

    a. intentional

    b. cognitive

    c. behavioral

    d. evaluative

4. "Putting your best foot forward" would be an example of

    a. impression management function

    b. social identification function

    c. the affective component of attitudes

    d. an attempt to avoid stereotyping

5. Stephen buys Nike shoes because Bo Jackson advertises them. His favorable attitude about Nike shoes has most likely been acquired by

    a. operant conditioning

    b. classical conditioning

    c. observational learning

    d. persuasion

6. From a social psychology point of view, which statement best explains why Candice Bergen is the spokesperson for Sprint Telephone Systems?

    a. she is high in telephone expertise

    b. she is high in trustworthiness and expertise in another field

    c. she is able to deliver a persuasive speech

    d. she is physically attractive

7. If a person delivering a persuasive communication has the background, education, and training to qualify her to speak on the topic, we say that the communicator is high in

    a. expertise

    b. trustworthiness

    c. knowledge

    d. effectiveness

8. Which of the following is an example of an external attribution for a behavior?

    a. saying that you failed an exam because the instructor was unfair

    b. blaming your lack of ability for your consistently high golf scores

    c. calling another driver a jerk for cutting you off in traffic

    d. All of the above are external attributions.

9. Mark is dating a cheerleader and explains his choice by saying that she is pretty and fun to be around. His friend Stephen is also dating a cheerleader, but Mark says that Stephen dates her because she has a great car. Mark is demonstrating the

    a. self-serving bias

    b. actor-observer bias

    c. fundamental attribution error

    d. just world hypothesis

10. The _____ model of interpersonal attraction suggests that for a relationship to prosper, both members must receive an equal ratio of rewards to costs.

    a. social exchange

    b. reinforcement

    c. equity

    d. attachment

11. The fact that familiarity is more likely to breed attraction rather than contempt is explained by the

    a. attachment theory

    b. proximity theory

    c. social identification function

    d. mere exposure phenomenon

12. A study done by Walster at the University of Minnesota found that
    a. similar personality characteristics were more important than physical attractiveness
    b. attachment patterns determined whether people dated again after the initial pairings
    c. physical attractiveness was the most important characteristic for both men and women in determining whether they would date a person again
    d. men were more concerned with physical attractiveness and women cared more about other personality characteristics

13. When given freedom to choose partners, people choose the most physically attractive partner available unless
    a. they are very attractive themselves
    b. they are more concerned with personality characteristics
    c. there is a rich person available
    d. there is a chance of rejection

CHAPTER 14 — SOCIAL PSYCHOLOGY
TOPIC 14B — SOCIAL INFLUENCE

LEARNING OBJECTIVES

Because our perception of the world is often unclear and ambiguous, we tend to rely on others for assistance. The social influence provided by others is an important determiner of our behavior. Students should be able to:

1. Discuss the methodology and findings of the Sherif and Asch studies.
2. Discuss Milgram's studies of obedience.
3. Explain how the presence of others affects helping behavior and list the three factors that account for these effects.
4. Describe how social influence affects quality of performance.
5. Describe how social influence affects group decision-making.

LEARNING TOPIC 14B VOCABULARY

On your own paper, write the definition for each of the following key terms. Your learning will be facilitated by writing the definition in your own words rather than copying the exact definition from your text.

CONFORMITY	AUDIENCE INHIBITION
PLURALISTIC IGNORANCE	DIFFUSION OF RESPONSIBILITY
PSYCHOSOCIAL LAW	SOCIAL LOAFING
SOCIAL FACILITATION	SOCIAL INTERFERENCE
GROUP POLARIZATION	GROUPTHINK
VIOLENCE	

MATCHING

Match the following key terms from your textbook with the appropriate definitions.

____ 1. violence	____ 2. conformity
____ 3. groupthink	____ 4. audience inhibition
____ 5. group polarization	____ 6. pluralistic ignorance
____ 7. social interference	____ 8. diffusion of responsibility
____ 9. social facilitation	____ 10. social loafing
____ 11. psychosocial law	

a. Changing one's behavior so that it is consistent with the behavior of others.
b. Reluctance to intervene and offer assistance in front of others.
c. A condition in which the inaction of others leads each individual in a group to interpret a situation as a nonemergency, thus leading to general inactivity.
d. The tendency to allow others to share in the obligation to intervene.
e. The view that each person who joins a social situation adds less influence than did the previous person to join the group.

f. The tendency for a person to work less hard when part of a group in which everyone's efforts are pooled.

g. Improved performance due to the presence of others.

h. Impaired performance due to the presence of others.

i. The tendency for members of a group to give more extreme judgments following a discussion than they gave initially.

j. A style of thinking of cohesive groups concerned with maintaining agreement to the extent that independent ideas are discouraged.

k. Behavior with the intent to do physical harm to another.

TRUE-FALSE PRACTICE TEST

_____ 1. Conformity is always undesirable and negative.

_____ 2. Asch's initial hypothesis was that individuals would not change their judgments when a situation was provided so that there was little question of the accuracy of their judgment.

_____ 3. Asch found that conformity increased as the size of the incorrect majority increased.

_____ 4. Asch found that subjects were more likely to trust their own judgment if one other person among the confederates agreed with them.

_____ 5. Milgram initially hypothesized that the Nazis' obedience might actually be a part of their character rather than a situational or external attribute.

_____ 6. The astonishing results of Milgram's study indicated that the subjects responded to the authority figures and were not at all distressed when required to administer what they thought were painful shocks.

_____ 7. People tend to rely on others for help in determining social reality when ambiguity is present.

_____ 8. Follow up research done by Milgram indicated that women are less likely than men to be obedient.

_____ 9. Following his study, Milgram provided reasonable care for his subjects, doing all that was necessary for them.

_____ 10. There are really no realistic or reasonable excuses for failure to help in an emergency.

_____ 11. According to Latane and Darley, the victim is unlikely to get help in an emergency because of all the steps in deciding to render assistance and the potential costs of intervention.

_____ 12. The psychosocial law suggests that each person added to a group increases the likelihood that the target person will not respond to the emergency.

_____ 13. A meta-analysis of many research studies on the bystander effect concluded that a person is more likely to help when he or she is alone rather than in a group.

_____ 14. Social loafing tends to decline when individuals believe that their effort is special or that it can be identified and evaluated.

_____ 15. Group polarization refers to the fact that group discussion usually leads to a more conservative conclusion than the opinions of the individuals in the group.

FILL-IN PRACTICE TEST

1. Modifying behavior under pressure in order to be consistent with the behavior of others is known as _____.

2. Sherif used the _____ _____ to show how social norms can develop and induce conformity in an ambiguous situation.

3. Yielding to the perceived pressure of peers is conformity, but yielding to the perceived pressure of an authority figure is _____.

4. The Yale psychologist who became interested in and did research on obedience was _____.

5. After a study such as Milgram's, it is very important that subjects be _____, explaining to them the deceptions involved and why they were necessary.

6. First attempts at explaining why no one intervened to help Kitty Genovese used labels such as _____ _____ and alienation.

7. According to Latane and Darley, the first step in bystander intervention is for the bystander to _____ the situation.

8. The tendency to be hesitant to do things in front of others is referred to as _____ _____.

9. _____ _____ is the belief on the part of the individual that only she or he doesn't know what to do and everyone else is doing nothing for a good reason.

10. The _____ law specifies that each person that is added to a group has less impact on the target individual than the previous person to join the group.

11. _____ _____ refers to the tendency to work less as the size of the work group increases.

12. When the presence of others improves an individual's performance, it is called _____ _____.

MULTIPLE CHOICE PRACTICE TEST 1 TOPIC 14B

1. In the study of social influence, psychologists are most interested in how
   a. an individual influences another individual
   b. an individual influences a group of people
   c. groups of people influence individuals
   d. groups of people influence other groups of people

2. A confederate in a research study is someone who is
   a. "in on the experiment" and assists the researcher
   b. in the control group
   c. in the experimental group
   d. observing the study in order to maintain ethical standards

3. Asch's study differed from Sherif's in that
   a. Asch's study was more ethical
   b. Asch's study presented a less ambiguous situation
   c. Sherif's study was more conclusive
   d. Sherif's study dealt with obedience

4. Asch is to conformity as Milgram is to _____.
   a. obedience
   b. perception
   c. social influence
   d. authority

5. Milgram's initial goal in his obedience research was to determine whether obedience differed among
   a. different ethnic groups
   b. different socioeconomic groups
   c. people with different amounts of education
   d. people in positions of authority

6. If we judge the subjects of Milgram's study to be cold, callous, and unfeeling, we probably are being victimized ourselves by
   a. social identification function
   b. internal attributions
   c. impression management
   d. attribution error

7. Milgram found that obedience could be decreased by
   a. decreasing the distance between the subject and the learner
   b. decreasing the distance between the experimenter and the learner
   c. increasing the distance between the subject and the learner
   d. increasing the distance between the subject and the experimenter

8. It is very unlikely that Milgram's studies will ever be repeated because
   a. it is unnecssary when research results are so conclusive
   b. some of the subjects in the learner role were permanently impaired
   c. ethical standards have been raised and would prohibit such a study today
   d. no one would voluntarily participate in such a study

9. Which of the following people is most likely to render aid in an emergency?
   a. a single bystander
   b. a single bystander with experience in similar emergencies
   c. a member of a large crowd of bystanders
   d. the first person who happens by

10. Scottie participates in speed skating events. His father, Bob, has been keeping records of his performances and notes that he skates faster when competing against other skaters as opposed to skating against the clock. The best explanation for this is

    a. bystander effect

    b. social facilitation

    c. social interference

    d. social loafing

11. A jury enters the jury room to deliberate with all of its members having moderate confidence in the defendant's guilt. After deliberations, and having found the defendant guilty, indeed, the jurors are even more convinced of the defendant's guilt. This illustrates the phenomenon known as

    a. group polarization

    b. groupthink

    c. social facilitation

    d. opinion drift

12. When group members are really more interested in maintaining a positive atmosphere and reaching consensus, _____ is likely to occur.

    a. group polarization

    b. groupthink

    c. social facilitation

    d. opinion drift

MULTIPLE CHOICE PRACTICE TEST 2 TOPIC 14B

1. Sherif's study of conformity showed that an individual's judgment

    a. remains the same even when others disagree

    b. remains the same only if he dislikes the people who disagree

    c. changes to become more like that of others

    d. cannot be predicted on the basis of influence from others

2. One potential problem with Sherif's study is that the situation was

    a. ambiguous

    b. unethical

    c. not possible to replicate

    d. not realistic

3. Asch's research on conformity shows that

    a. individual judgments, once made, remain independent regardless of what others say

    b. even on a task involving a simple judgment, individual judgments may be significantly altered by what others say

    c. the effect of what others say on the judgment of the individual is independent of the difficulty of the task involved

    d. in ambiguous tasks, individual judgments cannot withstand the pressure of what others in a group may say

4. In Milgram's study of obedience, _____ percent of the subjects obeyed the authority figure and administered the highest level of shock.

    a. 25

    b. 35

    c. 50

    d. 65

5. The behavior of the subjects in Milgram's study can best be explained by

    a. external attributions

    b. internal attributions

    c. attribution error

    d. ambiguous attributions

6. One positive outcome resulting from the murder of Kitty Genovese is that

    a. police protection in Queens was increased

    b. people became more likely to intervene or call for help

    c. the 911 emergency numbers were established

    d. research was begun that helped understand why no one intervened to help her

7. Latane and Darley conducted research because they were not willing to believe that

    a. people refuse to help because of difficult situations

    b. people refuse to help because of personal characteristics

    c. people actually refused to help at all

    d. only trained emergency personnel are willing to help others

8. Rachel finds herself stranded on the highway after her car breaks down. Even though there are many cars on the he highway, no one is stopping to offer her help. The most probable cause for this, according to research is

    a. pluralistic ignorance

    b. bystander apathy

    c. diffusion of responsibility

    d. conformity to inaction

9. Fara went to a movie that was attended by a large crowd. When the feature began, the screen was split and what should have been at the bottom was at the top. Fara wondered if she should go and tell the manager, but she kept thinking that someone else would go or perhaps the projectionist would notice the problem. Consequently, she did nothing and the movie ran for almost ten minutes without being corrected. This occurrence can best be explained by

    a. pluralistic ignorance

    b. audience inhibition

    c. social facilitation

    d. diffusion of responsibility

10. The opposite of social facilitation would be
    a. social loafing
    b. social interference
    c. bystander effect
    d. audience inhibition

11. Zajonc explained the confusing effects of social interference and social facilitation as relating to
    a. arousal
    b. motivation
    c. practice
    d. anxiety

12. Which of the following is NOT a correct match?
    a. Zajonc - social facilitation
    b. Janis - groupthink
    c. Milgram - obedience
    d. Asch - bystander effect

Dr. G's Best Study Tips #14

SOCIAL COGNITION: STUDYING WITH OTHER PEOPLE

There appears to be three options for studying in terms of a social context: studying with better students, studying with students at about your same level, and tutoring or helping weaker students. Let's examine these options in a little more detail.

Your first step should be an honest evaluation of yourself as a student or "studier." Do you have good skills? Are you self-motivated? Are you well-organized? Are you able to stay on task or easily distracted? Do you make good grades? What do you have to offer a study partner? Once you have answered some of these questions, you are ready to think about whether you would benefit from a study group or study partner and what kind of person/people you should seek.

If you are a weak student, you should seek out a stronger student who will help you to select the main points, get organized, motivated, and stay on task. I believe there is little to be gained by assembling a group of weak students.

A strong student can really benefit by tutoring or helping others. Research indicates that peer tutors benefit more from the experience than the person who receives the tutoring. The best explanation for this is that the process of organizing the information and understanding it well enough to explain it to someone else, enhances the tutor's own understanding and memory.

If you are an average student, you should seek out other average students or stronger students as study partners. Whatever your level, the following guidelines should be helpful.

1. Try to meet several people on the first day of class and get their phone numbers. You will want to call them about notes and assignments if you should be unable to attend class.

2. Look around to see who is taking notes. Try to find someone who appears to be organized. Listen for someone who asks intelligent, thought-provoking questions or offers relevant, interesting comments in class. Another hint: good students tend to sit near the front of class.

3. Once you have formed a study group, always have a definite plan as to what you want to accomplish when the group meets. If necessary, set an agenda just like a business meeting and stick to it. Do NOT let the study session turn into a "bull" session.

4. Go to the group well-prepared. Read assignments and write out questions ahead of time. Make notes about issues you want to clarify or discuss with the group. This should not be a substitute for individual effort, rather a way to enhance your own preparation.

5. Reward yourselves if you are successful. Raise your test grades? Then go out and celebrate.

CHAPTER 15 — APPLIED PSYCHOLOGY TOPIC 15A
— INDUSTRIAL-ORGANIZATIONAL PSYCHOLOGY

LEARNING OBJECTIVES

Industrial-organizational psychologists work to improve the effectiveness and efficiency of business and industrial-organizations. They are concerned with fitting the right person to a given job and how best to fit the job to the person. Students should be able to:

1. Explain what is involved in doing a job analysis.
2. Describe some of the information sources that can be used in making personnel decisions.
3. Describe the rationale for using assessment centers in selecting and promoting employees.
4. List some of the factors that need to be considered in the design, implementation, and evaluation of a training program.
5. Summarize some of the factors that affect motivation of workers to do a good job.
6. Define job satisfaction and the quality of work life.
7. Describe the relationship between job satisfaction and job productivity.
8. Describe three approaches to improving safety and discuss their effectiveness.

LEARNING TOPIC 15A VOCABULARY

On your own paper, write the definition for each of the following key terms. Your learning will be facilitated by writing the definition in your own words rather than copying the exact definition from your text.

JOB ANALYSIS	PERFORMANCE CRITERIA
ASSESSMENT CENTER	IN-BASKET TECHNIQUE
TRAINING	EXPECTANCY THEORY
EQUITY THEORY	JOB SATISFACTION
QUALITY OF WORK LIFE	

MATCHING

Match the following key terms from your textbook with the appropriate definitions.

____ 1. training   ____ 2. in basket technique

____ 3. expectancy theory   ____ 4. assessment center

____ 5. equity theory   ____ 6. performance criteria

____ 7. job satisfaction   ____ 8. job analysis

____ 9. quality of work life

a. A complete and specific description of a job, including the qualities required to do it well.
b. Specific behaviors or characteristics that a person should have in order to do a job as well as possible.
c. A personnel selection procedure in which persons are tested, interviewed, and observed in a number of situations by a team of evaluators.
d. An assessment technique requiring applicants to respond to a variety of situations that might be encountered in a typical workday.

e. A systematic and intentional process of altering the behaviors of employees to increase organizational effectiveness.

f. The view that workers make logical choices to do what they believe will result in their attaining outcomes of highest value.

g. The view that workers are motivated to match their inputs and outcomes with those fellow workers in similar positions.

h. An attitude; a collection of feelings about one's job or job experiences.

i. A group of factors concerning one's work that influence one's attitude toward one's job.

TRUE-FALSE PRACTICE TEST

_____ 1. A job analysis describes the actual behaviors done on the job in more detail than a job description.

_____ 2. Most job analyses involve the use of both hard and soft criteria.

_____ 3. The goal of a job analysis is to find the best available person to do a job as well as possible.

_____ 4. A job analysis is really the first step in the selection, training, and motivation process.

_____ 5. Research indicates that interviews are very successful techniques for selecting the right employee for the job.

_____ 6. Unstructured interviews tend to be more valid than structured interviews.

_____ 7. One problem with structured interviews is that they take away the interviewer's freedom to explore different issues.

_____ 8. An I/O psychologist might be called on to construct a test to assess some unique ability or characteristic for which a valid measure does not already exist.

_____ 9. In the decade of the 70s, training was the most frequently used approach to improving productivity.

_____ 10. One crucial decision to be made about training is whether or not it is really needed.

_____ 11. Although evaluating a training program is important, usually one evaluation immediately after the training session is sufficient.

_____ 12. Motivation is of concern to the I/O psychologist because being able to do a job well and wanting to do a job well are not the same thing.

_____ 13. One reason why employees are not motivated is that so few believe that they are actually compensated for their work performance.

_____ 14. According to equity theory, the reality of fairness is more important than the perception of fairness.

_____ 15. The concept of concern for worker satisfaction, safety, and quality of work life are products of the twentieth century.

FILL-IN PRACTICE TEST

1. A _____ _____ is a systematic study of the tasks, duties, and responsibilities of a job and the knowledge, skills, and abilities needed to perform it.

2. A list of characteristics that a person should have in order to do a job as well as possible is called _____ _____.

3. The _____ is the most widely used employee selection procedure in this country.

4. When applicants are asked to role play the task they may be hired to do, it is referred to as _____ _____.

5. When choosing a test for use in personnel selection, _____ of the test is a very important consideration.

6. The first nongovernmental use of the assessment center approach was by _____.

7. In the _____ technique, applicants are provided a number of tasks, memos, and assignments of the sort they might encounter in a typical day at the office.

8. _____ is a systematic intentional process of altering behavior of organizational members in a direction which contributes to organizational effectiveness.

9. _____ proposed a system for implementing effective training programs.

10. The first step in designing and implementing a training program is _____ _____.

11. According to _____ theory, workers behave rationally and logically, making decisions based on their judgments, beliefs, and expectations.

12. According to _____ theory, what matters most to workers is their perception of the extent to which they are being treated fairly compared to other workers.

13. _____ _____ refers to a person's attitude toward work, usually a pleasurable or positive feeling.

14. The _____ approach to safety is based on the notion that some people are more accident prone than others.

15. The _____ approach to safety is based on the idea that safety can be enhanced by designing safe equipment and procedures.

MULTIPLE CHOICE PRACTICE TEST 1 TOPIC 15A

1. Which of the following would NOT be the concern of an industrial-organizational psychologist?
    a. selecting personnel
    b. training individuals for jobs
    c. motivating people with good skills to work more efficiently
    d. counseling people with work related problems such as stress

2. Which of the following is NOT one of the functions served by an application form?
    a. It can be used as a rough screening device.
    b. It can help determine how an employee will fit in with fellow workers.
    c. It can supplement the interview.
    d. It provides biographical data.

3. Which of the following statements about interviews is NOT true?
   a. Interviews are subject to bias on the part of the interviewer.
   b. Research indicates that interviews have poor validity.
   c. There is no way to improve an interviewers skills or techniques.
   d. The success of the interview depends in part on the skill of the interviewer.

4. The type of psychological test considered to be most useful in personnel selection is
   a. personality tests
   b. achievement tests
   c. tests of motivation
   d. tests of mechanical aptitude

5. It is expected that training and retraining employees will become even more critical in the years ahead due to
   a. the decrease in the number of people entering the workforce
   b. the number of people retiring from the workforce
   c. the increased complexity of job tasks due to new technology
   d. all of the above

6. To be of any real value, a training program must
   a. include hands on learning opportunities
   b. increase job satisfaction
   c. be evaluated for both short-term and long-term effectiveness
   d improve worker motivation

7. Which of the following components are part of a successful training program?
   a. assessment of organizational needs
   b. development of job analysis and performance criteria
   c. training objectives
   d. all of the above

8. Which of the following is NOT part of the process of motivation?
   a. arousing
   b. focusing
   c. directing
   d. sustaining

9. Which of the following provides the best analogy for Vroom's expectancy theory of work motivation?
   a. "What's good for the company is good for the worker."
   b. "If she gets a 15-minute break, I want one too."
   c. "Tell me what and I may; tell me why and I will."
   d. "All we ask is that you do your best."

10. Which of the following statements about job satisfaction is NOT true?

    a. There is no relationship between job satisfaction and the age of the worker.

    b. Sex differences in job satisfaction are virtually nonexistent.

    c. Racial differences in job satisfaction are small, but whites tend to be higher in job satisfaction than nonwhites.

    d. Satisfaction is positively related to the perceived level or status of one's job.

11. Which of the following statements best explains the relationship between job satisfaction and worker productivity?

    a. in some instances the two may be correlated

    b. increased job satisfaction causes increased productivity

    c. decreased job satisfaction results in reduced productivity

    d. there is no relationship between job satisfaction and productivity

12. Which of the following is NOT a model approach to safety used to reduce industrial accidents?

    a. the personnel approach

    b. the industrial-social approach

    c. the engineering approach

    d. the safety-training approach

MULTIPLE CHOICE PRACTICE TEST 2 TOPIC 15A

1. All psychologists are interested in the ABCs, affect, behavior, and cognitions. Which of the following distinguishes the work of an industrial psychologist from psychologists in other fields?

    a. an interest in the ABCs as applied to work settings

    b. using the ABCs to train good employees

    c. applying the ABCs to institutions

    d. a focus more on behavior and less on affect and cognition

2. The two steps in writing a job analysis are

    a. interviewing people in the job and reporting their ideas about the job

    b. making a complete description of what the person is expected to do and translating the duties into measureable criteria

    c. measuring what the person actually does and determining what changes should be made

    d. making a survey of the supervisors and compiling the survey results

3. Which of the following functions of a job application is believed by some industrial-organizational psychologists to be the best source for predicting success on the job?

    a. It can be used as a rough screening device.

    b. It can help determine how an employee will fit in with fellow workers.

    c. It can supplement the interview.

    d. It provides biographical data.

4. Which of the following can be positively influenced by training?
    a. quality of work
    b. quantity of work
    c. accent reduction
    d. all of the above

5. When I/O psychologists use psychological tests, it is usually to:
    a. screen out job applicants who have psychological disorders
    b. find psychological traits known to be correlated with job success
    c. ensure that only the most intelligent applicants will be considered for the job
    d. help determine which criteria of the job analysis are going to be most useful

6. The techniques most commonly used to increase productivity are:
    a. employee training programs
    b. attempts to increase worker satisfaction
    c. improved employee selection methods
    d. programs to motivate employees to work harder

7. Which of the following would typically be used to evaluate a training program?
    a. ask participants how they feel about the training
    b. measure the behavioral changes that follow the training
    c. measure increases in profit or productivity
    d. all of the above

8. In order for goal setting to have a positive influence on a worker's behavior, which of the following criteria must be met?
    a. the employee must set the goal himself or herself
    b. the goal must be clear to the employee
    c. the employee must think of the goal as worth the effort
    d. both b and c

9. Which of the following is NOT true of goal setting as a means of motivating employees?
    a. Difficult but achievable goals increase productivity more than easy goals.
    b. Specific goals are better than general ones.
    c. Periodical feedback is not necessary with highly motivated workers.
    d. It doesn't especially matter who sets the goal, as long as the employee thinks it is reasonable and worthwhile.

10. Which of the following workers is likely to experience the highest level of job satisfaction?
    a. a young black man with a high status job
    b. a middle-aged white woman with a high status job
    c. a young white man with a low status job
    d. a middle aged black man with a high status job

11. Factors such as a sense of respect from supervisors, income adequacy, job security, self-esteem, challenge, and independence, opportunities for social interaction, and a sense of making a real contribution are part of

    a. quality of work life

    b. motivation

    c. goal setting

    d. job satisfaction

12. Which of the following work behaviors is most related to job satisfaction?

    a. productivity

    b. efficiency

    c. absenteeism

    d. motivation

CHAPTER 15 — APPLIED PSYCHOLOGY — TOPIC 15B
HEALTH, ENVIRONMENTAL, AND SPORT PSYCHOLOGY

LEARNING OBJECTIVES

One of the major goals of psychology is to apply what we have learned about our subject matter in the real world. In addition to the usual applications to mental disorders, learning, and other familiar areas, psychologists study physical health issues, environmental issues, and the world of sports and athletics. Students should be able to:

1. Summarize the relationship between the Type A behavioral pattern and coronary heart disease.
2. List some of the ways psychologists intervene to promote physical health.
3. Define environmental psychology and list some of the issues that environmental psychologists study.
4. Define the concepts of personal space and territoriality.
5. Explain the difference between population density and crowding.
6. List the positive and negative aspects of city living.
7. Describe the effects of noise, extreme temperature, and neurotoxins have on behavior.
8. Explain what environmental psychologists can do to have a positive impact on the environment.
9. Discuss some of the ways that psychologists can become involved in sports and athletics.

LEARNING TOPIC 15B VOCABULARY

On your own paper, write the definition for each of the following key terms. Your learning will be facilitated by writing the definition in your own words rather than copying the exact definition from your text.

HEALTH PSYCHOLOGY   TYPE A BEHAVIOR PATTERN

ENVIRONMENTAL PSYCHOLOGY   PERSONAL SPACE

TERRITORIALITY   POPULATION DENSITY

CROWDING   NEUROTOXINS

APPLIED BEHAVIOR ANALYSIS   SPORT PSYCHOLOGY

MATCHING

Match the following key terms from your textbook with the appropriate definitions.

____ 1. health psychology   ____ 2. environmental psychology

____ 3. territoriality   ____ 4. crowding

____ 5. applied behavior analysis   ____ 6. type A behavior pattern

____ 7. personal space   ____ 8. population density

____ 9. neurotoxins   ____10. sport psychology

a. The field of applied psychology that studies psychological factors affecting physical health and illness.
b. A collection of behaviors often associated with coronary heart disease.

c. The field of applied psychology that studies the effect of the general environment on organisms within it.

d. The mobile "bubble" of space around you reserved for intimate relationships into which others may enter only by invitation.

e. The setting off and marking of a piece of territory as one's own.

f. A quantitative measure of the number of persons per unit of area.

g. The subjective feeling of discomfort caused by a sense of lack of space.

h. Chemicals that affect psychological processes through the nervous system.

i. An approach, based on operant conditioning, that attempts to find solutions to human environment problems in the real world.

j. The application of psychological principles to sport and physical activity at all levels of skill development.

TRUE-FALSE PRACTICE TEST

_____ 1. Many of the components of Type A behavior are actually very positive, productive traits that are valued in our society.

_____ 2. Although a health psychologist would intervene with lifestyle behaviors associated with increased risk for certain diseases, there would not be similar intervention related to safety behaviors.

_____ 3. Smoking is one case where preventive measures seem clearly advantageous over changing established habits.

_____ 4. Personal space and territory are the same thing.

_____ 5. Environmental psychologists have concluded that living in a densely populated city produces negative consequences such as increased stress.

_____ 6. Noise is considered most stressful when it is loud, high-pitched, and unpredictable.

_____ 7. Total absence of noise can also prove stressful.

_____ 8. Although the presence of noise has been proven to disrupt performance on problem-solving tasks, the performance returns to normal as soon as the noise stimulus is removed.

_____ 9. It seems clear that extreme temperatures have adverse effects on behavior.

_____ 10. Although some environmental toxins affect physical health, there are none known that affect mental health or behavior.

FILL-IN PRACTICE TEST

1. _____ psychology is the study of psychological or behavioral factors affecting physical health and illness.

2. A person who is competitive, achievement-oriented, and impatient, probably could be characterized as _____ behavior pattern.

3. _____ could be considered to be the single greatest behavioral health risk.

4. _____ psychology is the subfield that studies how the general environment affects the behavior and mental processes of those living in it.

5. The imaginary bubble of space that surrounds a person and into which others may enter comfortably only by invitation, is called _____ _____.

6. The smallest amount or bubble of personal space is between actual contact and about 18 inches and is referred to as _____ distance.

7. A distance of 4 to 12 feet is referred to as _____ distance.

8. _____ involves the setting off and marking of a piece of territory as one's own.

9. A teenager's bedroom is a prime example of _____ territory.

10. The number of persons or animals per unit of area is referred to as _____
_____.

11. Substances that have harmful effects on the human nervous system are called
_____.

12. The specific techniques of applied behavior analysis derive from the work of
_____.

13. _____ psychology is the application of psychology to sport and physical activity at all levels of skill development.

14. _____ _____ , a writer, might legitimately be referred to as the "mother of the environmentalist movement".

15. Psychologists are likely to help athletes with the _____ aspects of their game.

MULTIPLE CHOICE PRACTICE TEST 1 TOPIC 15B

1. Which of the following is not one of the four basic assumptions for involving psychologists in the medical realm of physical health?
    a. Behavioral interventions are as expensive as medical treatment.
    b. Certain behaviors increase the risk of disease.
    c. Changes in behaviors can reduce the risk of disease.
    d. Changing behavior can be safer and easier than treating certain diseases.

2. The relationship between the Type A behavior pattern and coronary heart disease is now somewhat questionable, but still being studied. One potential problem with past research has been
    a. finding volunteers with coronary heart disease who were willing to participate in research
    b. accurately identifying Type A behavior
    c. ruling out other factors related to CHD
    d. finding that Type A behavior correlates to other diseases as well

3. According to Wright, it may be a subcomponent of Type A behavior that is the actual risk factor in CHD. Which of the following is NOT one of the suggested subcomponents?
    a. time urgency
    b. anger/hostility
    c. chronic activation
    d. multiphasia

4. Health psychologists have been most helpful in improving the health of the general population by:

   a. helping people bring about changes in dangerous aspects of their lifestyles

   b. pointing out which toxins in the environment are most dangerous

   c. determining which medications are most useful in treating various diseases

   d. discovering cause and effect relationships between certain personality variables and specific diseases

5. Most smokers who quit permanently use

   a. the cold turkey method

   b. hypnosis

   c. behavior modification and nicotine gum

   d. no formal program or intervention

6. Which of the following activities are health psychologists likely to engage in?

   a. investigate the relationships between psychological variables and disease

   b. use psychological methods to help ease the symptoms of physical illness

   c. help people change behaviors in order to prevent health problems

   d. all of the above

7. Which of the following is the least influential factor related to personal space?

   a. who the intruder is

   b. your age

   c. your sex

   d. your cultural background

8. You are being audited by the IRS and have never met the auditor. Which of the descriptors below indicates the amount of personal space with which you are most likely to be comfortable. (Note that being in Brazil is not an option.)

   a. intimate distance

   b. personal distance

   c. social distance

   d. pubic distance

9. My family has rented a pavillion in a local park to use for a family reunion. This is an example of

   a. primary territory

   b. secondary territory

   c. public territory

   d. private territory

10. Which of the following are functions of various territories that we devise?

    a. They provide a sense of structure and continuity.

    b. They help us claim some sense of identity.

    c. They regulate and reinforce our need for privacy.

    d. All of the above.

11. When comparing the costs and the benefits of city life, it appears that
    a. city life is definitely inferior to country living
    b. city life is worse for those who don't have other options
    c. city life really has no advantages over country life
    d. city life would be fine if the noise and air pollution problems were solved

12. Two important factors in whether noise disrupts performance are
    a. predictability and control
    b. pitch and predictability
    c. control and frequency of the noise
    d. ear protection and frequency of exposure

13. The common perception that high temperatures are associated with more aggressive behavior and displays of violence is
    a. a myth promoted by policemen to get more recruits during summer months
    b. an opinion not supported by research
    c. largely supported by research
    d. none of the above

MULTIPLE CHOICE PRACTICE TEST 2 TOPIC 15B

1. Most psychologists whose goal is that of applying principles in the real world are those whose major concern is:
    a. diagnosis and treatment of disorders
    b. efficiency and productivity of business and industry
    c. psychological correlates of physical health
    d. way in which behaviors have an effect on the environment

2. Which of the following does not show evidence of being linked to personality factors?
    a. heart disease
    b. depression
    c. anxiety
    d. cancer

3. What percentage of the leading causes of death in the United States are believed to be behaviorally determined?
    a. 80
    b. 70
    c. 50
    d. 25

4. Smoking, misuse of alcohol, nutrition, physical fitness, control of stress, and family planning are a few of the areas where health psychologists have been able to help by using
   a. medications
   b. behavior modification
   c. group therapy techniques
   d. preventive interventions

5. The one behavioral change that would save more lives than any other is
   a. wearing seat belts
   b. exercise
   c. quitting smoking
   d. ending drug abuse

6. One reason why patients do not follow doctors' orders is that
   a. they have no confidence in the doctor
   b. they have no confidence in the treatment
   c. expensive medications can pose a financial burden
   d. they do not like the medication

7. Which of the following is the correct order for the various types of personal space, in terms of distance from near to far?
   a. intimate distance - personal distance - social distance - public distance
   b. personal distance - social distance - intimate distance - public distance
   c. intimate distance - social distance - public distance - personal distance
   d. public distance - intimate distance - social distance - personal distance

8. Which of the following measures of personal space most likely exists between most psychology professors and their students during lecture?
   a. intimate distance
   b. personal distance
   c. social distance
   d. public distance

9. The major difference between territoriality and personal space is that territoriality:
   a. cannot be broken down into types or subcategories
   b. does not lead to distress when it is "invaded"
   c. is a fixed location and does not move around with the person
   d. is seldom defended by the individual

10. Population density is to overcrowding as
    a. objective measure is to subjective feeling
    b. public space is to intimate space
    c. personal space is to territoriality
    d. perception is to reality

11. Studies of children living near the Los Angeles airport indicated that they
    a. had adjusted to the noise through habituation
    b. were more easily distracted than children at quieter schools and had higher blood pressure
    c. were slightly more distractable but showed no physical effects
    d. appeared to have symptoms similar to children with attention deficit disorder

12. The anti-litter slogan for the state of Texas is "Don't Mess with Texas". This is an example of
    a. applied behavior analysis
    b. territoriality
    c. environmental cognition
    d. public territory

13. Sport psychologists are likely to assist athletes with the mental aspect of their performance. Which of the following statements regarding mental practice is NOT true?
    a. Mental practice can be helpful in reducing negative thoughts about performance.
    b. Mental practice can be helpful for athletes who participate in team sports as well as individual performers.
    c. Mental practice can play an important role in setting realistic performance goals.
    d. Mental practice is not helpful in perfecting actual physical tasks such as a golf swing or tennis backhand.

Dr. G's Best Study Tips #15

ADD SOME COLOR TO YOUR STUDYING

You may already be aware that the single most effective study strategy is highlighting or underlining in textbooks. Here are some hints for making this technique even more effective.

1. Don't underline mindlessly. Read carefully before you highlight or underline anything. Then limit your marking to those things you do not know. There is no sense marking a key term if it is one with which you are already familiar.

2. Use color coding to identify different kinds of information. When you go back for a study session, you may find that you wish to review only key terms on one occasion and important people in psychology on another. To prepare for this, use one color to highlight key terms and another for important figures.

3. Another area that might be identified with a different color is important research studies and their results.

4. Can you think of additional ways to segment information for studying? If so, incorporate them into your new color coding system.

5. When you study each segment that you have color coded, you should begin to identify information that you know and other segments that still need more study. Develop a system for separating these by marking what you know with an asterisk or a check mark. When you study again, focus on the material which is not marked. In this manner, you are constantly making your learning task smaller and revealing to yourself the proven results of your previous study sessions.

STATISTICAL APPENDIX

LEARNING OBJECTIVES

After psychologists measure the affect, cognitions, and behaviors of organisms, they have to deal with the numbers they have accumulated. That's where the use of statistics helps to summarize, describe, and make judgments about measurements. Students should be able to:
1. Define a frequency distribution and a histogram, and explain what each is used for.
2. List and define three measures of central tendency.
3. Define standard deviation.
4. Explain what is meant by "test of statistical significance".
5. Explain the normal curve and the percentage of cases at each standard deviation.

LEARNING VOCABULARY

On your own paper, write the definition for each of the following key terms. Your learning will be facilitated by writing the definition in your own words rather than copying the exact definition from your text.

FREQUENCY DISTRIBUTION	HISTOGRAM
CENTRAL TENDENCY	VARIABILITY
MEAN	MEDIAN
MODE	RANGE
STANDARD DEVIATION	INFERENTIAL STATISTICS
NORMAL CURVE	STATISTICALLY SIGNIFICANT DIFFERENCES

MATCHING

Match the following key terms from your textbook with the appropriate definitions.

____ 1. normal curve   ____ 2. inferential statistics

____ 3. range   ____ 4. standard deviation

____ 5. histogram   ____ 6. variability

____ 7. frequency distribution   ____ 8. central tendency

____ 9. mode   ____10. mean

____11. median   ____12. statistically significant difference

    a. An ordered listing of all X values, indicating the frequency with which each occurs.
    b. A bar graph, a graphic representation of a frequency distribution.
    c. A measure of the middle, or average, score in a set.
    d. The extent of spread or dispersion in a set or distribution of scores.
    e. The sum of all X scores divided by the number of X scores.
    f. The score of an ordered set above which and below which fall half the scores.
    g. The most frequently occurring X value in a set.
    h. The highest score in a distribution minus the lowest score.
    i. A type of average of the deviations of each X score from the mean of the distribution.

j. Statistical tests that tell us about the significance of the results of experimental or correlational studies.

k. Differences between descriptive statistics not likely to have occurred by chance if the descriptive statistics were describing the same group.

l. A commonly found, symmetrical, bell-shaped frequency distribution.

TRUE-FALSE PRACTICE TEST

_____ 1. Graphs of frequencies of scores are among the most common types of graphs used in psychology.

_____ 2. The mean, median, and mode are all measures of variability.

_____ 3. The normal curve is a rare, asymmetrical frequency distribution.

_____ 4. The range and the standard deviation are measures of variability.

_____ 5. The normal curve could be thought of as a line graph for a frequency distribution.

_____ 6. Scores in a distribution that form a normal curve tend to bunch around the standard deviation.

_____ 7. In a normal curve, all the measures of central tendency, the mean, median, and the mode would be the same numerical value.

_____ 8. The mean divides the normal curve exactly in half.

_____ 9. Mean IQ is 115.

_____ 10. All normal curves have the same amount of variability.

FILL-IN PRACTICE TEST

1. A _____ _____ lists all the numbers or scores and indicates the frequency with which each occurs.

2. A graphical representation of a frequency distribution is called a/an _____.

3. The _____ is the middle score in a distribution.

4. The _____ is the central tendency measure that is most often used in statistics.

5. The most frequently occurring value in a data set is the _____.

6. The _____ _____ is a measure of variability that tells us the average amount by which scores deviate from their mean.

7. _____ statistics are tests that tell us about the significance of the results of experiments.

8. A commonly found, symmetrical bell-shaped frequency distribution is called the _____ _____.

9. Differences between descriptive statistics not likely to have occurred by chance are said to be _____ _____.

10. A measure of variability based on the highest and lowest values in the distribution is the _____.

MULTIPLE CHOICE PRACTICE TEST

1. Statistics can best be described as
   a. tools
   b. lies
   c. another form of mathematics
   d. much ado about nothing

2. Which of the following is NOT a measure of central tendency?
   a. mean
   b. median
   c. mode
   d. standard deviation

3. Averages are referred to as measures of
   a. variability
   b. correlation
   c. reliability
   d. central tendency

4. To determine how much dispersion is in a particular set of scores, researchers focus on
   a. variability
   b. correlation
   c. reliability
   d. central tendency

5. The range is a measure of variability that has the weakness of
   a. being a large number
   b. only considering two values in the set
   c. causing the overestimation of variability
   d. causing the underestimation of variability

6. Formulas that allow the researcher to calculate the likelihood that particular experimental or correlational results arose by chance are referred to as
   a. descriptive statistics
   b. inferential statistics
   c. advanced statistics
   d. measures of central tendency

7. Results that seem unlikely to have occurred by chance are said to be
   a. positively correlated
   b. nonstatistical
   c. negatively correlated
   d. statistically significant

8. Which of the following is/are factors that influence a test of significance?

    a. size of the mean difference
    b. sample size
    c. variability
    d. all of the above

9. In a normal curve, the symmetry allows us to know that _____ percent of the values in the distribution fall between one standard deviation below the mean and one standard deviation above the mean.

    a. 34
    b. 50
    c. 68
    d. 84

10. If mean IQ is 100 and the standard deviation is 15, what percent of people will have IQs between 85 and 100?

    a. 10
    b. 28
    c. 34
    d. 50

Dr. G's Best Study Tips #16

USE IT OR LOSE IT

Below you will find a list of the fifteen study strategies that have been presented in the previous chapters. Perhaps they will not all be equally helpful to you. It is certain, that none will be helpful unless tried and evaluated. After you have given each strategy a fair trial, write a one sentence evaluation in the space provided. Try to identify several strategies that have helped you the most and make them part of your regular study routine.

1. Time management.

2. Dealing with distractions.

3. Getting to know your textbook.

4. How to read a textbook.

5. Using the Premack Principle to reinforce studying.

6. Getting along with your professor.

7. Using mnemonic strategies.

8. Using 3 x 5 cards.

9. Being a star in class.

10. Suggestions for taking notes.

11. Taking objective tests.

12. Taking essay exams.

13. Stressed about the test.

14. Studying with other people.

15. Adding some color to your studying.

ANSWER KEY

CHAPTER 1 TOPIC 1A

MATCHING

1. B	2. L	3. J	4. I	5. N
6. P	7. G	8. F	9. D	10. S
11. A	12. Q	13. K	14. C	15. E
16. M	17. O	18. H	19. R	

TRUE-FALSE PRACTICE TEST

1. F	2. T	3. T	4. F	5. F
6. F	7. T	8. F	9. T	10. T
11. F	12. T	13. F	14. T	15. T

FILL-IN PRACTICE TEST

1. John Locke	2. interactive dualism
3. philosophy, science	4. affect
5. cognition	6. behavior
7. operational	8. Fechner
9. Wilhelm Wundt	10. William James
11. John Watson	12. behaviorism
13. psychoanalysis	14. whole
15. Galton	

MULTIPLE CHOICE PRACTICE TEST 1

1. C	2. B	3. A	4. A	5. D
6. C	7. D	8. A	9. B	10. C
11. A	12. B	13. C	14. B	15. C

MULTIPLE CHOICE PRACTICE TEST 2

1. C	2. B	3. D	4. D	5. A
6. C	7. C	8. A	9. C	10. D
11. A	12. B	13. C	14. B	15. D

CHAPTER 1 TOPIC 1B

MATCHING

1. J	2. N	3. P	4. E	5. Q
6. T	7. S	8. G	9. A	10. D
11. C	12. I	13. K	14. M	15. R
16. O	17. L	18. F	19. H	20. B

TRUE-FALSE PRACTICE TEST

1. T	2. F	3. F	4. F	5. T
6. T	7. T	8. F	9. T	10. F
11. F	12. F	13. T	14. F	15. F

FILL-IN PRACTICE TEST

1. correlation
2. positive
3. negative
4. experiments
5. experiment
6. independent
7. dependent
8. extraneous
9. experimental
10. control
11. random assignment
12. single-blind
13. double-blind
14. meta-analysis
15. debriefing

MULTIPLE CHOICE PRACTICE TEST 1

1. B	2. A	3. C	4. A	5. D
6. C	7. B	8. D	9. A	10. D
11. D	12. B	13. C	14. B	15. C

MULTIPLE CHOICE PRACTICE TEST 2

1. B	2. D	3. A	4. A	5. B
6. C	7. C	8. D	9. A	10. D
11. B	12. C	13. C	14. A	15. C

CHAPTER 2 TOPIC 2A

MATCHING

1. J	2. T	3. P	4. K	5. Z
6. FF	7. DD	8. V	9. X	10. BB
11. N	12. R	13. B	14. G	15. F
16. O	17. AA	18. Y	19. W	20. EE
21. CC	22. Q	23. L	24. M	25. S
26. U	27. A	28. I	29. H	30. GG
31. HH	32. E	33. C	34. D	

TRUE-FALSE PRACTICE TEST

1. F	2. F	3. T	4. T	5. T
6. F	7. F	8. T	9. F	10. T
11. T	12. T	13. T	14. F	15. T
16. F	17. T	18. T	19. T	20. F

FILL-IN PRACTICE TEST

1. gene
2. dominant gene
3. neuron
4. nucleus
5. axon
6. myelin
7. myelin
8. axon terminals
9. neural impulse
10. ions
11. resting potential
12. refracting
13. neural threshold
14. synapse
15. neurotransmitters
16. endorphins
17. memory
18. central nervous system
19. hormones
20. Berger

MULTIPLE CHOICE PRACTICE TEST 1

1. A	2. D	3. C	4. A	5. B
6. C	7. C	8. D	9. B	10. A
11. B	12. C	13. A	14. D	15. D

MULTIPLE CHOICE PRACTICE TEST 2

1. A	2. D	3. D	4. B	5. A
6. B	7. C	8. D	9. C	10. A
11. B	12. D	13. C	14. B	15. A

CHAPTER 2 TOPIC 2B

MATCHING

1. T	2. Z	3. J	4. Q	5. O
6. A	7. I	8. F	9. M	10. R
11. S	12. K	13. B	14. G	15. U
16. Y	17. P	18. L	19. N	20. V
21. W	22. C	23. H	24. D	25. X
26. E				

TRUE-FALSE PRACTICE TEST

1. T	2. T	3. F	4. F	5. T
6. F	7. T	8. F	9. T	10. T
11. F	12. F	13. T	14. F	15. T

FILL-IN PRACTICE TEST

1. spinal cord
2. spinal reflexes
3. cross laterality
4. pons
5. limbic system
6. hippocampus
7. cerebrum
8. occipital
9. corpus callosum
10. split-brain procedure
11. epilepsy
12. Parkinson's disease
13. l-dopa
14. hypothalamus
15. thalamus

MULTIPLE CHOICE PRACTICE TEST 1

1. C	2. B	3. D	4. A	5. B
6. B	7. C	8. C	9. D	10. A
11. B	12. C	13. D	14. D	15. B

MULTIPLE CHOICE PRACTICE TEST 2

1. B	2. B	3. A	4. D	5. C
6. A	7. B	8. D	9. B	10. C
11. C	12. A	13. D	14. B	15. A

Chapter 3 Topic 3A

Matching

1. JJ	2. K	3. V	4. R	5. II
6. U	7. M	8. S	9. E	10. J
11. G	12. BB	13. X	14. W	15. HH
16. O	17. P	18. T	19. A	20. H
21. F	22. B	23. Q	24. CC	25. EE
26. Y	27. Z	28. AA	29. FF	30. C
31. I	32. D	33. L	34. GG	35. DD

True-False Practice Test

1. T	2. F	3. F	4. T	5. T
6. T	7. T	8. F	9. F	10. F
11. T	12. F	13. T	14. F	15. T

Fill-in Practice Test

1. sensation
2. psychophysics
3. subliminal perception
4. difference threshold
5. sensory adaptation
6. dark adaptation
7. decreases
8. nanometer
9. iris
10. retina
11. cones
12. light
13. yellow
14. cornea
15. monochromatic

Multiple Choice Practice Test 1

1. D	2. A	3. C	4. C	5. C
6. B	7. D	8. B	9. B	10. D
11. C	12. D	13. C	14. C	15. A

Multiple Choice Practice Test 2

1. C	2. B	3. D	4. D	5. A
6. C	7. A	8. A	9. B	10. C
11. D	12. D	13. A	14. B	15. D

Chapter 3 Topic 3B

Matching

1. C	2. I	3. R	4. M	5. A
6. F	7. K	8. D	9. N	10. Q
11. B	12. G	13. E	14. J	15. H
16. L	17. P	18. O		

True-False Practice Test

1. T	2. T	3. F	4. T	5. T
6. F	7. F	8. F	9. F	10. T
11. T	12. F			

FILL-IN PRACTICE TEST

1. amplitude		2. decibels	
3. timbre		4. white noise	
5. pinna		6. ossicles	
7. taste		8. smell	
9. pheromones		10. cutaneous	
11. vestibular		12. kinesthetic	
13. placebo		14. endorphins	
15. pain			

MULTIPLE CHOICE PRACTICE TEST 1

1. D	2. C	3. D	4. A	5. A
6. B	7. D	8. C	9. B	10. A

MULTIPLE CHOICE PRACTICE TEST 2

1. B	2. C	3. A	4. C	5. B
6. D	7. C	8. A	9. D	10. D

CHAPTER 4 TOPIC 4A

MATCHING

1. D	2. I	3. K	4. T	5. M
6. Q	7. A	8. G	9. N	10. S
11. P	12. J	13. B	14. H	15. L
16. C	17. R	18. F	19. O	20. E

TRUE-FALSE PRACTICE TEST

1. F	2. T	3. F	4. F	5. T
6. T	7. F	8. F	9. T	10. F
11. F	12. T	13. T	14. T	15. T

FILL-IN PRACTICE TEST

1. perception		2. motion
3. top-down		4. Gestalt
5. closure		6. binocular
7. retinal disparity		8. illusion
9. phi phenomenon		10. autokinetic
11. ganzfeld		12. shape constancy
13. size		14. illusion
15. accommodation		

MULTIPLE CHOICE PRACTICE TEST 1

1. D	2. C	3. C	4. A	5. A
6. B	7. D	8. C	9. A	10. D
11. C	12. B	13. A	14. C	15. D

MULTIPLE CHOICE PRACTICE TEST 2

1. A	2. B	3. D	4. C	5. B
6. C	7. C	8. A	9. B	10. D
11. D	12. C	13. A	14. B	15. D

CHAPTER 4 TOPIC 4B

MATCHING

1. K	2. S	3. O	4. C	5. J
6. F	7. T	8. Q	9. M	10. R
11. A	12. E	13. G	14. P	15. B
16. I	17. D	18. L	19. H	20. N

TRUE-FALSE PRACTICE TEST

1. F	2. F	3. T	4. T	5. T
6. F	7. F	8. F	9. T	10. T
11. T	12. T	13. T	14. F	15. T

FILL-IN PRACTICE TEST

1. insomnia	2. delta
3. REM	4. NREM
5. Freud	6. atonia
7. microsleeps	8. meditation
9. mantra	10. psychoactive
11. tolerance	12. withdrawal
13. psychological	14. stimulants
15. alcohol	

MULTIPLE CHOICE PRACTICE TEST 1

1. B	2. A	3. C	4. B	5. D
6. C	7. A	8. B	9. D	10. D
11. A	12. D	13. C	14. C	15. C

MULTIPLE CHOICE PRACTICE TEST 2

1. C	2. B	3. A	4. A	5. B
6. D	7. D	8. C	9. A	10. D
11. B	12. C	13. C	14. A	15. C

CHAPTER 5 TOPIC 5A

MATCHING

1. J	2. P	3. D	4. H	5. B
6. F	7. K	8. N	9. A	10. I
11. C	12. M	13. O	14. L	15. G
16. E				

TRUE-FALSE PRACTICE TEST

1. T	2. T	3. F	4. T	5. F
6. T	7. F	8. F	9. T	10. F
11. F	12. F	13. F	14. T	15. F

FILL-IN PRACTICE TEST

1. conditioning
2. reflex
3. acquisition
4. extinction
5. salivation
6. spontaneous recovery
7. suppressed
8. discrimination
9. phobic disorder
10. systematic desensitization
11. Wolpe
12. counterconditioning
13. Watson
14. habituation
15. aversion

MULTIPLE CHOICE PRACTICE TEST 1

1. B	2. C	3. C	4. A	5. A
6. B	7. B	8. D	9. C	10. A
11. D	12. A	13. B	14. D	15. D

MULTIPLE CHOICE PRACTICE TEST 2

1. C	2. A	3. A	4. D	5. C
6. D	7. C	8. B	9. C	10. A
11. D	12. B	13. D	14. B	15. A

CHAPTER 5 TOPIC 5B

MATCHING

1. X	2. R	3. K	4. U	5. M
6. V	7. F	8. J	9. A	10. H
11. C	12. I	13. W	14. D	15. O
16. T	17. L	18. B	19. Q	20. E
21. P	22. G	23. N	24. S	

TRUE-FALSE PRACTICE TEST

1. T	2. F	3. T	4. T	5. T
6. F	7. T	8. F	9. F	10. T
11. F	12. F	13. T	14. T	15. T

FILL-IN PRACTICE TEST

1. cognitive
2. operant
3. consequences
4. Thorndike
5. Skinner box
6. base rate
7. shaping
8. acquisition
9. spontaneous recovery
10. reinforcement
11. primary
12. secondary
13. intermittent
14. punishment
15. instinctive drift

MULTIPLE CHOICE PRACTICE TEST 1

1. C	2. A	3. D	4. B	5. A
6. B	7. D	8. C	9. B	10. A
11. D	12. C	13. B	14. A	15. D

MULTIPLE CHOICE PRACTICE TEST 2

1. B	2. A	3. C	4. A	5. B
6. B	7. C	8. C	9. D	10. B
11. D	12. C	13. A	14. B	15. D

CHAPTER 6 TOPIC 6A

MATCHING

1. O	2. T	3. D	4. J	5. G
6. K	7. A	8. L	9. R	10. M
11. C	12. I	13. B	14. N	15. S
16. P	17. F	18. Q	19. E	20. H

TRUE-FALSE PRACTICE TEST

1. F	2. T	3. F	4. F	5. T
6. T	7. F	8. T	9. T	10. T
11. F	12. T	13. F	14. T	15. T

FILL-IN PRACTICE TEST

1. encoding
2. sensory
3. working
4. chunk
5. maintenance
6. elaborative
7. procedural
8. semantic
9. episodic
10. metamemory
11. subjective
12. ACT
13. anterograde
14. retrograde
15. serotonin

MULTIPLE CHOICE PRACTICE TEST 1

1. D	2. A	3. B	4. A	5. B
6. C	7. D	8. A	9. B	10. C
11. D	12. D	13. D	14. C	15. D

MULTIPLE CHOICE PRACTICE TEST 2

1. C	2. C	3. B	4. C	5. D
6. B	7. A	8. B	9. D	10. B
11. B	12. A	13. C	14. A	15. B

CHAPTER 6 TOPIC 6B

MATCHING

1. J	2. O	3. E	4. H	5. I
6. M	7. D	8. A	9. N	10. B
11. G	12. L	13. F	14. C	15. K

TRUE-FALSE PRACTICE TEST

1. F	2. T	3. T	4. F	5. F
6. T	7. T	8. F	9. T	10. T
11. T	12. F	13. T	14. F	15. T

FILL-IN PRACTICE TEST

1. recall
2. recognition
3. recall
4. nonsense syllables
5. implicit
6. explicit
7. procedural
8. procedural
9. flashbulb
10. schemas
11. mnemonic devices
12. narrative chaining
13. schema
14. overlearning
15. retroactive

MULTIPLE CHOICE PRACTICE TEST 1

1. C	2. A	3. D	4. B	5. D
6. A	7. C	8. C	9. B	10. A
11. B	12. C	13. D	14. A	15. C

MULTIPLE CHOICE PRACTICE TEST 2

1. A	2. B	3. C	4. D	5. A
6. A	7. C	8. D	9. D	10. D
11. A	12. A	13. A	14. B	15. B

CHAPTER 7 TOPIC 7A

MATCHING

1. O	2. N	3. A	4. F	5. H
6. L	7. K	8. C	9. B	10. M
11. D	12. G	13. E	14. I	15. J

TRUE-FALSE PRACTICE TEST

1. T	2. T	3. T	4. T	5. T
6. F	7. F	8. T	9. T	10. T
11. F	12. T	13. T	14. F	15. T

FILL-IN PRACTICE TEST

1. concept
2. attribute-rule
3. formal
4. conjunctive
5. disjunctive
6. prototype
7. psycholinguists
8. phonemes
9. semantics
10. morpheme
11. syntax
12. pragmatics
13. babbling
14. holophrastic
15. overregularization

MULTIPLE CHOICE PRACTICE TEST 1

1. C	2. B	3. D	4. D	5. D
6. B	7. C	8. A	9. B	10. C
11. C	12. D	13. B	14. A	15. A

MULTIPLE CHOICE PRACTICE TEST 2

1. A	2. B	3. A	4. C	5. B
6. C	7. B	8. C	9. C	10. C
11. C	12. D	13. A	14. B	15. C

CHAPTER 7 TOPIC 7B

MATCHING

1. K	2. A	3. E	4. J	5. H
6. G	7. I	8. B	9. F	10. D
11. C				

TRUE-FALSE PRACTICE TEST

1. T	2. F	3. F	4. T	5. T
6. F	7. T	8. F	9. F	10. T
11. F	12. F	13. T	14. T	15. T

FILL-IN PRACTICE TEST

1. representation
2. strategy
3. algorithm
4. heuristic
5. means-ends
6. hill climbing
7. mental set
8. availability
9. representativeness
10. divergent
11. convergent
12. incubation
13. verification
14. preparation
15. illumination

MULTIPLE CHOICE PRACTICE TEST 1

1. D	2. B	3. D	4. A	5. C
6. A	7. B	8. C	9. B	10. C
11. C	12. D	13. D	14. B	15. A

MULTIPLE CHOICE PRACTICE TEST 2

1. C	2. C	3. A	4. B	5. A
6. A	7. C	8. D	9. C	10. B
11. B	12. A	13. D	14. B	15. C

CHAPTER 8 TOPIC 8A

MATCHING

1. G	2. O	3. F	4. A	5. C
6. E	7. H	8. I	9. M	10. N
11. L	12. B	13. J	14. D	15. K

TRUE-FALSE PRACTICE TEST

1. T	2. F	3. T	4. T	5. F
6. T	7. F	8. T	9. T	10. F
11. T	12. T	13. T	14. T	15. F

FILL-IN PRACTICE TEST

1. measurement	2. g-factor
3. s-factors	4. psychological test
5. reliability	6. test-retest
7. correlation	8. validity
9. concurrent	10. content
11. norms	12. Alfred Binet
13. verbal	14. WAIS-R
15. Army Alpha	

MULTIPLE CHOICE PRACTICE TEST 1

1. C	2. D	3. C	4. A	5. B
6. D	7. A	8. B	9. D	10. D
11. C	12. A	13. B	14. D	15. B

MULTIPLE CHOICE PRACTICE TEST 2

1. B	2. A	3. D	4. C	5. A
6. C	7. D	8. B	9. C	10. B
11. D	12. C	13. A	14. B	15. A

CHAPTER 8 TOPIC 8B

MATCHING

1. F	2. C	3. A	4. E	5. B
6. D				

TRUE-FALSE PRACTICE TEST

1. T	2. F	3. T	4. T	5. F
6. F	7. T	8. F	9. F	10. T
11. T	12. T	13. F	14. T	15. T

FILL-IN PRACTICE TEST

1. correlation
2. seven
3. 100
4. cross-sectional
5. longitudinal
6. vocabulary
7. fluid intelligence
8. crystallized intelligence
9. intellectually
10. 130
11. Terman
12. Termites
13. developmentally delayed
14. Down's syndrome
15. phenylketonuria

MULTIPLE CHOICE PRACTICE TEST 1

1. B	2. A	3. C	4. A	5. C
6. C	7. C	8. B	9. A	10. B
11. D	12. D	13. A	14. C	15. D

MULTIPLE CHOICE PRACTICE TEST 2

1. D	2. A	3. D	4. B	5. C
6. D	7. A	8. D	9. C	10. B
11. A	12. C	13. C	14. C	15. D

CHAPTER 9 TOPIC 9A

MATCHING

1. D	2. K	3. C	4. I	5. J
6. B	7. A	8. F	9. L	10. E
11. G	12. H			

TRUE-FALSE PRACTICE TEST

1. F	2. T	3. T	4. T	5. F
6. T	7. F	8. T	9. T	10. T
11. T	12. F	13. F	14. T	15. T

FILL-IN PRACTICE TEST

1. plasticity
2. zygote
3. prenatal
4. implantation
5. embryonic
6. fetus
7. viability
8. fetal alcohol syndrome
9. neonate
10. vision
11. visual cliff
12. schema
13. assimilation
14. accommodation
15. conservation

MULTIPLE CHOICE PRACTICE TEST 1

1. A	2. C	3. B	4. D	5. B
6. A	7. A	8. C	9. A	10. B
11. B	12. D	13. B	14. D	15. D

MULTIPLE CHOICE PRACTICE TEST 2

1. A	2. D	3. B	4. C	5. C
6. A	7. B	8. B	9. C	10. D
11. C	12. D	13. B	14. C	15. D

CHAPTER 9 TOPIC 9B

MATCHING

1. H	2. B	3. D	4. G	5. A
6. F	7. C	8. E		

TRUE-FALSE PRACTICE TEST

1. T	2. T	3. F	4. T	5. T
6. F	7. T	8. F	9. F	10. F
11. T	12. F	13. F	14. T	15. T

FILL-IN PRACTICE TEST

1. growth spurt	2. puberty
3. formal operations	4. identity crisis
5. adolescent egocentrism	6. personal fables
7. integrative	8. induction
9. middle adulthood	10. sandwich generation
11. stagnation	12. Havighurst
13. ageism	14. plasticity
15. old-old	

MULTIPLE CHOICE PRACTICE TEST 1

1. D	2. C	3. D	4. B	5. A
6. B	7. C	8. A	9. B	10. C
11. C	12. C	13. A	14. B	15. D

MULTIPLE CHOICE PRACTICE TEST 2

1. C	2. B	3. B	4. C	5. A
6. D	7. C	8. D	9. B	10. A
11. C	12. C	13. A	14. D	15. B

CHAPTER 10 TOPIC 10A

MATCHING

1. S	2. A	3. M	4. B	5. E
6. D	7. T	8. K	9. Q	10. P
11. V	12. N	13. C	14. H	15. R
16. U	17. L	18. O	19. F	20. I
21. G	22. J			

TRUE-FALSE PRACTICE TEST

1. T	2. F	3. F	4. F	5. T
6. F	7. T	8. T	9. T	10. F
11. T	12. T	13. T	14. F	15. T

FILL-IN PRACTICE TEST

1. theory
2. personality
3. psychoanalysis
4. conscious
5. basic instincts
6. eros
7. thanatos
8. defense mechanisms
9. Carl Jung
10. archetypes
11. habits
12. trait
13. common traits
14. role-playing
15. interview

MULTIPLE CHOICE PRACTICE TEST 1

1. C	2. A	3. D	4. B	5. A
6. D	7. C	8. D	9. B	10. A
11. A	12. B	13. A	14. A	15. D

MULTIPLE CHOICE PRACTICE TEST 2

1. D	2. C	3. C	4. D	5. A
6. B	7. C	8. A	9. B	10. A
11. C	12. B	13. D	14. D	15. D

CHAPTER 10 TOPIC 10B

MATCHING

1. T	2. Q	3. M	4. A	5. G
6. K	7. B	8. L	9. P	10. F
11. J	12. C	13. I	14. N	15. S
16. R	17. D	18. H	19. O	20. E

TRUE-FALSE PRACTICE TEST

1. T	2. T	3. T	4. F	5. T
6. F	7. F	8. T	9. T	10. F
11. T	12. T	13. T	14. F	15. T

FILL-IN PRACTICE TEST

1. Klinefelter's syndrome
2. steroids
3. androgens
4. estrogens
5. erogenous zones
6. aphrodisiac
7. homosexuals
8. impotence
9. frigidity
10. gender identity
11. gender roles
12. androgyny
13. syphilis
14. AIDS
15. verbal

MULTIPLE CHOICE PRACTICE TEST 1

1. C	2. A	3. D	4. D	5. B
6. C	7. A	8. B	9. C	10. C
11. C	12. D	13. B		

MULTIPLE CHOICE PRACTICE TEST 2

1. C	2. D	3. B	4. C	5. C
6. A	7. D	8. D	9. C	10. B
11. A	12. D			

CHAPTER 11 TOPIC 11A

MATCHING

1. I	2. Q	3. A	4. K	5. R
6. B	7. L	8. F	9. M	10. O
11. E	12. C	13. J	14. N	15. H
16. G	17. P	18. D		

TRUE-FALSE PRACTICE TEST

1. T	2. F	3. F	4. T	5. T
6. T	7. F	8. T	9. T	10. F
11. T	12. T	13. F	14. T	15. F

FILL-IN PRACTICE TEST

1. arousal
2. instincts
3. McDougall
4. secondary
5. primary
6. hierarchy
7. safety
8. incentives
9. set point
10. sensation seeker
11. cognitive dissonance
12. bulimia
13. Thematic Apperception Test
14. fear of success
15. affiliation

MULTIPLE CHOICE PRACTICE TEST 1

1. B	2. C	3. C	4. A	5. B
6. D	7. D	8. C	9. A	10. C
11. B	12. B	13. A	14. A	15. D

MULTIPLE CHOICE PRACTICE TEST 2

1. B	2. A	3. B	4. C	5. D
6. A	7. D	8. C	9. B	10. B
11. B	12. C	13. A	14. B	15. C

CHAPTER 11 TOPIC 11B

MATCHING

1. G	2. D	3. A	4. B	5. E
6. C	7. F			

TRUE-FALSE PRACTICE TEST

1. T	2. T	3. F	4. F	5. F
6. T	7. T	8. T	9. F	10. T
11. T	12. F	13. F	14. T	15. T

FILL-IN PRACTICE TEST

1. epinephrine
2. opponent process
3. Zajonc
4. parasympathetic
5. sympathetic
6. stressor
7. frustration
8. approach-approach
9. avoidance-avoidance
10. change
11. hassles
12. Holmes
13. cognitive reappraisal
14. anxiety
15. frustration

MULTIPLE CHOICE PRACTICE TEST 1

1. A	2. A	3. C	4. A	5. B
6. B	7. B	8. D	9. C	10. D
11. C	12. D	13. A	14. D	15. D

MULTIPLE CHOICE PRACTICE TEST 2

1. D	2. D	3. B	4. D	5. B
6. B	7. A	8. C	9. A	10. B
11. A	12. C	13. B	14. B	15. C

CHAPTER 12 TOPIC 12A

MATCHING

1. L	2. G	3. R	4. M	5. B
6. N	7. P	8. T	9. Q	10. S
11. O	12. A	13. K	14. D	15. I
16. H	17. C	18. J	19. F	20. E

TRUE-FALSE PRACTICE TEST

1. T	2. T	3. F	4. F	5. T
6. F	7. F	8. T	9. T	10. F
11. T	12. T	13. T	14. T	15. F

FILL-IN PRACTICE TEST

1. diagnosis
2. DSM-III-R
3. etiology
4. insanity
5. anxiety
6. neuroses
7. anxiety
8. fear
9. generalized anxiety
10. compulsions
11. post traumatic stress
12. somatoform
13. hypochondriasis
14. conversion
15. psychogenic fugue

MULTIPLE CHOICE PRACTICE TEST 1

1. C	2. B	3. A	4. A	5. D
6. A	7. B	8. C	9. D	10. C
11. A	12. A	13. C	14. B	15. C

MULTIPLE CHOICE PRACTICE TEST 2

1. D	2. A	3. B	4. D	5. C
6. A	7. C	8. B	9. B	10. A
11. B	12. D	13. D	14. D	15. A

CHAPTER 12 TOPIC 12B

MATCHING

1. H	2. G	3. F	4. E	5. D
6. C	7. B	8. A		

TRUE-FALSE PRACTICE TEST

1. T	2. T	3. F	4. T	5. F
6. T	7. F	8. T	9. T	10. F
11. F	12. T	13. F	14. T	15. F

FILL-IN PRACTICE TEST

1. psychotic
2. Alzheimer's disease
3. degenerative
4. mood
5. mania
6. bipolar disorder
7. dysthymia
8. schizophrenia
9. unipolar
10. neologisms
11. process
12. reactive
13. dopamine
14. catatonic
15. disorganized

MULTIPLE CHOICE PRACTICE TEST 1

1. D	2. D	3. A	4. B	5. B
6. C	7. B	8. A	9. C	10. B
11. D	12. A	13. C	14. D	15. C

MULTIPLE CHOICE PRACTICE TEST 2

1. B	2. C	3. D	4. D	5. A
6. D	7. D	8. D	9. A	10. C
11. A	12. D	13. C	14. D	15. B

CHAPTER 13 TOPIC 13A

MATCHING

1. B	2. G	3. C	4. A	5. F
6. E	7. D			

TRUE-FALSE PRACTICE TEST

1. T	2. T	3. T	4. T	5. F
6. T	7. T	8. T	9. F	10. T
11. F	12. F	13. F	14. T	15. T

FILL-IN PRACTICE TEST

1. exorcism
2. Hippocrates
3. middle ages
4. 18th
5. Bedlam
6. Pinel
7. Benjamin Rush
8. Dorothea Dix
9. Clifford Bars
10. 20th
11. psychosurgery
12. lobotomy
13. shock treatments
14. psychoactive drugs
15. schizophrenia

MULTIPLE CHOICE PRACTICE TEST 1

1. A	2. D	3. B	4. C	5. A
6. C	7. B	8. B	9. D	10. C
11. D	12. A	13. B	14. D	15. B

MULTIPLE CHOICE PRACTICE TEST 2

1. C	2. C	3. C	4. D	5. A
6. D	7. B	8. B	9. A	10. C
11. B	12. D	13. B	14. A	15. A

CHAPTER 13 TOPIC 13B

MATCHING

1. P	2. R	3. J	4. O	5. L
6. I	7. C	8. F	9. B	10. H
11. A	12. K	13. Q	14. M	15. E
16. N	17. D	18. G		

TRUE-FALSE PRACTICE TEST

1. F	2. T	3. T	4. T	5. T
6. F	7. T	8. F	9. T	10. T
11. F	12. F	13. F	14. T	15. T

FILL-IN PRACTICE TEST

1. research
2. medicine
3. latent
4. transference
5. countertransference
6. client-centered
7. behavior
8. contingency management
9. contingency contracting
10. cognitive
11. cognitive restructuring
12. depression
13. group
14. communication
15. meta-analysis

MULTIPLE CHOICE PRACTICE TEST 1

1. C	2. A	3. A	4. B	5. C
6. A	7. B	8. C	9. A	10. B
11. D	12. D	13. B	14. A	15. D

MULTIPLE CHOICE PRACTICE TEST 2

1. D	2. C	3. B	4. C	5. C
6. B	7. B	8. A	9. D	10. B
11. A	12. D	13. A	14. D	15. A

CHAPTER 14 TOPIC 14A

MATCHING

1. H	2. I	3. P	4. O	5. F
6. A	7. D	8. G	9. L	10. C
11. K	12. M	13. B	14. E	15. J
16. N				

TRUE-FALSE PRACTICE TEST

1. F	2. T	3. T	4. F	5. F
6. F	7. T	8. T	9. T	10. T
11. T	12. T	13. T	14. F	15. T

FILL-IN PRACTICE TEST

1. individual
2. social influence
3. stereotype
4. norms
5. attitude
6. persuasion
7. distraction
8. central route
9. peripheral route
10. internal
11. external
12. fundamental attribution
13. reinforcement
14. attachment
15. reciprocity

MULTIPLE CHOICE PRACTICE TEST 1

1. A	2. C	3. B	4. C	5. C
6. D	7. A	8. B	9. D	10. A
11. B	12. C	13. D		

MULTIPLE CHOICE PRACTICE TEST 2

1. D	2. C	3. C	4. A	5. B
6. B	7. A	8. A	9. B	10. A
11. D	12. C	13. D		

CHAPTER 14 TOPIC 14B

MATCHING

1. K	2. A	3. J	4. B	5. I
6. C	7. H	8. D	9. G	10. F
11. E				

TRUE-FALSE PRACTICE TEST

1. F	2. T	3. T	4. T	5. T
6. F	7. T	8. F	9. T	10. F
11. T	12. T	13. F	14. T	15. F

FILL-IN PRACTICE TEST

1. conformity	2. autokinetic effect
3. obedience	4. Milgram
5. debriefed	6. bystander apathy
7. notice	8. audience inhibition
9. pluralistic ignorance	10. psychosocial
11. social loafing	12. social facilitation

MULTIPLE CHOICE PRACTICE TEST 1

1. C	2. A	3. B	4. A	5. A
6. D	7. A	8. C	9. B	10. B
11. A	12. B			

MULTIPLE CHOICE PRACTICE TEST 2

1. C	2. A	3. B	4. D	5. A
6. D	7. B	8. C	9. D	10. B
11. A	12. D			

CHAPTER 15 TOPIC 15A

MATCHING

1. E	2. D	3. F	4. C	5. G
6. B	7. H	8. A	9. I	

TRUE-FALSE PRACTICE TEST

1. T	2. T	3. T	4. T	5. F
6. F	7. T	8. T	9. T	10. T
11. F	12. T	13. T	14. F	15. T

FILL-IN PRACTICE TEST

1. job analysis	2. performance criteria
3. interview	4. situational testing
5. validity	6. AT&T
7. in-basket	8. training
9. Goldstein	10. needs assessment
11. expectancy	12. equity
13. job satisfaction	14. personnel
15. engineering	

MULTIPLE CHOICE PRACTICE TEST 1

1. D	2. B	3. C	4. B	5. A
6. C	7. D	8. B	9. C	10. A
11. A	12. D			

MULTIPLE CHOICE PRACTICE TEST 2

1. A	2. B	3. D	4. D	5. B
6. A	7. D	8. D	9. C	10. B
11. A	12. C			

CHAPTER 15 TOPIC 15B

MATCHING

1. A	2. C	3. E	4. G	5. I
6. B	7. D	8. F	9. H	10. J

TRUE-FALSE PRACTICE TEST

1. T	2. F	3. T	4. F	5. F
6. T	7. T	8. F	9. T	10. F

FILL-IN PRACTICE TEST

1. health	2. TypeA
3. smoking	4. environmental
5. personal space	6. intimate
7. social	8. territoriality
9. primary	10. population density
11. neurotoxins	12. Skinner
13. Sport	14. Rachel Carson
15. mental	

MULTIPLE CHOICE PRACTICE TEST 1

1. A	2. B	3. B	4. A	5. D
6. D	7. D	8. C	9. C	10. D
11. B	12. A	13. C		

MULTIPLE CHOICE PRACTICE TEST 2

1. A	2. D	3. B	4. D	5. C
6. C	7. A	8. D	9. C	10. A
11. B	12. A	13. D		

STATISTICAL APPENDIX

MATCHING

1. L	2. J	3. H	4. I	5. B
6. D	7. A	8. C	9. G	10. E
11. F	12. K			

TRUE-FALSE PRACTICE TEST

1. T	2. F	3. F	4. T	5. T
6. F	7. T	8. T	9. F	10. F

FILL-IN PRACTICE TEST

1. frequency distribution
2. histogram
3. median
4. mean
5. mode
6. standard deviation
7. inferential
8. normal curve
9. statistically significant
10. range

MULTIPLE CHOICE PRACTICE TEST 1

1. A	2. D	3. D	4. A	5. B
6. B	7. D	8. D	9. C	10. C